What People Are Saying About
Chicken Soup for the Working Woman's Soul...

"A bit of sunshine on a hectic day lifts the spirit. *Chicken Soup for the Working Woman's Soul* is the essence of sunshine—great stories to lift one's spirits."

Kay Koplovitz
founder, USA Networks
principal, Koplovitz & Company
author and entrepreneur

"These moving stories from working women remind us that we're not alone in the challenges we face, and they inspire us with their accounts of persistence, success and faith."

Dionne Fedderson and Sylvia Hopkins
vice presidents, Childhelp USA

"Which hat are you wearing right now? Working woman, mother, wife, girlfriend or the little girl inside you? *Chicken Soup for the Working Woman's Soul* reflects this incredibly wide range of our lives and challenges us as women with wit, wisdom, determination and compassion. These stories confirm that our lives are always full of infinite possibilities."

Sharon Lechter
coauthor, *Rich Dad Poor Dad* and the *Rich Dad* series

"There are wonderful, heartwarming messages in the touching stories within *Chicken Soup for the Working Woman's Soul*. They zero in on the juggling required today as women meet their challenges with skill, wit, care and wisdom. This book truly hits on the things that matter most in life!"

Sharon Dupont-McCord
real estate broker, Coldwell Banker Success Realty

"Wow, I can relate! All of us working women struggle to find that delicate balance between our personal and professional lives. *Chicken Soup for the Working Woman's Soul* gives us comfort that we are not alone and that the bumpy road we travel is paved with love, laughter and inspiration."

Robin Sewell
television personality

"Wonderful! These stories go straight to the heart of what it means to be a working woman today. They uplift, surprise, and nourish—and leave a warm glow in the heart that helps us to find and savor the special moments in our own lives."

Michelle Kerrick
partner, Deloitte & Touche

"With all the demands of work and family, it's never been more challenging to be a woman. *Chicken Soup for the Working Woman's Soul* is an inspiring guide, counselor and coach—and offers liberal doses of laughter and joy, too. It's a must-read for women everywhere."

Jan Donnelly
cofounder & CEO, *CareerWomen.com*

"The inspiring tales in *Chicken Soup for the Working Woman's Soul* remind us of the common bonds we share as working women in shaping the destinies of our children, our friends and our colleagues."

Melissa Wahl
executive director, National Association
for Female Executives

"*Chicken Soup for the Woman's Soul* holds up a mirror that shows us what we already know in our hearts: seek the good, spread love, make a difference, and never, never give up on our dreams!"

Stephanie B. Greer
vice president, private client manager
Wells Fargo Investments

"These motivating and emotional stories remind us of the importance of finding that delicate balance between our professional and personal lives."

Tricia J. Callaway
marketing program manager, Hewlett-Packard

CHICKEN SOUP FOR THE WORKING WOMAN'S SOUL

Chicken Soup for the Working Woman's Soul
Humorous and Inspirational Stories to Celebrate the Many Roles of Working Women
Jack Canfield, Mark Victor Hansen, Patty Aubery, Chrissy Donnelly and
Mark Donnelly

Published by Backlist, LLC,
a unit of Chicken Soup for the Soul Publishing, LLC. www.chickensoup.com

Front cover design by Lisa Camp
Originally published in 2003 by Health Communications, Inc.

Back cover and spine redesign by Pneuma Books, LLC

Distributed to the booktrade by Simon & Schuster. SAN: 200-2442

Publisher's Cataloging-in-Publication Data
(Prepared by The Donohue Group)

Chicken soup for the working woman's soul : humorous and inspirational stories to celebrate the many roles of working women / [compiled by] Jack
Canfield ... [et al.].

p. : ill. ; cm.

Originally published: Deerfield Beach, FL : Health Communications, c2003.
ISBN: 978-1-62361-007-4

1. Women--Employment--United States--Anecdotes. 2. Women employees--
United States--Interviews. 3. Anecdotes. I. Canfield, Jack, 1944-

HD6095 .C485 2012
331.4/0973   2012944059

PRINTED IN THE UNITED STATES OF AMERICA
on acid free paper

21 20 19 18 17 16 15 14 13 12   01 02 03 04 05 06 07 08 09 10

CHICKEN SOUP FOR THE WORKING WOMAN'S SOUL

Humorous and Inspirational Stories to Celebrate the Many Roles of Working Women

Jack Canfield
Mark Victor Hansen
Patty Aubery
Chrissy and Mark Donnelly

Backlist, LLC, a unit of
Chicken Soup for the Soul Publishing, LLC
Cos Cob, CT
www.chickensoup.com

Contents

3. TEAMWORK

4. SPECIAL MOMENTS

5. OVERCOMING OBSTACLES

6. A MOTHER'S WORK

7. MAKING A DIFFERENCE

8. LIVING YOUR DREAM

CONTENTS xi

Introduction

Because of working women like yourself, the world is a wonderful place. Every day presents a new opportunity to make a contribution that counts, whether it be at home or out in the workforce. Each labor of love is an occasion to celebrate life, with all its wonder, mystery and uncertainty. With time, even the rough spots in a working woman's day have the power to become memories that later strengthen the spirit and uplift the soul.

This book offers insight to such moments and memories. It contains stories that celebrate the commitment you and others like you demonstrate daily as you care for family, friends, coworkers and others. Within these pages you'll find stories of faith and fortitude, truth and tenacity, persistence and passion. You'll learn how women like yourself tackle the most difficult challenges with generosity and grace. The cycles of giving and receiving are revered, and time and time again we learn that often, the gift of giving is its own reward.

Whether you are an executive or a mother (or maybe you are both), you know the skills, the mental energy and the physical stamina it takes to accomplish all that needs to be done in a day. Sometimes you wonder where it all comes from, but then the heart speaks and reminds you of what's worthwhile. It is in rituals and routines that we find momentum and motivation, and that in turn leads us to new heights and inspiring innovations. Bit by bit, solid foundations for strong futures are built. These are the success stories that await you in *Chicken Soup for the Working Woman's Soul.* Written by working women with enthusiasm and dedication to their chosen career paths, they offer comfort and hope to women everywhere.

While reading through the hundreds of stories that were submitted for this book, we were amazed at the continual challenges working women face. But even more amazing are the creative solutions and the uplifting attitudes that pervade these pages. Despite demanding jobs, sometimes difficult people, and growing responsibilities, working women press on, conquering each day and making every moment count. In this way they better their own lives, and in the process, touch the lives of countless others in positive ways. It is our sincere hope that you, too, will be touched by these stories of support, encouragement and inspiration. May they bring you a smile, an idea, the recollection of a fond memory or two, and perhaps even newfound appreciation for who you are as well as amazement at all you do!

Thank you for reading *Chicken Soup for the Working Woman's Soul.*

1

ALL IN A DAY'S WORK

*F*all in love with what you are going to do for
a living.
To be able to get out of bed and do what you
love to do for the rest of your day is beyond
words.
I'd rather be a failure in something that I
love than be successful in something I hate.

George Burns

The Interview

Dreams are powerful reflections of your actual growth potential.

Denis Waitley and Reni L. Witt

The job of a lifetime, that's what it was, secretary for the district attorney. I couldn't wait for my interview. This was the kind of position I'd dreamed of, what all those years of college and entry-level positions were for.

The night before my interview, I spent two hours going through my closet to pick out just the right outfit. *What would I say to him?* I curled up into my pillowy bed and stared at the ceiling, unable to sleep. *How should I act?* Nervous, I shut my eyes and tried to get some rest, but I kept tossing and turning.

Finally, the alarm clock woke me. I tried to open my eyes, but something was wrong. My face felt stiff, strange. My hands flew to my cheeks.

"No!" My lips were unable to open all the way.

I ran to the bathroom and looked at myself in the bathroom mirror, horrified. My face was contorted like a stroke victim's. My eyes were misaligned. I couldn't move the right side of my face. I could barely recognize myself. *What was happening to me? What nightmare did I wake up into?*

My mother came into the room, "What's wrong?" Her eyes bulged as she withdrew in terror.

"What's happening to me?" I slurred to her.

"I'll take you to the emergency room," she finally gasped.

We were rushed in. The nurse took one look at me and called in a specialist. There, under the blazing white lights, my mother and I waited.

After several hours of tests, the doctor finally explained, "You have Bell's palsy. It is a condition in which your face muscles tighten because of stress. You need to get plenty of sleep, and in a few days your face will return to normal."

"But I have a job interview this afternoon," I sadly remembered.

"I'm sorry," the doctor said, concerned. "You should reschedule, maybe for later in the week."

During the long car ride home, all I could think about was how bad it would look to reschedule. Certainly, that would dampen my chances. Nobody reschedules with the district attorney. All the other applicants would have the advantage then, I concluded.

I looked at my watch and made the decision, "Mom, drop me off on Jacob Street. I'm going to the interview."

"Honey, I don't think you should. You look . . . strange," she said, ever so gently.

I knew she was right. He probably would take one look at me and judge me by my appearance rather than by my experience and talent. I probably shouldn't go. But if I didn't, I'd always wonder if I could have gotten my dream job.

"No, Mom, take me there."

Reluctantly, she took me where I wanted to go. I walked right into the formidable office with the mahogany furniture and pillars of white marble, not letting my own self-consciousness or any disease stop me. Not now, not when I had worked so hard for so long to be given this opportunity.

I went to the woman sitting behind the front desk and said, as well as I could, "Nicole Jenkins to see Mr. Robertson."

She stared at my face. "He's expecting you. Go right in."

I entered the room to her right and saw a gray-haired man sitting behind the large desk reading a file.

Suddenly my nerves got the best of me, and I had to sit. I took the chair in front of him.

"Hello," he said. "Miss Jenkins?"

"Yes. Please excuse me. I'm having a Bell's palsy attack. My doctor explained to me that it would last a few days. I came right from the hospital."

"You're very dedicated to come when you're not feeling up to speed," he responded, after a pause.

"Yes, Sir."

He spent a few minutes looking over my application. "Is everything on here correct?" He held it out to me.

I glanced over the paper, "Yes, but I failed to mention I type seventy-five words per minute."

"Wonderful," he smiled. "Out of one hundred points, you had our highest score on the application test. You scored well above average on grammar and computer programs."

"It comes easily for me," I honestly replied.

"Well, you are certainly qualified. You have an impressive background with related experience. I see here you worked for the navy."

"Directly with legal affairs," I reiterated.

"When are you available?"

"Two weeks."

He gazed down at his desk calendar. "The 27th then, be here at 9:00 A.M."

I gasped. "You're hiring me!"

"Yes, you're perfect for the position."

I stood. "Thank you for believing in me. I won't let you down."

"I know," he smiled, rising from his desk to shake my hand. "Not only have you got the skills I'm looking for, you also have the character."

Nicole Jenkins
as told to Michele "Screech" Campanelli

Ask and You Shall Receive

You may have the loftiest goals, the highest ideals, the noblest dreams, but remember this, nothing works unless you do.

Nido Qubein

You never walk into a job interview expecting to meet your greatest advocate, lifelong mentor and cherished friend. In 1981, I was a year out of MBA school, living in New York, and looking for a job in Colorado. I heard about a company headquartered in Boulder, Colorado, and managed to get an interview with two of their executives while they were in New York. Biff was in charge of the department in which I wanted to work. Tom was his boss. We met over lunch, and I did my best to impress them with my one year of experience. I don't know what I said during that interview, but when Biff got back to Colorado, he wrote Tom a memo that said, "I wouldn't touch her with a ten-foot pole."

Tom offered me a job anyway. I started as his executive assistant, and Tom immediately began training me in his way of doing things—skills that I continued to draw upon every day of my corporate life. He was especially strict about the one-page rule. Memos had to be no more than one page or he wouldn't read them. The summary had to be in the first paragraph.

"It's a memo," he said, "not a mystery. I don't want to wait until the end to find out how it turns out." It became a challenge to see how I could summarize an assignment in as few words as possible. The apex of our game came when I interviewed each of Tom's direct reports on a point of contention between them. Tom wanted to know why they couldn't agree on how to handle a new service. My memo read as follows: "Gary wants a piece of the pie. Bill wants a bigger piece of the pie. Roger wants the whole pie and permanent possession of the pan." Tom didn't say anything about the memo to me, but years later he would sound like a proud father reciting my memo from memory and laughing more with each telling.

After a three-month probationary period, I was eligible for my first salary and performance review. Tom took me to lunch at a local restaurant and asked me to review myself. I wasn't prepared for that and was disappointed not to get some real feedback on my performance. I did my best to recall projects I had completed, plans for additional training and goals for the future. Tom then asked what I thought my raise should be. I was thoroughly prepared for that question and immediately gave him an answer. He cleared his throat and nodded thoughtfully.

"What percentage is that?" he asked. I told him in complete confidence that the number was indeed a reasonable figure. "If your salary increased by that percent every year for ten years, how much would you be earning?" I took out my calculator and Tom waited while my fingers tap-danced across the keys. The total came to horrifying digital life, and I smiled, asked for his patience, and did the calculations again. I'm certain Tom knew exactly what the number would be, and that it would fall somewhere in the low eight figures.

I couldn't read the number out loud. "It would be kind of high," I said, "but I did take a pay cut to come here, and I think it would still be fair." We finished lunch and returned to the office without another word on the subject. I was certain I'd blown it. A few minutes later, Tom's secretary, MaryJane, came into my office and laid a memo on top of my desk. It was from Tom, typed by MaryJane and impressively short. The title was longer than the memo: Monetary Considerations: Luncheon Discussion Thursday, September 3rd. I can only imagine the fun he had dictating that into his recorder. The body of the memo was exactly seven words, an achievement in brevity I have never surpassed. It said, "Ask and you shall receive." Cordially, Tom.

As Tom's assistant, I was privy to some of the salary negotiations he conducted. I learned that you don't always get as much as you ask, but you'll never get more. At my three-month review luncheon in 1981, I told Tom my goal was to be vice president, in charge of strategic planning and marketing. Seven years later, I was.

Jane Imber

"When I complimented you on your work, Ms. Miller, I didn't expect you to spoil it all by coming in here and asking for a *raise!*"

Reprinted by permission of Bob Zahn.

Love and War

People always want to know who won.

When I tell them my husband and I met when we were opposing attorneys on a case, that's always their first question.

"Who won?"

"You decide," I say. Then I tell them the rest.

I was an aggressive young associate, newly hired by my law firm and anxious to prove myself. John was a seasoned pro who worked for another law firm in the same building. When I found out he was opposing counsel, I was nervous. I'd seen his name on countless appellate decisions and knew he was far more adept at this type of case than I was. I decided that what I lacked in skill and experience, I would make up for with hard work and bravado.

I devised a campaign of daily badgering: discovery requests, legal motions, correspondence, phone calls. If I wasn't satisfied with how quickly he responded, I walked down the hall and pestered him in person. I was relentless—a terrier yipping at his heels. My client and my boss loved it.

But somewhere along the way I started to like him. Maybe it was the way he overlooked my obvious lack of sophistication and treated me like a serious adversary. Maybe it was our verbal sparring that often left me walking away with a stupid grin, as though we'd been flirting instead of arguing. Whatever the reason, after a few months on the case, I decided my adversary was a decent guy. If we'd met under difference circumstances, I might want to see where the flirting could go. But since we were opposing counsel, ethics prevented us from becoming personally involved. Romance was out of the question.

One Friday afternoon John left his office without giving me a set of documents I needed to review over the weekend. I tracked him down at home and demanded he turn over the materials to me that day.

"All right," he said, "I'll have them at my house tonight."

Skeptical, but not wanting to back down, I said, "Fine. I'll be there at 7:00."

That night changed everything.

Some people claim an instant familiarity with a place or a stranger, convinced they must have been there or known each other before. Walking into John's house, what I felt was not déjà vu, but more a sense of how things could be. I felt instantly at home, as I never have any place before or since.

The house was small, with wood floors and walls decorated with a strange combination of quilts and antlers. The furniture looked lived-in without being shabby. The place was modest, warm and comfortable—not at all like some of the palatial showcases I'd seen other lawyers strut through.

Seeing him in that environment, I felt more comfortable around John, too. Even though it was his house, it felt like neutral ground. I didn't have to act so tough anymore. I sank onto his couch and felt myself relax.

"So what's your story?" I asked, and he gave me a brief sketch of his life.

My answer to the same question was much briefer: "Work. That's all I do."

"I used to be like you," John said. "Trust me—it can't last. You need other things." He told me he was happiest when he was backpacking or sailing, running the power tools in his workshop, or simply puttering in his vegetable garden on the weekends. What a curious idea. I had always thought weekends were for more work.

I wished I were there under other circumstances. I wanted to talk longer. I wanted to know him better. But eventually duty called. I stood and held out my hand for the papers.

"I don't have them yet. Let's take a ride."

He drove me in his nine-year-old Honda station wagon (more bonus points—a modest car) to a house a few miles away.

"Come on," John coaxed. I followed him to the door.

John's client answered. It's hard to say who was more shocked, the client or me.

"You know Elizabeth," John said. His client raised an eyebrow, but politely shook my hand. Then he handed John the papers I'd wanted. John handed them to me.

Years later John confessed that what he'd really wanted to say when his client opened the door was, "Look! I have captured their queen!"

And it was true, he had.

My way had always been to rush into a relationship then see it flame out a month or so later. That couldn't happen this time. Being on opposite sides of a case forced me to get to know him slowly. I had the chance to see his character in action—his integrity, loyalty, honesty. By the time our romance began, I was already sold.

We had two choices: Wait until the case was over to pursue a relationship, or plunge ahead. If we weren't going to wait, one of us would have to withdraw from the case.

The next day I told my boss. He promptly fired me.

John's client still swears he paid John to date me, just to get me off the case. He says they both knew I was trouble.

Another lawyer took over for me and eventually the case settled. By then John and I had already been married three years. Good thing we didn't wait.

John and I have been married ten years now. We still live in the house where I felt so at home that night. There are still quilts and antlers on the wall, and we've only just now replaced the couch where I sat one Friday evening and wished I could know this man better. I still badger my husband at times, and he digs in his heels when I'm wrong. Ours is a marriage of negotiations and compromise, of flirting when we seem to be arguing. A worthy opponent, it turns out, makes a wonderful spouse.

So who won?

No doubt about it: I did.

Elizabeth Rand

"It was a purely professional decision, Harris. I hope my firing you won't affect our marriage in any way."

Reprinted by permission of Harley Schwadron.

The Commanding Secretary

Working as a secretary at an international airport, my sister had an office adjacent to the room where security temporarily holds suspects.

One day security officers were questioning a man when they were suddenly called away on another emergency. To the horror of my sister and her colleagues, the man was left alone in the unlocked room. After a few minutes, the door opened and he began to walk out. Summoning up her courage, one of the secretaries barked, "Get back in there, and don't you come out until you're told!"

The man scuttled back inside and slammed the door. When the security people returned, the women reported what had happened.

Without a word, an officer walked into the room and released one very frightened telephone repairman.

Russel M. Perman

"Why, I'd just love to pick up your dry cleaning, would you like to rotate my tires?"

Reprinted by permission of George Abbott.

Getting Away

I don't get out much. Like most moms, I'm too busy doing mom stuff to take time for myself.

It wasn't always like this. Before I had kids, I had a career. Though I spent more hours nurturing my professional image in those days, it still seemed there was time left over for me. I'd make time to rejuvenate at a spa or unwind on a daylong shopping spree. Relaxing was a crucial component to the corporate image I was polishing.

Now, the only thing I polish is the furniture.

Having swapped the corner office at work in order to write from the corner bedroom at home, I now consider a trip to the grocery store without the kids to be a getaway. The business lunches I enjoyed at fancy restaurants were so long ago that the navy blue business suit I'd worn to them has gone out of style. I've cashed in the career and all the perks that come with it.

Oh, I'm not complaining. This is exactly where I want to be. So you can imagine the emotional tug-of-war I felt when my literary agent phoned to say that the publisher of my first book was sending me on an all-expense paid publicity tour from coast to coast!

At first the whole idea of a business trip seemed almost scary to me. The last time I was away from home all night I was giving birth. It's been a decade since I've gone anywhere without stuffing Goldfish crackers and an Etch-A-Sketch into my bag for the ride. I'd have to step out of my comfortable role as mother and step into the role of—*what?—businessperson? Out of my Reeboks and into heels? Out of the laundry room and into television studios? Can I pull that off?* I wondered. *Won't they catch on and realize I'm just a mom?*

But then I pondered the benefits of the trip. I'd be flying alone, dining alone and sleeping in luxury hotels alone. For an entire week, it would be just me. No school lunches to pack. No baseball practice. No four o'clock panic over what to make for dinner. I started to plan all the adult things I'd be able to do. I could visit each city's famous museums and stare as long as I wanted at each masterpiece without having to divert my eyes to keep tabs on my boys. I would browse through shops instead of racing through them, shouting, "Don't touch!" to my guys. And I would "dine" instead of "eat." It was beginning to sound better and better.

Finally, after making sure the refrigerator was full and the hamper was empty, I was on my way. As the plane took off, it also took my breath away. I was, for the first time in thirteen years, on my own—if only for a week. The curious thing about the trip was this: Instead of feeling like an adult, I actually felt more like a child! I could stare out the window of the plane in awe of the billowy clouds without having to tend to someone else. I could think uninterrupted thoughts. I didn't have to make my bed. I could drop my towel on the floor in the hotel bath and someone else would pick it up. I could order anything I wanted off the menu and not worry if I had enough money to pay the tab.

Even dessert. Twice if I wanted to.

Instead of driving my kids to school and practice and trying to stay on schedule, I had personal author escorts in every city who chauffeured me around. They were being paid to keep me on schedule. While they concentrated on the road I could take in the scenery, the flowers and the people—all things you miss when you're the pilot instead of the passenger.

But San Francisco's cable cars and Seattle's Space Needle left me missing my family. Flying over Mount St. Helen's and seeing New York's skyline on approach to JFK are sights that should be shared. The guy in the seat next to me was snoring.

During a layover in Denver, I watched an exhausted mother chase her toddlers through the terminal. She apologized as they knocked my luggage over. "It's okay," I smiled. "I'm a mom, too."

But after days without doing any mom stuff I didn't feel like one. I had morphed into this other person, but the spell was starting to wear off. I knew I'd be turning back into a pumpkin soon, and the weird thing was, I was looking forward to it.

It became clear to me that for moms, coming home is what getting away is all about. Whether it's cruising the Caribbean or cruising the aisles of the grocery store alone, I know now how important it is to get away.

When I returned home my children looked angelic. The exploding hamper was a challenge, not a chore. I looked forward to filling up the empty refrigerator. I was refreshed. I was home.

A week later, up to my ears in mom stuff, I decided to write another book.

Kimberly A. Porrazzo

Career Day

It was only 7:45 A.M., but already I was multitasking. I stood at the kitchen sink, simultaneously slapping together cheese and mustard sandwiches for Max's lunch, while frantically brainstorming ways to put an exciting new spin on the twelve-hundred-word article due later that day. "We'd really like something compelling," my editor had said. The topic was thrush. Who said my work wasn't challenging?

Then the cry came out. "Mom, I need you!" Max called from his seat in front of the computer. "It's a 'mergency!"

Okay, so I know that moms are supposed to be ultra-responsive to their kids' every need, but this was the fourth "'mergency" this morning.

"There's a problem with Stuart-Little-dot-com," he told me. "The Snowball coloring book isn't loading."

"It'll have to wait, Max," I told him. "We have to get going. I have to get to work."

Then I added the kicker. "My work is more important than Stuart-Little-dot-com."

Max looked extremely skeptical. He stared at me in silence, but "That's what you think, Mom" flickered in his wide blue eyes.

Still, despite what my son may think, my work is important. Validation of that fact came the very same night, in the form of a phone call from a total stranger.

"Mary Dixon Lebeau?" the voice asked, stumbling over my last name. "Hi. This is Linda Goodparent from the Cross County Elementary School. I'm on the Careers Day committee, and some of the committee members said you'd be a good choice to represent the newspaper on Career Day."

That was more like it. Here were my people—people who have read and chuckled over my column and wanted me to share the wonder of writing with their children.

Perhaps they knew me from my feature writer days, when I tracked down the best of the "feel good" stories and brought Pee Wee hockey teams, foreign exchange students and anti-drug campaigns into their homes on a weekly basis.

Maybe they had followed me since the beginning of my work at the paper. Maybe they recognized me as a talented reporter, one whose eagle eye and precise writing skills held corruption in our schools and on our planning boards at bay, keeping our county safe for all of its citizenry.

Or maybe Dave Barry was busy.

"Sure, I'd love to. Just send me all the details."

"Great!" Ms. Goodparent sounded really enthusiastic. Then she paused. "Now, what is it you do at the newspaper, exactly?"

Hmm, I had a feeling I wasn't dealing with a fan.

So that's how I found myself at this particular Career Day, explaining beats and deadlines and inverted pyramids to the ten-and-under set. The agenda was simple—each of the guests would give a brief, under-five-minute explanation of their work, then answer questions from the crowd. Later, we would take our places at booths in the cafeteria, and the kids could wander around and learn more about the jobs that most interested them.

The line-up that day included a legal secretary, a truck driver, a dentist, a minor-league hockey player, a policeman and me. "You'll be speaking last," the teacher informed me. I thought this was an honor—like the rest of the speakers were the "warm-up acts" and I was the main attraction.

Later, however, I learned I was last because the attention span of an average third-grader is approximately twenty minutes. "We want to make sure they're fully awake when the policeman talks," the teacher said.

We each gave our mini-explanation. One by one, the volunteers talked about the importance of their jobs. They did a great job, too. In fact, the minor-league hockey player even had me convinced that skating across fake ice in pursuit of a puck is essential to the American way of life.

Finally, it was my turn. I tried to explain how reporters are the eyes of the people at every meeting, every event and every crime scene. "If you know what's going on, down the street or across the country, it's because a reporter was there," I finished. Thirty-seven little faces stared back at me as their teacher applauded. (Sure, the policeman had a more enthusiastic response, but he demonstrated the use of handcuffs. No one told me we were allowed to bring visual aids!)

Then it was the question-and-answer time. A little blonde asked the legal secretary how fast she types. A skinny kid with a runny nose inquired about goalie pads. "Did you ever meet O.J.?" an inquisitive tot asked the policeman.

No one asked me anything. I attributed that to the outstanding job I did in the initial presentation. After all, if they already know everything, who needs questions?

"Does anyone have a question for Ms. Lebeau?" the teacher prodded.

"I thought all reporters were superheroes, like Clark Kent," one tike commented. I shook my head. "They should've had a pirate here. Or a cowboy," he said. I could see his point.

Things weren't much better on the homefront. My sons have their future ambitions picked out already—one wants to be a veterinarian, because of his passion for reptiles and rodents. One wants to go to law school after a career with the WWF.

And Max wanted to be an artist—or at least I thought. (He's already practicing the "starving" part by refusing to eat any meal that doesn't come with a prize in the box.)

But then my youngest son surprised me. "Mom, I think I want to be a writer, just like you," he told me the other night. I smiled.

And I kept smiling, even as I scrubbed his latest bestseller off the bedroom wall.

I'm sure Dave Barry started the very same way.

Mary Dixon Lebeau

The Birthday Tiara

If you want to change attitudes, start with a change in behavior.

Katharine Hepburn

For my thirtieth birthday, I threw myself a soirée to celebrate. My friend Sarah arrived early, sat me down and handed me a white cake box. A crown drawn in gold ink decorated the top. My heart leapt. After all, this was from Sarah, someone who gave the most meaningful gifts.

I peeled back the lid. Nestled amidst star-splattered tissue paper was my very own crown. Brightly colored candles sprouted from a framework of iridescent pipe cleaners.

"It's a birthday tiara," said Sarah. "And you have to wear it."

I laughed. She knew I needed permission.

And so, for one night, I felt like a celebrity surrounded by adoring fans. But after the festivities, I packed up my treasure and stowed it away. I'd had my night of stardom.

Several years later, I remembered my tiara. I decided to display it amidst the children's books in my study.

Glancing up from my computer, I'd notice it and smile.

Then came another birthday. My thirty-fourth. They were all beginning to feel the same. After I opened my gifts from my husband John, I told myself, *This will just be a nice day.*

I said my morning prayers. Sitting up from where I had reclined on the rug, I spied the crown. *Should I?* I thought. *No. That's silly.*

But then I heard a louder voice. *John's gone to work . . . I'm home alone . . . Why not?*

I plunked it on my head. Chuckling, I smiled ear to ear. I felt lighthearted as I got ready for work, like I'd been zapped with a tiny current of energy and joy. Was that me twirling around the kitchen?

Singing goodbye to the kitties, I grabbed my car keys and purse. Then a voice in my head yelled, *Stop! You're not wearing that out, are you?*

I froze. *What would people think?* I must be nuts.

But wait, said the new, fun-loving me. *It'll be an experiment. To see how many motorists notice.*

I was bitterly disappointed when not a soul looked my way during my commute. *Now what?* I thought, sitting in the parking lot at work. *Do I wear it in?*

Stares of disbelief greeted me at the museum staff entrance. The security supervisor trailed me, a grin on his face. He pummeled me with questions like, "What is that thing? Does it light up? How old are you?" I answered the first two and ignored the third.

My female colleagues embraced my new look. "I love it," they exclaimed, showering me with accolades. "You have to wear it for your school group."

I met the fourth-graders from Fairfax and immediately addressed a few open mouths and wide eyes. "Does anyone know why I'm wearing this?"

A hand shot up. "You wanna look silly?" blurted out a youngster.

A chorus of giggles met my feigned hurt look.

Another student, as if to make amends for his rude classmate, asked if they could sing that "Happy Birthday song" to me.

"At the end of the tour," I promised, tickled.

Walking next door to meet my friend Brittney for lunch, I thought about my headpiece. *It's really like a hat,* I rationalized. *Hey! I can wear those now!* I'd always been envious of the stylish creations worn by older women at church.

I shared with Brittney what I'd observed so far. "Women congratulate me. I think they all secretly long to wear one. Children stare or ignore it. They're the most polite. Men try and guess my age, then ask, 'Does it light up?' I'm getting sick of that one. Guys and their toys!"

"It's lit from within," said Brittney. Girls are so gushy.

My tiara slipped off that afternoon. I insisted my stylist wear it while she cut my hair.

"You don't need it, Miriam," teased her boss. "You already think you're a queen."

By the time I drove to meet my husband at his office, I'd practically forgotten what was on my head. But he noticed.

"You've worn that all day?" he asked in disbelief.

"Yup," I replied. "And I'm not taking it off now."

He threatened to bail out on our evening together, but I was armed. "It's my birthday. One day out of 365."

He knew he was beat.

At the restaurant I was greeted with the typical responses I'd heard all day. Except for one. En route to the restroom, a very vocal woman shouted at me, "When you gonna light your candles?"

"I can't," I told her, amused. "They're plastic." Her face fell in disappointment.

It was after midnight when I finally returned my tiara to its spot on the bookcase. Another birthday had come and gone. But a very different one. Why? Because I had made it so. I had risked. Tiptoeing at first, tempted to turn back, I had ventured beyond the safe and secure. I'd found courage within myself. As one friend remarked, I was "gutsy and glorious." And this was only the start.

Deborah M. Ritz

Not Just Another Rat

*Our character is what we do when we think no
one is looking.*

H. Jackson Brown Jr.

It was still dark outside, and my breath floated like a
frosty cloud in the cold air. I was feeling sorry for myself
again. There was a reason they called it a rat race.

Day in and day out, the same old thing. Up and out of
the house before daylight. An hour and a half commute to
the office. Eight to nine hours at work, and then the same
commute home, still dark outside. The short winter days
made me wonder: *Did the sun ever come out during the day?* I
wasn't sure anymore—if it did, I certainly missed it.

I made my way to the train station on that bleak
Monday morning. My week stretched out before me like a
deep black hole. The week might be new, but I was feeling
old and worn-out. The brief weekend respite hadn't provided much relief, what with the laundry that had piled
up, not to mention the supermarket and the dry cleaners
and the myriad other errands that ate into what was supposed to be our family time together. We barely had a

chance to play a quick game of Scrabble before it was time to set the alarm clock and start the week once more.

The train was late again. Any attempt at relaxing thoughts was quickly replaced by memories of the piles of paper sitting on my desk. So much to do, and the days were never long enough. I tuned out the crowd around me and began to mentally sort through the priorities that would beckon as soon as I arrived at the office. E-mails and faxes, reports and meetings. The day would be full, more so because it was the beginning of the week. I cringed as I remembered how often I had put things off "'til next week." Well, "next week" was here. Note to self: thinking about things "tomorrow" may have worked for Scarlett O'Hara, but it only created grief for me.

The shifting crowd brought me back to the moment. The train was pulling in, and the army of commuters was of one mind: Grab an empty seat at any cost. Men and women were equal-opportunity pushers, propelling each other to the edge of the platform. Even as I allowed myself to be swept along, I also resolved to seize the first available seat I could find. With a firm grip on my briefcase I pushed along with the best of them, and landed my prize. Sitting would allow me to get a jump on some paperwork, perhaps a memo or two. Any head start would help.

Was this what my life had deteriorated to? The highlight of my day was that I got a seat on the train? Surely my aims were loftier than that. We were working so hard, my husband and I. Our goal was to pay off the mortgage, and set aside savings to prepare for retirement. We were almost there. Just another year or two of my imitation of superwoman, and then I could relax. Just another year or two . . .

That's when I saw her. The young woman looked vaguely familiar. Had I seen her at the train station before, or did I simply recognize the look on her face? The look that reflected resignation at having missed out on a seat again. The look that said, ever so clearly, "I don't have the energy to do this anymore." I knew just how she felt, but I also knew that I had work to do. Memos to answer, reports to write. I had a seat, and she didn't. Nobody said life was going to be fair.

But there was more than just her face. Even under her bulky winter coat, I could see that she was expecting a baby. Her pregnancy was rather far along, and it was all that she could do to hold on to the metal bar as the train lurched into motion. I felt a pang of guilt, and then argued with myself. *Surely there were enough men on the train who could see her condition. Chivalry wasn't dead yet, was it?* But no one moved. It seemed as if everyone on the train was studiously avoiding the view of this young woman as they buried their heads in their newspapers, or pretended to be deeply engrossed in their conversations.

I put the memos and the legal pad back in my briefcase, stood up, and motioned to get her attention. The work could wait. There certainly was enough of it, and one or two more memos wouldn't make much of a difference in my schedule. If I had any second thoughts, they were wiped away by the look on her face. A new look—one of relief and thanksgiving. Words didn't need to be exchanged, but as she said thank you I realized that this small act of kindness was as much for me as it was for her. A reminder that even though I was part of the rat race, I didn't have to become a rat.

It was still Monday morning, but the emerging sunrise told me it was going to be a beautiful day.

Ava Pennington

Trooper

After working for a law firm in downtown Houston for ten years, I changed careers and have "graduated" to working with horses every day, and spend a lot of time in my truck delivering or picking them up. About every six to eight weeks I travel to Tennessee via the freeways of east Texas, Louisiana, Mississippi and Alabama. I believe the most beautiful freeway along the route that I take is Interstate 59 right around Hattiesburg, Mississippi. Magnolia trees are plentiful, along with a thick forest of pine trees on both sides of the two-lane southbound freeway, as well as northbound, so that the opposite side of the freeway is completely camouflaged.

In fact, the last time I drove this freeway, it was so secluded and quiet, I had the road completely to myself. I had been driving alone for about seven hours and was feeling kind of stiff and tired, so I decided to "get comfortable." I carefully checked front and back for any other vehicles—no traffic for miles. The truck was in cruise in the left lane, and I wanted to remove a particularly binding undergarment, which is relatively easy to do in a safe manner while cruising. Double-checking and once again not finding a soul in sight, I removed my shirt and set it on

my lap close to the door, removed the offending undergarment and tossed it to my right (where it fell to the passenger floor area), and proceeded to carefully retrieve my
shirt to put it back on.

All of a sudden, out of nowhere, a state trooper passed
me on the right. For some reason, his taillights came on
just as he blew past me, and he suddenly slowed down to
coast even with my passenger door. Meanwhile, much to
my horror, I found that my shirt was hung up on the door
handle, and I had no way and nothing to cover myself
with. I was unsuccessfully trying to untangle the shirt
without accidentally opening the door while simultaneously watching the road and keeping an eye on him. After
what seemed like an hour, he flashed his lights and hand-
motioned for me to pull over. (I swear he took his own
sweet time communicating this command to me!)

After he dropped back behind me, I immediately moved
to the right lane, still trying to untangle the shirt and wondering how to hide myself. (I didn't think I had been
speeding, and the only thing I could imagine was that I
would have a hard time explaining to my kids that I had
been thrown in jail in Mississippi for public indecency!) I
finally came to a stop, put the truck in park and jammed
the shirt back on over my head. I took deep breaths in an
effort to return my face to its natural color before he
walked up to my window. As he approached to ask for my
driver's license and insurance card, I noticed that Mr.
Trooper was very young and very good-looking. Since my
face was still burning three shades of red, I tried not to
make eye contact as I handed him my license and,
Ohmigosh, an expired insurance card. I wasn't sure if it was
my imagination, but it seemed he was trying really hard
not to break out laughing.

He made me get out of the truck and walk all the way
back to the end of the horse trailer. After quizzing me on

where I was going, who I was going to see, etc., he asked me if I realized that I had managed to commit three infractions. I was shocked, but braced myself for the embarrassment. The first, he said, was speeding. Fortunately, I didn't deny it, and he informed me that it was only five miles over the limit and he would just drop it. The second was I had no license plate on my horse trailer. I thought he was kidding, but when I looked up, I realized that it had blown off. The third, he said, while allowing a slow smile to light up his face, and while I braced myself for total humiliation, was that I had been driving in the left lane. I was so relieved that it was not related to my barreling down the freeway seventy miles per hour naked that I actually laughed and demanded to know what kind of people were Mississippians to build freeways with two lanes and not be allowed to use the left one? With that mysterious little smile, he patiently explained that the left lane was for passing only, which was the law in other states as well, including Texas. He graciously never mentioned my nudity and even though my insurance card was expired, he just smiled and pretended not to notice.

Mr. Hunka Trooper returned my driver's license and worthless insurance card and told me he was not going to cite me. I drew a deep breath of relief as he told me to be safe and have a good day. I thanked him, wished him the same, briefly entertaining and dismissing the thought of giving him a quick hug when he zapped me.

"By the way, your shirt is on backward and inside out," said my smug little Trooper Guardian Angel with a twinkle in his eye as he climbed back into his patrol car.

Laura Kidder

The Lady Behind the Slinky

Imagination is the highest kite one can fly.

Lauren Bacall

Betty James, seventy-five, comes to work every morning here at the Slinky factory in Hollidaysburg, Pennsylvania, a tiny blip of a town tucked in a deep fold of the Allegheny Mountains. Betty stands just over five feet tall, gets her hair done once a week and walks with so much dignity she reminds you of Queen Elizabeth, except with a more relaxed sense of humor.

Betty is the one who made the Slinky what it is today, although this was not exactly what she set out to do with her time here on earth.

No big neon signs announce "Home of the Slinky" or anything, but 120 people work in shifts around the clock making Slinkys, shipping thirty-six thousand a day to toy stores on every continent except Antarctica.

Just one set of double doors away from Betty's office are the *whir, clank, cha-ching* and other industrial music put out by the eight Slinky machines. These are the exact same machines that have always made Slinkys, and number one, as it is called, is still notoriously slow. Barrels of water, used to clean the steel wire, sit under the Slinky machines, each stenciled with a request: "No Spitting in Barrels."

Most American toy manufacturers long ago headed offshore in search of cheap labor. But not Slinky.

Another strange thing is that the Slinky company has remained so small. You'll find no R&D department here at James Industries, no PR office and not a single MBA walking these halls. "We're not big-time," says Betty. "We like it the way it is. Slinky is like a child, and you don't exploit your child."

Betty James is definitely not a tycoon. People might say she lets her heart make too many of her decisions. She still makes the Slinky the same size, with the same fine American steel; she could have used cheaper steel or made the toy smaller, and, really, who would notice? Also, people wonder why Betty doesn't raise prices. When Slinky first came out, it retailed for $1. Now, nearly a half-century later, you can still get one for about $1.89.

"My theory is, if it's a child's toy, make it affordable," says Betty. "That's just what I go by."

Betty embodies the spirit of the Slinky, rolling through the years according to the way life pushes and pulls. Her mother died when Betty was eight, and that's when her father took off. She was raised by a grandmother and an aunt.

Studying early-childhood education at Pennsylvania State University, Betty met Richard James. He was a handsome engineer, class of 1939. They fell madly in love, married and moved to Philadelphia, where Richard worked as a shipyard engineer for fifty dollars a week. One of his jobs was to test the horsepower on battleships, using a meter with a torsion spring inside.

One day, Richard saw one of these springs fall off his desk. It rolled over itself in the most fascinating way. He took it home to Betty and said, "I think I can make a toy out of this." But it needed a name.

"So I said, 'I'll try to find a word for slithering,'" Betty recalls. "That's how Slinky came. It just seemed to depict everything."

The Slinky didn't sell at first. Then Gimbels department store in Philadelphia gave Betty and Richard the use of a counter one evening to demonstrate the toy. This was in 1945. "We had four hundred Slinkys made, and I said to Richard, 'Now you go ahead and I'll get a friend, and if nobody's buying, we'll come over and buy some to stimulate people.'

"So my friend and I get off the elevator, and I'm looking around and I don't see anybody. But over in one corner there's this mob of people, and they all have dollars in their hands, and it was, Wow! Go for it! We sold out in ninety minutes. And that's how we started."

Richard would bring the Slinkys home, and Betty would wrap them in yellow paper. "That was what we called packaging." Soon they opened a larger factory with twenty employees, then an even larger one.

In their marriage's early years, Betty was happy having babies. She'd always dreamed of having a family. And Richard was happy being rich and famous. Maybe too happy. Betty didn't like what was happening to him.

"He announced one night, 'I'm leaving. I'm going to South America. Do you want to run the company or sell it?' And I said, 'I'll run it.'"

Richard moved to Bolivia to join a religious cult. He died there, in 1974.

Betty soon learned that Richard had donated a big hunk of the family fortune to that cult. And he had been ignoring the business. "We were bankrupt," says Betty, "but I was too dumb to know it." With six kids to raise, she *had* to make the company work.

The first thing she did was protect the children. She

bought a big, old house in Hollidaysburg, where she had aunts and uncles who could help out. She fixed the house and had the children's bedrooms all done up to exactly match the bedrooms in their house in Philadelphia, right down to the stuffed animals. "The children had been through enough trauma," says Betty.

She remembers crying every Sunday night for a year when she would leave her children to make the four-hour trek to Philadelphia. She would stay through Thursday, trying to revive the Slinky factory and reduce the stack of unpaid bills Richard had left her.

She rented a factory near Hollidaysburg, and four years later, the Slinky company finally made some money. Betty not only paid every bill, she included a thank-you note. "They had waited. And I was thankful, so I told them so," she says.

With the company springing back, Betty needed her own factory. But she had no land. The people of Hollidaysburg came to the rescue. They wanted the factory. They needed jobs. A local pharmacist called Betty and said, "Meet me down by the railroad line on Beaver Street." She went. He asked how much land she needed.

"Well," Betty recalls, "I didn't know an acre from a half-acre. So I said, 'I have six kids. How about six acres?' And he said, 'Fine. Is a dollar too much?' And I handed him a dollar."

Betty takes almost no credit for turning the Slinky company around. She says it was the people who helped her: the creditors, the townspeople and, most notably, her controller, Bob Lestochi, whom she hired many years ago. He is still with the company.

James Industries is a private company and does not reveal annual sales, but the Standard & Poor's Register estimates five to ten million dollars.

People with calculators in their pockets and advanced degrees are dumbfounded when they hear that Betty

James didn't sell the Slinky to some toy conglomerate years ago. She could have made zillions, and gone to sit poolside at some lovely condo on the coast of Florida for the rest of her life. It's not as if she hasn't had offers. "Oh, I have been wooed by some of the best," says Betty.

The closest she ever got was when CBS, the TV network, put in a bid. "They were offering me everything," says Betty. She almost did it. But then she took up a CBS executive's offer to visit the toy showroom. "So I went down, I looked, and then I called the man back. I said, 'I'm not going to sell to you. I think your toys look cheap. And I don't want to put my toy in there with yours.'

"I would have been much better off if I'd sold it," she admits. "But you know, these people working here, they're good people. And we're their livelihood. I have to think of them. Because I like them. Not all of them, you know, but most of them. And I have everything I need. I am happy."

Tom, her oldest son, is Slinky's sales manager. The rest of Betty's children are off doing other things, but the family, including her sixteen grandchildren, remains very close.

"You know, you fall and you land on your feet," Betty says. "And you don't count on standing up for long. Because life is at its best uncertain. Happy people are people who focus on what's important: other people. In fact, that might be the secret to happiness in old age right there. Being loving, and being loved. I can't think of anything more important."

Jeanne Marie Laskas

A Speedy Job

My sister answered an advertisement for a typist to work on a book on weather forecasting. She gave her typing speed as: "Approximately 55 w.p.m., with occasional gusts of 60 to 65 w.p.m."

She got the job.

Evelyn L. Lesch

"It says on your résumé that you can type
260 words per minute. No offense,
Mrs. Ballas, but I find that pretty hard to believe."

The Real Lesson

To love what you do and feel that it matters—
how could anything be more fun?

Katharine Graham

As a speech-language pathologist, I spent many years teaching students in a classroom setting. These students had such significant speech and language impairments in their native language that they required a smaller class size and instruction in classroom curriculum to be taught by someone with a background in the development of language.

While rewarding, at times this job could be exhausting. Imagine working all day with people who have difficulty getting their point across and understanding your point. These students needed instruction in the language that was to be used in the lesson before the lesson could ever be taught. Many days I was filled with frustration for I never got to the "real" lesson. I never got to the subtraction lesson. I was too busy teaching what the words "more," "less," "take away" and "equal" meant to students that did not naturally have these words in their everyday vocabulary. The lessons in my lesson plan book, the "real" lessons for the day, never seemed to take form.

On the Wednesday before Thanksgiving break, I got a "real" lesson from one of my students. I was busy trying to teach the "real" meaning behind the holiday of Thanksgiving. This is a holiday about feelings and emotions. Feeling and emotion words are difficult for language-impaired students. These words fall into a gray category. They are abstract. They are not simple to explain. Yet we never really think about having to teach a child what "happy," "sad," "exhausted" or "thankful" really means.

On this particular day, I was experiencing all of these emotions: *happy,* that a four-day weekend was coming, *sad* that my "real" lesson about Thanksgiving was getting lost in a sea of unexplained words, *exhausted* from the cooking and preparing we had done all week for our big classroom Thanksgiving feast, and *thankful* it would all be over in thirty minutes when the 2:30 bell rang.

In an attempt to teach the real lesson of this holiday, I read books to the students about the first Thanksgiving. We had to have elaborate discussions at the end of every sentence, sometimes in the middle, to explain vocabulary words such as: cranberries, mashed potatoes, cornucopia, pheasant, and so on. Most confusing were some of the Indian names. How could a full sentence be someone's name? Boy Who Runs with Wolf; Little Laughing Coyote. In an attempt to explain this, I gave each student an Indian name that fit their likes and dislikes. First this required a lesson on the words "like" and "dislike" and once again I was blown off course from the real lesson. I persevered, however, and each person got a name that fit his or her personality.

Now it was time to go to the long table we had set with our feast. With the announcement, "It's time for our

Thanksgiving feast," the students ran to the table. As if they were siblings fighting for parental attention, the seat at the head of the table became the most desired spot in the classroom. To end the arguing, I firmly announced, "My Indian name is 'She Who Sits at the Head of the Table' and I will be sitting at the head of the table." With this announcement, the students took their seats.

In an attempt to teach the real lessons of Thanksgiving, that we should be grateful for what we have, we should be thankful for the things that really matter, for the people that love us and care for us, I called each person by his or her Indian name and asked each to tell what he or she was most thankful for on this Thanksgiving. A surge of emotions, *sadness, disappointment, exhaustion,* surfaced as the responses were all material items. "Boy Who Runs Quickly" was most thankful for his Nintendo. "Girl with a Smile" was most thankful for her Barbie Dream House. Nobody got the real lesson. Had I even taught the real lesson or was all my instruction just a bunch of words with no meaning for these students? Had I wasted my time with hands-on activities to help these children know the emotional words associated with Thanksgiving: love, happiness, gratitude, thankfulness? I knew the answer to this question as each Indian boy and girl said they were most thankful for a meaningless object. No one was thankful for their mother, father, sister, brother, friends, not even a family pet. These were good, sweet kids with no way of expressing emotions I knew they had experienced. I knew they loved their parents. They were thankful for their families, the roof over their heads and the food in their stomachs, but no one had the words or the ability to recall the words and present them in the correct sequence for others to understand how they felt.

My last student, my quietest student, my most

language-impaired student, Christopher,* responded in a quiet simple voice. He found the words. He put them in the correct order. He connected them to an emotion. He showed me I had taught the real lesson. This quiet Indian boy stated, "I am most thankful for 'She Who Sits at the Head of the Table.'"

Ruth Reis Jarvis, M.A., C.C.C.

---

*Name has been changed.

The Red Purse

Love and kindness are never wasted.
They always make a difference.
They bless the one who receives them,
and they bless you, the giver.

Barbara DeAngelis

I know we are not supposed to judge people, but where Kennie was concerned, I found it impossible.

I decided he was the wrong person in the wrong kind of work.

I'm a swing-shift nursing supervisor, and it's my job to evaluate workers' performances at a convalescent hospital.

Kennie was a new employee, tall and very strong, not bad looking, with his blond hair cut to the collar and dark green eyes. After a few weeks' probation, I had to admit he was clean, punctual and reasonably efficient. But I just didn't like him.

Kennie looked like a hood. I knew the neighborhood he came from—a cesspool of gangs, drugs and violence. His language was street talk, his manner wry, his walk springy and controlled like a boxer's, and his expression closed off like the steel door on a bank vault. He seemed too large and carefully controlling of a powerful will to be able to fit into the highly specialized teamwork of a convalescent hospital.

The vast majority of our patients come to us in the final stages of terminal disease or with the most terminal of all diseases—old age. They come to us crippled, weakened, confused and defeated, no longer able to function out in the world. Many have lost the faculty of rational thought, a casualty of failing health and a world that often seems brutal and indifferent.

Mary B. was one of those. Attendants call her Mary B. because she was one of four Marys in the West Wing. At ninety-four years old, Mary B. was frail as a cobweb. She outlived her husband and sisters, and if she had any children, they had long since abandoned her. She was in almost constant motion as long as she was awake.

Mary B. had an obsession that someone had taken her purse. She searched for it all hours of the day and night. Unless tied to her bed or wheelchair, she would go through the door onto the street, into the men's wards, through the laundry room and into the kitchen, mindlessly searching and never giving up. When restrained, she wanted her wheelchair in the hallway, where she stopped everyone who came near.

"Can you lend me a comb?" she asked. "I've lost mine. It was in my red purse. My money is gone, too. Where is my purse? Where is my purse?"

Every day it was the same, until Mary B.'s queries became background noise, like the sound of carts loaded with hot trays rumbling down the halls, the hum of air conditioning or the static of the intercom.

We all knew Mary didn't have a purse. But on occasion someone would stop to listen to her out of kindness and concern, although we were furiously busy. Still, most of us maneuvered around her with, "Sure, Mary, if I see your purse I'll bring it back."

Most of us—but one.

The last thing I expected of Kennie was that he would listen to Mary B., but strangely, he always had a word for her.

What is he up to? I wondered, watching him. My first suspicion was that he might be working here to steal drugs. I thought I had spotted a potential troublemaker.

Every day as Mary B. stopped him to ask about her purse, and as Kennie promised to look for it, my suspicions grew. Finally I concluded that Kennie was planning something involving Mary. *He's going to steal drugs,* I told myself, *and somehow hide them around Mary. Then some accomplice will come in and sneak them out of the hospital.* I was so sure of all this that I set up more security systems around the drug-dispensing department.

One afternoon, just before supper, I saw Kennie walking down the hall with a plastic grocery bag in his hand. It was obviously heavy.

This is it, I told myself, scrambling from behind my desk. I started after him, but realized I needed more evidence. I halted behind a laundry cart, piled high with baskets.

It was tall enough to conceal me, but I still could see Kennie clearly as he strode down the hall toward Mary B. in her wheelchair.

He reached Mary and suddenly turned, looking over his shoulder. I dodged out of sight, but I could still see him peering up and down the hall. It was clear he didn't want anyone to see what he was doing.

He raised the bag. I froze . . . until he pulled out a red purse.

Mary's thin old hands flew up to her face in a gesture of wonder and joy, then flew out hungrily like a starved child taking bread. Mary B. grabbed the red purse. She held it for a moment, just to see it, then pressed it to her breast, rocking it like a baby.

Kennie turned and glanced sharply all around. Satisfied no one was watching, he leaned over, unsnapped the flap, reached in and showed Mary a red comb, small coin purse and a pair of children's toy spectacles.

Tears of joy were pouring down Mary's face. At least, I guessed they were.

Tears streaked my face, too.

Kennie patted Mary lightly on the shoulder, crumpled the plastic grocery bag, threw it into the nearby waste-can, then went about his work down the hall.

I walked back to my desk, sat down, reached into the bottom drawer and brought out my battered old Bible. Turning to the seventh chapter of Matthew I asked the Lord to forgive me . . .

At the end of the shift, I stood near the door used by the aides coming to and leaving work. Kennie came bouncing down the hall carrying his coat and radio.

"Hi, Kennie," I said. "How's everything going? Do you think you'll like this job?"

Kennie looked surprised, then shrugged. "It's the best I'll ever get," he grunted.

"Nursing is a good career," I ventured. An idea was growing. "Uh, have you ever thought of going on to college for a registered nursing degree?"

Kennie snorted. "Are you kidding? I ain't got a chance for anything like that. The nurse's aide course was free or I wouldn't have *this* job."

I knew this was true. Kennie set down his radio and pulled on his coat. "Take a miracle for me to go to college," he said. "My old man's in San Quentin, and my old lady does cocaine."

I clenched my teeth but still smiled. "Miracles do happen," I told him. "Would you go to college if I could find a way to help you with the money?"

Kennie stared at me. All at once the hood vanished, and I caught a glimpse of what could be. "Yes!" was all he said. But it was enough.

"Good night, Kennie," I said as he reached for the door handle. "I'm sure something can be worked out."

I was sure, too, that in Room 306 of the West Wing, Mary B. was sleeping quietly, both her arms wrapped around a red purse.

Louise Moeri

2

BALANCING WORK AND FAMILY

*There is no doubt that it is around family
and the home that all the greatest virtues,
the most dominating virtues of human society, are created, strengthened and
maintained.*

Winston Churchill

Getting My Priorities Straight

The great dividing line between success and failure can be expressed in five words: "I did not have time."

Robert J. Hastings

One of today's most precious commodities is time. No matter how many gadgets we buy, books we read or classes we take, there is no quick fix to busyness.

As a working mother, I constantly juggle the demands of work, personal interests, household errands and my children's school activities—games, practices, music lessons, rehearsals and performances. These activities are designed to enrich my children's lives and develop their skills, talents and values.

However, mothers can be so busy juggling that they lose sight of the true purposes for the child's participation in these activities. From infancy, children seek parental approval and attention. Parents heap tons of encouragement and praise as the baby learns to crawl, pull up, walk, speak, hit the ball—the list goes on and on. As the child grows older, simple learning tasks are replaced with other activities such as sports, cheerleading or music. Parents are always on the sidelines or in the audience cheering, cajoling, clapping and encouraging.

However, sooner or later, a working mother is faced with a major conflict between some personal or business commitment and her child's game, play, concert or other event. She can't be in two places at once. Her heart is ripped into pieces trying to decide what to do; what is best for her child; what would a good mother do; how to make a bad situation into a win-win for everyone.

I experienced one of those decisive situations when my daughter's school district hosted its annual "String Fest," where five school orchestras are packed into a gymnasium along with a sea of family and friends. The participants were to arrive about forty-five minutes earlier than the event's start time so that the musicians could tune and warm up their instruments. As often happens, the event occurred during a crunch period for both my husband's and my jobs. We arranged for my teenage son to drop off his sister at the appointed time.

My daughter, who was very much aware of my time-management efforts, attempted to cut me some slack by saying, "Mom, you don't have to come tonight. Just be there on time to take me home." I couldn't have asked for a better solution. I wouldn't have to fight the rush-hour traffic for my thirty-two mile commute. I could work a couple more hours. By then the traffic would be light, and I could make it to the gymnasium in record time. Besides, how many concerts had I already attended? I could afford to miss this one, right?

After pondering my choices, I decided it was not okay with me if I was absent. Even though my daughter had given me her permission to miss the concert, it did not justify my absence. I felt guilty enough for my not taking her to the concert. I left work and arrived just before the concert began. I found a seat in the bleachers several rows directly across from my daughter's orchestra. I had her in my line of sight, but in the ocean of faces, she would never see me.

As I watched, the warm-up session ended and my daughter put her violin aside. I saw my daughter's eyes as they began to scan the audience row by row, looking for a familiar face. When her eyes found me, I was waving my arms in that embarrassing way mothers do, and we exchanged smiles. Her body language said it all. I had "made her night." No promotion, raise, bonus or anything could ever pay for that moment. It was an image that is forever etched in our hearts and memories and could never be recorded with a camera or camcorder. It was just two hearts exchanging love across the gymnasium.

Sybella V. Ferguson Patten

"Instead of learning to organize my priorities
I've become comfortable with panic."

Reprinted by permission of Mark Litzler.

Just a Few More Minutes

The best thing to spend on your children is your time.

Louise Hart

"Just a few more minutes . . . please, Mommy!"

Although my own children were grown, I found myself turning instinctively in the direction of the little voice. He was trailing after his mother, looking reluctantly over his shoulder at a display of remote-control toys in the large department store.

He couldn't have been more than four years old. With chubby cheeks and wispy blond hair going in several directions, he trotted behind his mother down the main aisle of the department store. His boots caught my eye. They were green. Really green. Bright, shiny, Kermit-the-Frog green. Obviously new and a little too big, the boots stopped just below his knees, leaving a hint of dimpled legs disappearing into rumpled shorts. Perfect boots for the rainy transition from summer to fall.

He stopped abruptly at a display of full-length mirrors, lifting one foot at a time, grinning and admiring his boots until his mother called for him to catch up to her. Dressed in a suit, heels clicking on the tile floor, she was tossing items into her cart as she and her son made their way to the checkout lanes at the front of the store.

I smiled at the picture he made clumping noisily behind his mother. I found myself wondering if she had just picked him up from daycare after a busy day in an office somewhere. I sighed as I selected an item and put it in my own cart. My days of trying to juggle a full-time job and two small children had been busy, sometimes even hectic, but I missed them.

Finishing my own shopping, I forgot about the little boy and his mother until I stepped outside the store. There a panorama unfolded before me. The rain had slowed to a drizzle, perforating the numerous puddles in the parking lot. Several mothers with their small children were hurrying in and out of the department store. The children were, of course, making beelines to the puddles that dotted their way from the cars to the store's entrance. The mothers were right behind them, scolding.

"Get away from that puddle!"

"You'll ruin your shoes!"

"What's the matter with you? Are you deaf? I said, GET OUT OF THAT PUDDLE!"

And so it continued. The children were being pulled away from the puddles and hurried along. All except for one . . . the little green-booted boy.

He and his mother were not rushing anywhere. The boy was happily splashing away in the largest puddle in the parking lot, oblivious to the rain and to the people coming and going. His wispy hair was plastered to his head and a huge smile was plastered on his face. And his mother? She put up her umbrella, adjusted her packages and waited. Not scolding, not rushing. Just watching.

As she fished her car keys out of her purse, the boy,

hearing the familiar jingling, paused in mid-splash and looked up.

"Just a few more minutes? Please, Mommy?" he begged.

She hesitated, and then she smiled at him.

"Okay!" she responded and adjusted her packages again.

By the time I got to my car, loaded my packages and was ready to ease out of my parking space, the green-booted boy and his mother were walking toward their car, smiling and talking.

How many times had my own children begged for "just a few more minutes"? Had I smiled and waited like the mother of the green-booted boy? Or had I scolded?

Just a few more minutes of giggling and splashing in the bathtub. So what if bedtime got pushed back a little?

Just a few more minutes of rocking a sleepy toddler. So what if toys were strewn around the room, littering the floor?

Just a few more minutes of life with them before they were grown and gone. So what if my career goals didn't fit my original timeline?

Just a few more minutes. Everything I have read about time management for working mothers can be summed up in one picture. The picture of that young mother standing under her umbrella, arms full of packages, smiling at a wet, green-booted boy who had asked her the universal time-management question for working mothers everywhere, "Just a few more minutes?"

Sara Henderson

A Working Mother's Prayer

Now I lay me down to sleep,
I pray, the Lord, I won't get beeped,
My cell phone will not start to ring,
My e-mail will not sound a "ding."

I wish for peace throughout my house,
For silence quiet as a mouse,
No little children in my bed,
No thoughts of work run through my head.

And, while I'm at it, may I ask
For help with one of my worst tasks,
Getting my children out of bed,
Without my screams that wake the dead?

Let there be coffee made for me,
My clothing pressed . . . nylons run-free.
And let this be a good hair day,
Don't let me see more strands of gray.

Let there be milk for breakfast-time,
My car keys out for me to find,

The children dressed with matching socks,
Backpacks are filled with each lunch box.

I pray for traffic to be light,
My kids will have no backseat fights.
They'll have their coats, mittens and hats,
I'm off to work . . . ten minutes flat.

And once I'm there, please let me see,
A parking space out front for me.
My phone light will not be bright red,
A sign of my great day ahead.

I'm on a roll . . . so I will ask,
For no complaints, no nasty fax,
I'm left alone, nothing goes wrong,
No interruptions all day long.

I know that I must end this prayer,
But one more thing . . . or do I dare?
I know I've asked you for a lot,
But may I add just one more thought?

Lord, if you could just see a way,
For me to have one perfect day,
I'd be forever in your debt.
(I'll take whatever I can get!)

Cheryl M. Kremer

This Is the Best Day of My Life

The purpose of life, after all, is to live it, to taste experience to the utmost, to reach out eagerly and without fear for newer and richer experiences.

Eleanor Roosevelt

Being a mother of five children who were all born within seven years tells me I am either very crazy or I love being a mother. For me it is the latter. From the moment I felt the first baby moving within my womb I was hooked. I knew my calling in life. I went to college; I did all the things that the modern woman is told to do. But, all I really wanted was to be a full-time domestic goddess (as Roseanne Barr used to say).

For many years I was a full-time mother; however, I did have to supplement my husband's income to make ends meet. So I would tend and fall in love with yet more children. Not children that I gave birth to but working mothers' children. I loved those kids like my own. This allowed me to stay home with my own and share my love for others' children. A working mom is a happy mom when her kids are happy. Well, I did my very best to make sure that their kids were happy.

When my last child started school I decided that I would substitute teach at the local schools. I loved it. Again I was allowed to be home with my kids when they were at home. What I didn't realize was that I would be able to go on field trips with my own children. I would have freedom that I hadn't had in a long time. I had never been able to do this when I ran home daycare. I felt that it was a fair trade-off to be home with my kids.

My son, who was eight at the time, brought home a note for a field trip to be signed. For years I had always checked the "No" box where they ask for chaperones. He pleaded with me to go. I already had a substitute job scheduled for that day. I thought about it for a while and I checked the "Yes" box. Jonathan was thrilled to say the least. I quickly notified the teacher that I wouldn't be able to sub on that day, and she would have to find someone else. She wasn't thrilled but she understood.

The field trip day arrived. We were going to ride the "Bell Carol" steamboat down the Cumberland River and then walk to the Spaghetti Factory for lunch. The anticipation was just about to kill my son. He beamed with pride as we walked into the school building together. He introduced me to his class. I was so touched by his tender words and pride in me.

The bus ride from LaVergne, Tennessee, to downtown Nashville is about thirty minutes on a good day. This can be a very long time with ninety-plus kids on a bus. Jonathan wanted me to sit by him. I chose not to be the disciplinarian to the children that I was sitting by that day. I let the teachers and their aides do that. I focused my entire attention on my son, and we talked the entire ride. We talked about many fun and silly things. I listened while he talked. Our eyes met, and he looked deep inside mine and said, "Mama, this is the best day of my life." My heart was filled with true joy. A soft tear or two rolled down my face and Jonathan asked me, "Mama, don't cry; Mama, why are you crying?" And I answered, "Because you have made this one of the best days of my life."

The true joy of motherhood comes from the simple things that we do for and with our children.

Dian Tune Lopez

Two of a Kind

I work at home, so my four-year-old twin daughters, Maggie and Katie, are used to seeing me operate a computer and fax machine. One afternoon I was watching them have fun on our indoor playset's small slide. Maggie proceeded to go down headfirst, giggling that she was "faxing" herself. Not to be outdone, Katie stood at the top of the slide and shouted, "Here comes page two!"

Paula Ferrato

"Hello, Mom, I forgot my homework.
Would you fax it to me at school?"

What Goes Around, Comes Around

Sitting at my desk one morning, I was deeply engrossed in an important project—trying to rebutton my shirt so each button lined up with the right hole. One side of my blouse was definitely hanging at an odd angle and I wanted to fix it before most of my coworkers arrived. Making sure I'm dressed properly is something I normally do at home in front of a toothpaste-speckled mirror, but this morning there'd been no time. This morning I had played the home version of army boot camp.

My goal: to leave the house and drive to work. The obstacles: a toddler and a nine-year-old boy. Every time I tried to make a strategic move, like tying my shoes or finding my keys, there was a child at my feet who desperately needed something. My nine-year-old claimed he had to have a sandwich for school because the cafeteria was serving the wrong kind of pizza. He likes "personal pizza," which is round, but this day it was square. Apparently, the round pizza tastes like it just came from the oven of Italy's finest bistro, while the square pizza is inedible.

"It's too tomatoey," he explained.

Then my two-year-old sneezed just after I placed a heaping spoonful of oatmeal in his mouth. This necessitated a change of my clothes, but there was no time to be choosy.

It was my turn to drive my nine-year-old and his friend to the bus. I grabbed a clean blouse from the dryer, threw it on, and ran out the door with the whole gang. We made the bus, and I dropped my toddler at the sitter's before racing to work. Is it any surprise my shirt was buttoned wrong? I'm just glad it was buttoned.

As I contemplated what I could have done to ease the morning mayhem, several colleagues arrived in the office, including my boss. He had a funny expression on his face, like he was trying to hold in a sneeze. But it wasn't a sneeze, it was a grin.

"I have good news and bad news," he said. All present opted for the good news first. It turns out he and his wife are expecting a baby this summer—thrilling news.

My colleagues and I, many of whom have children, told him we knew he'd be a great dad. He and his wife, a schoolteacher, have been married several years and have big hearts. Their house is already filled with the playful chaos of five formerly homeless cats.

After a round of congratulations, I remembered his early words. "What's the bad news?" I asked.

"The bad news is the same as the good news," he said. He'll take a block of time off when the baby's born—good news for him, but bad news, i.e., a tougher workload, for the rest of us.

I didn't see it as bad news. Like they say, what goes around comes around. When I gave birth to my younger son, I took a four-month maternity leave. My boss covered for me, and I'm more than happy to do the same for him. Besides, when he's a father he'll have a better understanding of what it's like to juggle work and childcare.

The announcement that he'll soon be crib shopping meant we had a new person to initiate into the ranks of parenthood. We began giving him a preview of how his life will change.

"You won't be going to the movies anymore because

you'll need to buy diapers—lots and lots of diapers," one colleague intoned.

"Yeah, and then when the baby is out of diapers you'll be able to go to the movies again, but they'll all be cartoons," warned another. "Your whole life will be rated G."

My boss laughed and said that's why stores rent videos. He pointed out that he and his wife can still enjoy the pleasures of dining out.

"For now," said a female coworker. "But once the baby's older you won't be asking about the soup du jour any more. You'll be reading the 'Happy Meal' menu and trying to get through a dinner without someone spilling their drink all over you."

"So let me get this straight," my boss said. "I'll spend all my money on diapers, and I won't ever go to the theater or eat out? Well, I can still ride my bicycle this summer."

A male coworker, an experienced father, slowly shook his head. "Nope, you won't be doing any of that. No more bike trips."

My boss gave him a smug look and announced he could always get a buggy that attaches to his bicycle.

"Sure, you could do that, but it'll be a waste of money," said the dad. "My son didn't sleep through the night for months. His sleep cycles were reversed. When's your baby due? June? Trust me, you'll be too tired to go biking."

At this point a female coworker, the mother of two teenage daughters, walked over to put her two cents in. "Actually, you should go home and go to sleep right now. That way, you might have a chance at getting through this whole fatherhood thing," she advised.

"And don't worry if you come to work with your shirt buttoned wrong," I added. "We'll understand."

Linda Tuccio-Koonz

"My babysitter's got the flu."

Notes Left by Two Working Parents

Monday

Sweetheart,

It's Claire's turn to bring snack to school today. There's celery in the fridge. Cut it up into two-inch chunks, spread peanut butter on them and place five raisins on each. Wrap in cellophane (not a dry-cleaner bag!) and be sure there are twenty-four plus one for her teacher Ms. Goodesteem. Tidy the family room if you get a chance. Did you call the plumber yet?

I love you,
Allison

Monday

Honey,

That was okra not celery. Claire saw me spreading Cheez Whiz on them and cried twenty minutes until I forked over twenty-four pieces of Halloween candy (who told the kids the candy was hidden in the vacuum bag?). By the time I untied your son's doubleknots with your graduation pen, the family room was a lost cause. Dinner is on time-bake. I have Rotary tonight. Was the pen important?

Hugs and kisses,
Ken

Tuesday
Ken,

   The toilet has been asking for the plumber. You forgot Alasdair's milk money again. He says he owes some fifth grader $3.25 plus interest for milk loans. I have a meeting tonight. The mess has spread to the dining room.
Love,
Allison

Tuesday
Allison,

   I couldn't find Alasdair's lunchbox so I used your hat. Call the principal about the loan shark. Replaced your graduation pen—disregard the year. I think you took my car keys this morning—the taxi's here, got to go.
Sincerely,
Ken

Wednesday
Hey,

   Your keys were in the juice pitcher. The kids won't go to the bathroom—when's the plumber coming? I enjoyed our talk last night. We have to abandon the downstairs to the clutter and take refuge upstairs tonight. Dinner is on your son's top bunk.

Allison

Wednesday

Al,

We didn't have a conversation last night—our bed was full of kids; I slept with the dog. What's the plumber's phone number? Did you know Tuesday was class picture day, and your son wore his 'I'm with stupid' T-shirt . . . apparently he stood next to his teacher.

Ken

Thursday

The neighbor called—something about your son and some jumper cables. I said you'd stop by tonight and talk to them. I spoke with the principal, picture retakes are next Monday . . . I burned the shirt. We owe the principal $4.50 for loaning our son milk money, too.

A.

Thursday

Yesterday was Alasdair's snack day; luckily, I had gum. I promise I'll call the plumber today.

K.

Friday

Wife,

I had a breakfast meeting this morning. I sand-bagged the bathroom last night, call the National Guard if it crests. Any idea where the cat is?

Me

Friday

Husband,

Provisions are low and something is moving in the

living room . . . could be the cat. Order pizza and watch out for the waterfall on the stairs.

P.S. Bring your sleeping bag, we're in the attic divvying up the rest of the Halloween candy.

Ken Swarner

"I'll tell you what I don't like about a working mother.
I don't like the lunches my dad packs."

Reprinted by permission of Martha Campbell.

A Child's Playground

A child's playground could be anywhere—a backyard, the sidewalk, a ball field, a nursing home. A nursing home?

That's exactly where I spent my afternoons as an eight-year-old. The red brick building, whose back door opened up into our church parking lot, had been the local medical clinic until a modern hospital opened just a mile down the road.

As the new hospital opened, my mother informed me of another business opening in its former residence. It would be called a convalescent center. Those were mighty big words for an eight-year-old.

"A what?"

"A convalescent center. It's like a hospital but only for older people."

I had no reason to question my mother on this subject, especially after learning that she would be working at the conva . . . well, nursing home, which is what everyone else called it. This would be her first job, at least since my memory was established, and would most likely alter my convenient everyday routine. Coupled with the departure of my sister, who married earlier that year, this was really going to shake up my world.

Luckily the nursing home was a short distance from school, which allowed me to walk there some afternoons. At first I enjoyed my visits as educational, learning about my mother's job and getting to know the patients. My mother walked me down the hall and into the individual rooms, introducing me to the occupants of each bed. Some I knew already, many I knew by name, and most I knew by association with their families.

Few of the patients were mobile, most not able to venture out of their beds or much further than a nearby chair. Many could not feed themselves or tend to their personal needs without at least some assistance. Others could not even express themselves well enough to make their wants and wishes known.

My mother thrived on assisting the less fortunate. As a first-grader, I often waited outside the cafeteria for her to pick me up and take me home for a special-order lunch. Waiting along with me were members of the poorer families who couldn't afford to buy or even bring lunch. Before long, she was providing them homemade meals and delivering right to their chairs.

Some afternoons, as we waited for our ride home, she would go out of her way to come inside the school auditorium and give them money to spend on candy or ice cream, a luxury not always afforded to her own children. When I objected, she replied with New Testament logic.

"We must always take care of those who can't care for themselves."

Always spreading cheer, Mother was an angel-in-waiting to many of the patients, just what the doctor ordered or should have, and I was the tag-along on her skirt tail. Peeping around from behind her, too shy to speak aloud, I would be introduced even to the ones who couldn't see beyond the foot of their bed or remember my name after I left.

Still, I enjoyed walking the halls behind my mother and seeing the wrinkled faces light up as she entered each room. When tired of being a shadow, I took a seat in the front waiting room which retained its clinical aroma and reminded me that the people here were either sick or in need of assistance. It was there that I met my friend.

She was old like all the others, though at age eight it's hard to tell the difference between fifty and ninety. To a child there is no degree of old, just old. The skin of her face was wrinkled and her hair was white, two of my prerequisites for old age. What made her different was the way she moved about, as though she were dutifully carrying out a task and stopping only long enough to check on the child sitting alone in the brown Naugahyde chair, rubbing my hands along the silver, metal arms that appeared more like the guardrails on the patients' beds.

Pausing in front of the chair and peering from up above me like the Grinch looking down over Whoville, she grabbed under my arms and hoisted me into the air before settling into the chair herself as I plopped into her lap. Story after story she told until I became antsy and bolted, sprinting down the hall to find my mother.

Occasionally my friend chased after me and I would discard my shoes, sliding down the hall in stocking feet until a heavy wooden door or a concrete wall blocked my path. When the hallway wasn't my track, it was my playing field. I sometimes brought my own playthings, like a rubber baseball or a miniature football, and she tossed these to me as I slid down the hall and made diving catches up against the wall.

Having to retrieve an errant pass or fumble, I frequently ventured into various rooms where I happened upon surprised but delighted patients who were pleased to be visited by an eight-year-old with football in tow. Lonely and longing to belong, many were happy to be visited by anyone.

Some of the patients I knew by name, their great-grandchildren were friends or classmates, but my friend had no relatives with whom I was acquainted. I knew her by sight, by voice, by action. Every day I thrilled to hear her stories, none of which remain with me in my mental scrapbook, and every day I delighted to play outdoor games inside this clinical stadium, displaying recently learned skills which I continued to develop.

One year later I grew from an atypical eight-year-old into a typical nine-year-old. At that age, one year represents a generation of transformations. The time came for my mind to wander and my interests to change. After school, play-time with friends and neighbors took priority and captured the place of my trips to the nursing home. My visits became sporadic and eventually ended completely.

In that year, I'd learned more about life than school had taught me about any subject matter. From the men and women in those rooms, I learned that what we need most is one another. From my mother, I saw that one caring soul can make a difference in the health and happiness of others. From my friend, I learned that age doesn't matter and the differences in people when measured by age is far less than we envisioned.

Never forgetting that year of fun and frolic in the nursing home, my mother kept me abreast of the latest proceedings on a regular basis. Occasionally, I would inquire about the status of certain individuals, particularly those who were related to my friends and classmates. Some were doing well, some weren't, and some had passed to a better place.

Remembering my friend and worried that she may have met that same fate, I asked my mother if that patient I used to play with was still alive. If so, I wanted to know how she was doing.

She gazed at me with a quizzical look on her face. "Which patient?"

"You know. The white-haired lady that used to play ball with me and tell me stories."

Quickly her appearance transformed to one of comical disbelief. "Son, she wasn't a patient. That lady was the director. She was my boss."

I was humiliated. Maybe I should have guessed because of her behavior, but I was basing things on how she looked, which to me was "old."

Through the years, my nursing home days found protective shelter far back into my recollection. High school passed and college arrived, while that year in the nursing home was hidden from my thoughts, only to be revived on the evening news.

The year was 1976, and I was back home for a few weeks, taking a break from college studies. One Saturday evening our family was relaxing in the den with the television on, not that anyone was watching closely.

Reading the paper, I only glanced up if something caught my attention. While sewing, Mother occasionally peeked up at the screen, only to go right back to her household chores.

Suddenly, she pointed at the screen and looked over at me. "Do you recognize her?"

Not really paying attention, I asked, "Who?"

"Her," and she pointed at the white-haired lady being interviewed by the newsman. "Do you remember her?"

"Not really," and that was an honest answer. I had seen her on TV before but as far as knowing her personally, I couldn't say that I did.

"That's the lady you used to play with at the nursing home. Remember now?"

I did. Her face and mannerisms were no different than they were thirteen years earlier. She still seemed young and active though she again looked old. A chill came over me as I realized this was the same woman that used to tell me stories as I sat in her lap, and chased me down the hall, laughing as I slid and crashed into the wall.

Now, here she was on the national news, doing what she had been for the past several months. They called her Miss Lillian. She was helping her son, Jimmy Carter, campaign for president.

Tony Gilbert

6-14

To help employees feel more in touch with their children, the company day-care center incorporated a creative new design concept.

Safe

Maturity begins to grow when you can sense your concern for others outweighing your concern for yourself.

John McNaughton

I am the mother of two wonderful, beautiful and intelligent boys. I am also a caseworker at a county child welfare agency. It is my job to investigate child abuse.

Several months before my son Thomas's third birthday he asked me what I did for work. I tried to think of a way to explain to him what I did but also shield him from the knowledge that children are physically, sexually and emotionally abused by their parents and others they trust. How could I explain to my son that sometimes it was my job to take children away from their parents because their mommy or daddy hurt them so badly that they needed to be taken to the hospital? How could my son understand what I did in my work? I finally decided to tell him that it was his mommy's job to keep little boys and girls safe. I did not go into any more detail. Over the next several weeks I would hear my son telling people that his mommy's work was to keep little boys and girls safe, and then he seemed to forget about it.

The day after Thomas's third birthday I decided to take the day off from work to spend time with Thomas and Alex, his twenty-one-month-old brother. After saying goodbye to their father I turned to my boys and said excitedly that Mommy didn't have to go to work, she was going to spend the whole day with her boys! I looked down at Thomas, expecting to see an excited look on his face, but instead I saw tears well up in his eyes and his lips begin to quiver. I bent down close to him and asked him what was wrong. He looked at me with tears streaming down his face and said, "Who will keep the little boys and girls safe if you don't go to work?" I could not believe that my son who just turned three the day before was worried about the little boys and girls he did not even know.

I took my son in my arms and gave him a big hug and explained to him that there were other people who worked with Mommy to help her keep the little boys and girls safe. We hugged each other for several more minutes as I tried to assure him that the little boys and girls would still be safe even if Mommy stayed home. When he finally felt secure he went off to play with one of his new toys.

I sat there on the floor for a few minutes longer and was just amazed by the concern and compassion my son felt for these children that he had never met. I hope my children never have to see the abuse of children that I have seen or face the difficult decision I make on a daily basis to keep children safe and alive. I never explained what "safe" meant to three-year-old Thomas, but I believe that he understands its meaning very well.

Andrea Durham

Household Chores

For the first few years after my marriage ended, I worked part of the time from home and added in a couple of part-time jobs to help make ends meet. Getting the housework done—never one of my favorite things, even when I was at home full time—tended to fall by the wayside.

As my eldest son's twelfth birthday approached, I thought of something that might help. Birthdays are major celebrations in our family. The night before the big day, I rummage through photo albums and boxes to find pictures that illustrate the birthday child's life—from birth to now. These are taped all over the side of the fridge. We have cake and ice cream and candles and many small presents to be opened and enjoyed.

That year, I added something extra. "Now that you are twelve, Matthew," I told him, "you are old enough for the Laundry Initiation." He laughed as I pinned a towel around his neck like a cape.

"To the laundry room!" I announced. The other three children followed us, but I held up my hand to stop them at the door. "I'm sorry," I told them, "but you have to be twelve years old for the Laundry Initiation." I closed the door firmly, with them on the other side.

I introduced Matthew politely to the washer and dryer and told him how the Magic Knobs work. Then I produced a basket of his laundry and demonstrated how to sort the clothes, and the settings to use for each type.

"Now," I told him, "you are a Laundry Master!"

From that day forward, Matthew did his own laundry. And as each of the other children turned twelve, they, too, were initiated and became Laundry Masters themselves.

I was amazed at how much it helped me to be relieved of that one responsibility. I helped them master other skills over the next few years: washing dishes, dealing with garbage and recycling, putting away groceries in an organized way. It didn't occur to me at the time that it was benefiting the children as well. Years later, when they went off to university, they regaled me with stories of their inept roommates who couldn't do laundry, wash dishes or prepare meals. They appreciated that I'd helped them learn the skills of everyday life.

Dan, my third child, was especially proud of his ability to prepare meals. That came about because some six years after starting out as a single parent, I finally got my first full-time job. I liked the work, but the office was an hour away and the days were long.

For the first few weeks, I'd arrive home at 6:45 or 7:00 at night and start preparing supper. I was hungry, the kids were hungrier, and by the time we actually sat down to eat everyone was tired. I found that they were snacking on buttered toast and bowls of cereal in the hours after school so often they didn't have room for the more nutritious meal I'd prepared.

So we came up with another plan. Each Sunday I would sit down and plan meals for the following week, based on the food we had in the house.

But who would do the cooking? Matthew had a

part-time job after school. Lisa was in rehearsal for the school play. It turned out that fourteen-year-old Dan was usually the first one to arrive home, and so he took the responsibility to prepare the meal for us each night.

We spent a couple of weekend evenings cooking together, and I taught him basic techniques. And for the rest of that year, he made supper for us every night.

Yes, there were a few disasters. We still laugh about the time he added the large can of lentils to the spaghetti sauce rather than the small one I'd intended to be used. You can definitely go too far when it comes to lentils.

Even with too many lentils, it was a great feeling for me to walk in the door and smell dinner cooking in the oven or simmering on the burner. We were able to start our evening around the table together, enjoying a simple but nutritious meal and sharing the events of the day.

A couple of years later, when I was no longer working full-time but doing freelance work and some part-time contracts again, I read an article about things that make us feel loved. The author commented that some people need to hear the words "I love you," others feel loved when they receive gifts and others need physical affection to really feel cared for. Intrigued, I asked my children what made them feel loved.

Dan's answer surprised me the most. "I felt loved when I made dinner every night when you were working full-time," he said.

"That made you feel loved?" I was incredulous. I'd often had moments of guilt over asking so much of my children, worrying that as a single parent I was overburdening them with chores.

"Yeah, it did," he said. "I liked learning to cook with you. And I felt that you trusted me to make the meals for the whole family. That was a big responsibility, and that made me feel loved."

I look at our household chores differently now. They are not painful and annoying tasks to be parceled out; they are part of what it means to be a family together. They are opportunities for each of us to demonstrate love for each other and to feel loved in return.

Teresa Pitman

The Girl Inside the Woman

I have an image in my head—an image of a woman (me) whose life is calm, ordered, nourishing. My days are spent on rich simplicities. I roll out a piecrust, arrange flowers in an ironstone pitcher, frame a favorite snapshot for the family-picture wall.

When my children come home from school we make cookies, play duets on the piano, and then sit around the kitchen table with popcorn and cocoa. The children confide in me, beg me to tell stories about my childhood. When I do, they take in the deep lessons and feel closer to me.

In my image, my work—writing—is something I do while the pies bake and the bread rises. It doesn't take me away from home or inconvenience anyone in my family. Issues of feminism do not exist. There are no angry words, no power struggles. The household runs smoothly, effortlessly. And at the end of each satisfying day I sit in front of the fire, holding hands with the man who is my partner.

The woman in this image is the woman I thought I would be. There was going to be no divorce (I am now married for the second time), no career conflict (I've tried in vain for twenty years to find a workable balance between home and career) and an infinite number of children (I have one daughter of my own, a stepson and a stepdaughter).

The image is a legacy from an old me—a girl who was raised in the 1950s. I am now a modern woman, living in a world very different from the one that fostered my expectations. I am a woman who for a time raised a child alone. A self-supporting woman who takes care of her own income taxes and car repairs. A woman for whom an egalitarian marriage is a necessity. It therefore surprises me that while driving in the rain on worn-out tires a voice in my head scolds, "What kind of a man would let his wife drive around on unsafe tires?" My intellect may be in this day and age, but my emotions have not yet caught up.

The old me is suspicious of the new, meet-the-deadline professional me, and worries: Am I a good mother? Do I spend too much time on my career? Am I cheating my family? Am I cheating myself? The modern me worries too: Maybe I should have accepted that full-time staff job even though it would have meant long hours and a grueling commute. I should be working more, earning more.

Where does the old image come from? It's a composite picture of moments from my childhood that I want to sustain and always thought I would re-create for myself and my children. And it is kept alive today by the idyllic, homey scenes that are so often shown in ads. For example, a TV commercial shows a mother looking through a rain-spattered window. She holds up a cup of coffee, and her tender smile is for the boy who tumbles off the school bus in a bright-yellow slicker. A voice in me says, *See? That is the way it's supposed to be.* I feel a sinking sense of loss, and a longing for a time when my mother was always there, totally loving and protecting.

Many women today think and feel as I do. But we can't carry it off. After all, we do not live in the same world our mothers lived in when they were our age. Back then, roles were better defined, certain morals and values were accepted as givens, things were calmer, simpler. Today we have to pick our way through a profusion of divergent values and options, with demands on us that we could not have anticipated when we were growing up and forming expectations for our lives.

Thirty years ago, our mothers enjoyed the camaraderie of women with shared goals. The large majority of women stayed home. Today only 7 percent of households fall into the traditional category—working father, a housewife and one or more children at home. The homogeneity that gave our mothers comfort does not exist for us. Today our lives are fractured and we are insecure, cautious of one another, defensive about the roles we've assumed.

Housewives, now a vanishing breed, say they often feel lonely and isolated. And women who've never had the opportunity to stay home tend to romanticize what their lives would be like as housewives. The woman in the old image has concerns that are homespun, family-centered. More is now expected of women. To the original list— cooking, cleaning, chauffeuring, sewing, laundering, being sexually attractive—has been added wage-earning, political awareness, physical fitness, sexual fulfillment and, above all, a new-woman gutsiness.

Thirty years ago there was no need to fret if we didn't understand the Common Market or know how to fix a fuel pump. But today if we need holes drilled or shelves installed, we know how to use a drill and hammer. We cannot let ourselves get away with playing helpless. And if the girl in us occasionally wants to sit back and let someone else do it, we feel embarrassed. We forget that men can have those feelings, too.

But then, the woman in the old image never admitted that men had those feelings at all. The way she related to a man—her man—was fairly clear-cut. She catered to his comforts. He thanked her with flowers, a new dress, a new washer-dryer. She fluttered her lashes, admired his muscles and stamped her foot when she was angry. She was adorable, always. He treated her as if she were fragile, and she treated him as if he were strong. If at times he didn't feel strong or she didn't feel fragile, they pretended anyway.

Most of us have no regret about saying good-bye to that system; we welcome the partnership approach to marriage. But conditioning dies hard. We grew up believing that we should look to our husbands for the final word. It's not so easy to assume an assertive posture, and we often slip up. Set out to persuade a man and find, to our horror, that we've slid into baby talk. Get into an argument and wind up in tears. Fix the furnace "all by myself" and we're waiting excitedly for his praise. We defer to a man and then resent him for "having the power"; we assert ourselves and worry that we've been too "pushy." We careen back and forth between old-image and new-image perceptions of men and of ourselves.

Yes, it is nice that he disposes of the dead mouse or finds out why the roof leaks. But we can no longer sit in the car while he changes the tire in the rain. We know that in order to be fully responsible we must participate fully. And this means we can't just be strong when it feels good, but also when it means getting cold, wet and grimy.

Still, going back to the old way—our husbands at the door with flowers—is appealing more often than we like to admit.

And even more appealing is the old image of men as the good providers. In the fifties, women could be fairly relaxed about money; the economy felt predictable, solid. But many mothers must work today to keep their families in the middle class. That fact can cause a painful conflict for the modern mother.

Children are a crucial part of the romance in the old image. Children are why we blow up birthday balloons, visit amusement parks, crank ice cream by hand. In the old image, mother was the center of her children's life. Perhaps that's why, during the twelve years I've been rearing a daughter, I've worried that my career has cheated her of things only a full-time, at-home mother can provide. What I have failed to see is that the world around us has been changing fast, and my daughter's reaction to my job is not the reaction I would have had if my mother had worked thirty years ago.

Yet many of us continue to worry. How can we deny our children the things our mothers gave us? It doesn't occur to us that children today may not need—or want-- as much of the close-range doting we had. Not that they don't need love, discipline, guidelines and attention, but that the kind of attention they need is not the kind our image has in mind for them. Even if we could re-create the old image for ourselves, it seems our children would find it quaint.

So we remain divided between the old and the new. We lurch back and forth between the two, looking for focus, clarity, definition. It would help if we could simply accept the ambivalence in us, since the ambivalence is not likely to go away. There will always be a part of us that swoons over a romantic novel. But we are also women with spunk who can do—and do—some of the toughest jobs on Earth. We are, like men, both strong and vulnerable. We are a blend of the old images and the new. Both parts of us are valuable. Both parts are worth hanging on to.

Peyton Budinger

First in Her Heart

A mother is she who can take the place of all others but whose place no one else can take.

Cardinal Mermillod

My daughter, Ariel, was two months old when I returned to my more-than-full-time job as a psychiatry resident. I'll always remember how anxious I felt the first time I put her in our nanny's arms. Before long, friends and relatives started barraging me with "working-mother conflict" questions: How was I balancing things? What time did I get home at night? Did I worry about the nanny horror stories I'd heard?

But the question that continued to haunt me for more than a year was the one I heard from women who had decided to stay home with their children: "Your baby still knows who her mommy is, right?" Remembering those words could turn my feelings of relief and gratitude that we'd found a great sitter to feelings of jealousy and insecurity as I let myself wonder: *Did Ariel know who her mommy was? Would she consider the woman with whom she spent eight waking hours a day—when I was only home for two or three—her mommy? Would she and I be able to bond?*

I should have known better. The child of a working mother myself, I was raised in a family where everyone had a career, and I've always heard stories about how my brother and I would rush from our nanny to our mother at the end of every day. My mother and I have always been close, speaking on the phone almost daily, sharing confidences, support and advice. But still, I worried. My mother, a nurse, had always worked fewer hours than I do, and she was never away overnight on call. My brother and I also spent lots of time with other relatives, who never let us forget who our mother really was.

When Ariel was seventeen months old, we decided to spend a few months in Pasadena, California, because my husband was offered a visiting professorship at a university there, and our nanny agreed to accompany us. I arranged to work at a local clinic that would give me more time off to spend with Ariel than I usually had. Yet I felt trepidation along with excitement. Our nanny would be living with us, and I worried that Ariel would get mixed up sometimes and call her Mommy. Would she run to me if she fell and got a boo-boo? Would she still bring me her books at bedtime? During our three months in California, Ariel never once confused Nanny and me. But when we spent time at the park, I occasionally heard some of the other toddlers calling an aunt or a friend Mommy. I realized that it's normal for young children to generalize; it says nothing about their attachment to their moms.

Ariel made it obvious that she loved her nanny—asking for her in the morning, giving her hugs and greeting her with a big smile when we returned from an outing—but she also knew that their relationship was different from hers and mine.

When I was at home, Ariel always wanted me to be the one to read to her or give her lunch. And although she'd wave bye-bye happily when I told her I was going to work, she'd protest loudly if I left for any other reason. One morning she cried when I said I was going for a run, but cheered up when I amended to it, "Mommy's going to work out." Ariel had come to think of work as an ordinary and expected event that separates us only temporarily, and apparently the only acceptable reason for my absence. I always try my best to convey to her that even when we are apart she remains my top priority. A working mom is still a full-time mom.

It's clear to me now that the women who had asked me whether Ariel knew I was her mommy weren't purposely trying to make me feel guilty; they were trying to reassure themselves that their decision to stay home was the best thing for their babies. Most of us want to do a superlative job, and there are no easy definitions of what that is. Unfortunately, at-home mothers and working mothers continue to throw darts at each other, and I'm convinced that it's out of insecurity. We all want to know that the choice we have made is the right one—and both choices involve sacrifices. All parents need to feel that the sacrifices are indeed worth it.

During these first two years of Ariel's life, I've come to a better understanding about what it means to be a mother. It's not the number of hours you devote to your child, nor the specific activities you share. It's more the way your child gets inside your very being and remains there twenty-four hours a day.

As creative, caring and responsible as our caregiver was, her relationship with Ariel was still defined by the fact that it was a job. She eventually left us to get married and start a family of her own. Our new babysitter used to work for friends who moved out of state. Sitters come and go in families, just as children come and go for sitters. But a mother is there forever: physically, for the first eighteen years or so, and spiritually, for the rest of a child's life.

Doris Iarovici, M.D.

"His parents want to make sure
they don't miss seeing him take his first steps."

A Hug for Your Thoughts

"Mom, you're always on the computer!" Laura grumbled.

"No, I'm not," I defended.

"Every day I come home from school you're working on the computer."

"Well, at least I'm here for you!"

My daughter, Laura, at twelve years old, was right. Day after day, in my home office, I would stare into space as my hands typed out the thoughts of a presentation or of research completed for an article. It seemed that my work as a writer and speaker cemented my fingers to the keyboard and my mind to valuable ideas. What Laura did not realize was that during her day away, I'd also be doing a load of laundry, answering incoming phone calls, cleaning up dirty dishes, crunching an editor's deadline, sorting the family mail, networking and marketing my speaking service. It was only around three in the afternoon that I'd finally collapse at my desk for a few precious moments of deep thought. Then she'd come in from school.

I prided myself on being available to my children. After all, I am a speaker on child behavior and parenting. But Laura's observation stung my conscience. Her perception of me must have been of a mom who was available but unapproachable. Hardly the image I wanted to project. My relationship with my children is more important than any other career.

"Laura," I called, "come here a minute."

Out of her bedroom, Laura strolled down the hall to my doorway. I had decided to have her alert me when I was obsessed with work. I wanted her to have the power to let me know when she thought I was being aloof.

"So you think I'm preoccupied?" I asked.

"Most of the time," came her honest reply.

After I explained my full schedule and the fact that I chose to office from home to be accessible to her and her sister, I offered Laura this compromise.

"Whenever you feel I'm ignoring you or you need my attention, I want you to hug me," I said. "Just come up and give me a little hug, and that'll be our signal that you need me."

Years later we still have that unspoken sign. I've become much more sensitive to my daughters' comings and goings. And on the days I'm not, Laura gives me a little squeeze to remind me of the real reason I work from home.

Brenda Nixon

Trouble Brewing

After an exhausting weekend, I woke up Monday morning and sleepily packed lunch for my eight-year-old. When I got home from work late that day, she handed me a note from her teacher, requesting I see her. "What's this all about?" I asked sternly.

Opening her lunch box, my daughter showed me the drink I had given her that morning. It was a can of beer.

Cynthia Briche

Mom's Special Day

Love doesn't make the world go 'round.
Love is what makes the ride worthwhile.

Franklin P. Jones

In the early eighties, when my two sons were toddlers, I put them in day care when I went to work. Like thousands of other working moms, I, too, was plagued by the articles and news stories about the negative impact of children growing up in day care. Despite the growing ranks of women in the workplace, society's message still seemed to be: "Mothers belong at home with their children." Period! End of discussion.

Although I was doing my best to balance wholesome family life with an aggressive career track, I was filled with guilt and self-doubt. *Am I ruining my kids for life by sending them to day care? Will they resent me? Should I be a stay-at-home mom?*

On Mother's Day 1993, at the traditional eighth-grade Mother's Day Tea, the answers to my questions came in a very unexpected way. To celebrate this day, the children had written poems about their mothers. I sat there, listening to poems describing cookie-baking, Halloween-costume-making, birthday-party-giving and car-pool-driving moms. There was laughter and plenty of tears as we all heard how our teenage children saw us.

Then it was Justin's turn. As he walked to the front of the room, I held my breath, and my stomach did a flip-flop. How would his poem describe me?

My Mom

> *How will you be remembered?*
> *A woman who owned her own business and became*
> *very successful,*
> *You will be remembered by the way you fulfilled all*
> *your dreams,*
> *How you spent time looking after kids while you*
> *reached the top—*
>
> *Two young boys, rowdy as monkeys.*
> *You were a great mom, a great wife, a great person—*
> *Mom, how on earth did you do it?*
>
> *Legends will be told about you, Mom.*
> *When I needed help, you were there.*
> *Your shoulder was a place where I could rest my head.*
>
> *What would I do without you?*
> *How would I survive?*
> *What I'm trying to tell you is, I love you, Mom.*

—Justin

In those few glorious moments, as I heard his words, all my doubts and fears about being a working mom were put to rest. Then and there, I knew, after years of baby-sitters, camps and day-care, that my son did not resent me. To the contrary, he let me know that through it all, I was always there when he needed me. He let me know that he was proud of me.

When he finished reading his poem, he looked over at me, sitting in the front row of the audience. He smiled that wide glimmering, silvery smile that only kids with braces are capable of. My first impulse was to race up and wrap my arms around him—like you would a small child—yet I resisted. Justin was a thirteen-year-old young man, and the process of "letting go" had begun. A thumbs-up from one proud mom said it all.

Connie Hill

Kiss

I'm in the military, and being on time is always an issue. I woke up late that morning, left late . . . the day was going horribly. My six-year-old son wasn't speedy enough for me which increased my frustration. We finally left for school and I was in no mood for chit-chat. Halfway there I felt bad for all my grumblings that morning. It wasn't his fault I got up late. *He's only six,* I thought, but didn't relent. We got to school, gave a quick hug and kiss and then I left. While thinking about what lay ahead for the day, still worrying about being late, I backed out of the school parking lot. Something told me to look up. There he was, my sweet precious child blowing a kiss in the window. It stopped me in my tracks. For all the grumbling I had done that morning, all the yelling to hurry up, that one blown kiss made me stop. *Who cared if I was late?* I certainly didn't, not by then at least. My boss and my job would wait. What really mattered here? It was a simple reminder to slow down, lighten up, keep it simple. My six-year-old reminded me time really didn't matter, only love. I'll try harder not to forget that lesson, Son—I love you, too.

Katherine Pepin

My Two-Piece Suit

I base most of my fashion taste on what doesn't itch.

Gilda Radner

When I was in high school, I knew that I wanted to be in public relations. I wasn't sure if I wanted to go into an agency or corporate setting, but what the heck, I had four years of college to figure that out. College was interesting and finally getting into my major was like the light at the end of the tunnel. This was me! I loved the classes, the writing, the teachers and the excitement of an internship with a public relations agency.

During my sophomore year, little did I realize that I had met the man I was to marry. He was older and was starting his own drywall construction company. We dated for a year and during my junior year I excitedly attended my first professional Public Relations Society of America Convention, briefcase intact, and had my head filled with grandiose thoughts of corporate America. I wanted to be the two-piece suit, single-minded, full-speed-ahead public relations woman of the year!

When I returned from the convention, I knew I had to break up with this man to pursue my dreams because I didn't want to stay local. I wanted to be able to relocate at a moment's notice. Chicago or New York were only a job offer away, and I couldn't be tied down. I had just been nominated for Public Relations Student of the Year at college and had an interview lined up with the marketing director for a major airline. *Could life get any better than this?*

Thanksgiving weekend I realized that a career was the most important thing in my nineteen-year-old life. I wanted to work the forty hours-plus, attend business meetings, have an expense account and drive a sports car as I sped to meet deadlines from demanding clients. With "corporate" stars in my eyes, I told my boyfriend about my dreams. I told him he wasn't able to be a part of that dream because of his newly formed company that was starting to take root. He slowly reached for an Old Spice cologne box and handed it to me. I looked at him thinking, *Okay, he doesn't know how to shop at a department store and buy a girl a gift.* I opened up the box and found a little black jewelry box with the most beautiful ring inside. I was shocked as he proposed to me after I had just told him I thought we should start seeing other people.

I have found out that life truly throws you a bouquet when you least expect it. Work is always going to be available, whether it's doing what you love, hope to love, or need to do to pay the rent. I was a twenty-year-old married girl finishing her senior year in college (that was the only way my parents gave us their blessing/approval to marry!). I graduated and went through the grueling proc - ess of interviewing even though I wasn't in New York. The interviews were full of rejections and praises as I was eventually hired as an advertising coordinator for a local trade magazine.

I liked my job and couldn't believe someone was

actually paying me to do something I enjoyed. My job allowed me to pursue my career, but again life was going to throw me another unexpected bouquet. I was pregnant and experiencing a gut-wrenching bout of morning sickness that lasted my first trimester. I stopped working for the magazine and helped my husband with his business. "Our" company was growing, and I went from ads to architectural blueprints! Not that I could read them, but I organized the office, did the books/payroll and paid bills. This wasn't a top-ten agency, there weren't any dress codes and there wasn't the glamour I had envisioned in my earlier days, but there was the excitement of seeing my name on our own business cards and immense pride in the man I loved who showed me working for ourselves wasn't so bad after all.

Our first son Nick was born, and I worked for my husband running the office. I'll never forget having to calculate from a book and pay the weeks' payroll in a hospital bed shortly after our second son, Kyle's, birth! At the same time, I was able to work at home and be the closest thing to a stay-at-home mom. Our business continued to grow, and so did our family. We were blessed with a daughter, Jacqueline. I loved being a mom, joining every play group in a one-mile radius of our home! By the time our oldest was four, we had outgrown our home office and relocated to a nearby business park. I had to take our children to a sitter, but I was only a phone call away.

I had my hands full with three kids. I looked forward to going to work part-time and that continued for the next two decades. I am living the realization of a dream as I walk into our office that has an office manager, superintendents, computers and phones in every office, a coffee machine with freshly brewed coffee, a copier and a warehouse of construction tools and trucks. I look at a company that was built with hard work, dedication and sacrifices through some of the lean years. It's not a PR firm, but it's a family business that has endured through perseverance, faith and patience. Our company proudly employs four out of five members of our household, and our daughter has already put in a few days of work this summer.

I got dressed one morning and looked at my favorite two-piece suit that I could never give away after all these years. It still hangs in my closet after twenty-one years of marriage and three teenagers. Our twenty-five-year-old company that started with such fragile roots has endured the highs and lows of construction and currently employs other men and women who have their own dreams. I haven't worn that two-piece suit lately, but when I look at it, I have no regrets in having walked down a totally different pathway than I had so eagerly anticipated. My business meetings turned into PTA and Safety meetings, my sports car turned into a Suburban, my expense account turned into a checking account, but demanding clients are definitely part of our daily business. Corporate America came to me and I thank God for that Old Spice box that gave me the best public relations job I could have ever asked for. I happily and proudly represent our company and beam with pride when someone asks me who I work for. Tomorrow, I may even wear that two-piece suit to work!

Elizabeth Neri Schorr

Vacuum Cleaner Marks—
Tracks to a Mother's Heart

Lost time is never found again.

Thelonious Monk

I perched on the edge of a tiny chair as my scissors marched around crisp paper, freeing yellow ducks from their construction-paper prison. I worried how I'd finish all the day's chores after work that night.

Homework, errands, supper and too many loads of laundry consumed my life. Forget relaxing. Who has time? I looked out the window of the teachers' lounge at the kindergarten children chasing each other through fifteen minutes of recess and wondered when my time to have fun would return.

"My son turned thirty yesterday," Chris said, startling me from my reverie.

"Does it make you feel old?" I asked, secretly wishing my own children weren't quite so young.

"Well, not as old as some other things," she said. "He doesn't live close by, and we couldn't see him on his birthday. I miss the cakes and presents on the day of his birth—it just isn't the same five days later."

I nodded. My mother, too, needed to connect with me on my birthday, the day when I was most her child.

The conversation drifted, and Chris asked me how it felt to be working again after so many years home with the children.

She understood my frustration and fatigue. She had enjoyed staying home with her children, but when she went back to work, she discovered something she hadn't considered: Her children learned things could be different and still good. If the cookies weren't made exactly the same or if supper happened at 6:00 P.M. instead of 5:00, no one starved. They learned where the bathroom cleaner was and how to use it.

"I remember those days well, Julia," she said with a sigh. "Some of them I wouldn't want to revisit at all. But some I look back on and chuckle."

I looked down at the ducks and sighed. *Here it comes,* I thought. *Another mother telling me to enjoy my children while they are still young.* "Before you know it they'll be gone, and then it'll be quiet," these moms often say. Honestly though, right then I'd have liked a bit of quiet. And I did enjoy my children; I just wished I didn't have to enjoy them quite so much some days.

"Vacuum cleaner marks," she said.

"Vacuum cleaner marks?" I asked, wondering if I'd missed something while I was feeling sorry for myself.

"The marks the vacuum cleaner leaves after you've done a whole room," she said with a laugh. "The last thing I did in each room was vacuum, and when I looked back, the carpet stood at attention with those lovely clean-looking lines. I knew it was clean when I saw that.

"When the kids came home from school they trotted across the room, leaving footprints in their wake. It took less than five minutes for my clean house to look lived-in again."

Unlocking my front door after work, I dreamed of my own home decorated with crisscross marks from the vacuum cleaner. But four children tumbled through the door after me, and the dream popped like a bubble from a sink of soapy water.

Later, a full bottle of pickles spilled on the carpet, homework forgotten at school, a fight about who got the blue cup last, and a ruined piece of artwork filled my evening.

I had almost forgotten about my conversation with Chris when shouts and thumps from the family room forced me to fling my dish towel over my shoulder and march in that direction like a general ready for battle. My footsteps reverberated through the house.

But I didn't want to deal with another fight. I really wanted to crawl under something and hide, escape from the myriad chores and constant squabbling echoing off walls. I dropped down onto the floor to retrieve a thrown book.

Instead, I leaned over and peered under the couch—a potential retreat from chaos. Although toys were crammed into every inch of space under there, I mentally calculated how fast I could yank them out and crawl under before anyone noticed.

"What ya doing, Mom?" questioned my four-year-old daughter. Her head cocked to one side, she looked like a cocker spaniel with her big blue eyes and pigtails that stuck out at odd angles.

"Looking for a place to hide," I said with a sigh as I flopped onto my back.

"Can I come?" She giggled and plopped down beside me. "Oh, Mommy, I don't think we'll fit under there."

I didn't want to tell her I was thinking of an escape route rather than a new game.

As she tucked herself under my arm, she grabbed a book and held it in front of my face with a "Please read it, just once." Dirty dishes scattered around the kitchen and a catalog of chores longer than my grocery list haunted me.

But, as I searched for an excuse, I became aware of something not often heard at my house—silence. The squabbling had stopped, and my three older children were moving closer. Like stray kittens who've been presented with a saucer of milk, they closed in on the coveted prize. I opened the book and began to read.

My voice washed over us like a blanket, chores and homework losing their importance with each turned page. Warm bodies, that minutes ago had been cold and angry, cuddled and curled around each other.

They snuggled in for one last story, and my mind drifted across the turbulent waves of the day and came to rest on the shore of contentment. Dishes undone, but reconnection achieved. Maybe we should end every day elbow to elbow and toe to toe.

And maybe I can wait a few more years for vacuum cleaner marks that last longer than five minutes.

Julia Rosien

Picture-Perfect Bologna

My mother-in-law's reputation as a cook extraordinaire is without blemish. Rumor has it if she swished her hand in a pan of dishwater, her guests would rave it was the best soup they ever tasted.

Her culinary skills were tested daily as she prepared three meals for fifty or more guests at the ranch-resort where she was employed as a cook. She didn't own a measuring cup or spoons. Her knack for blending just the right amount of ingredients made every meal she prepared a mouthwatering masterpiece.

Hers was the generation before fast-food restaurants, drive-throughs and cafeteria lunches for kids. She didn't know the luxury of grabbing a quick meal on the way home when her last ounce of energy was spent on the evening shift. Her kitchen chores extended into the wee hours after returning home to her family of eight children.

And so it was, late one night, when she began making sandwiches for the family's next-day lunches. She reached into the refrigerator for a jar of mayonnaise and the almost-empty package of bologna. She had packed so many lunches, she could make bologna sandwiches with her eyes closed. And a good thing it was, because most nights it was difficult to stay awake as she spread mayonnaise on the row of white bread slices. She tucked the last pieces of bologna into two sandwiches for her youngest son.

The following evening, during the sandwich-making ritual, her youngest son came into the kitchen.

"Mom, I want to talk to you about my lunch."

"You want something different than bologna?"

"No. Bologna's fine," he said. "It's about today's lunch."

"Oh?"

"Well, Mom . . . the first sandwich was good. It was the second one that was hard to chew."

"Why is that?"

"The first sandwich was real bologna. The second sandwich was the cardboard picture of bologna from the top of the package."

A picture-perfect bologna sandwich. Her reputation remains untarnished.

Diane M. Vanover

Ceiling Fans

It was a usual busy Saturday afternoon when I struggled to get household chores, writing work and other miscellaneous duties completed, all while taking care of my four-month-old son, Max. I was a career woman, a writer used to being able to drop everything to work on an idea, sketch out a story or make an e-mail contact. I was also a woman used to eating lunch when I wanted, calling friends for hour-long chats at the drop of a hat, going to a movie with my husband and cleaning the house whenever the urge hit me.

But all that had changed when I found out I was going to be a mother at the ripe "young" age of forty.

In fact, my whole life changed as I fell madly in love with this little boy, my son. But I had no idea just how much time and energy this little thing could, and would, demand from me, and how crazy my new schedule would become once the word "mom" was added to my growing résumé. Even with a husband working at home, it still was an exhausting lesson in juggling priorities and multitasking.

Before I knew it, I was getting used to doing twenty things at once, before dropping into bed at 9:00 P.M. or sooner, hoping to get enough sleep to do it all over again the next day. I had always been used to staying up as late as I wanted, doing whatever I wanted. This new way of life took my breath, not to mention most of my energy, away.

One particularly hectic afternoon, I plopped Max in the middle of our king-size bed on his back so he could watch the ceiling fan while I folded laundry at the edge of the bed. At first he fussed, wanting my attention, but after a while he began staring at the blades moving round and round, and before I knew it, he was in a trance, fascinated, a slight smile frozen upon his pink rosebud lips.

He moved his gaze to the ceiling itself, nothing but an expanse of off-white textured paint, and seemed equally enrapt. I wondered what was so interesting, what fascinated him so. I decided to lay down beside him and join him to see what all the fuss was about.

Now normally my attention would be everywhere but on the present moment, especially a present moment that didn't involve doing something "constructive." I would either be going over something I did in the past, or plotting out what I had to do in the future. I would be thinking about money, work, grocery shopping, losing weight, which relative had a birthday coming up. My body would be with Max, but my mind would be in a dozen other places as well.

But this time I found myself beginning to relax as we lay together on the bed, watching the whirring blades spin, feeling the soft breeze on our skin and tracing imaginary lines in the textured ceiling paint. As we lay there, we held hands and intertwined fingers, and Max gnawed on my knuckles with cool, wet gums. I kept feeling that I should get up and "do something," but Max refused to let go of my hand. He turned and looked at me with a smile that seemed to say, "Let it go for now, Mommy."

Suddenly, I felt myself totally embrace the moment. The fan, the breeze, Max's juicy wet mouth on my fingers, the laughter of our next-door neighbors splashing about in their pool. There was no thought of yesterday, or tomorrow, or even an hour from then. Only that moment.

It was as if time just opened up a huge chasm, and I fell headlong into it. The feeling only lasted a moment itself, but it jerked me back into my senses, reminding me just how much of my life I had been living in another time and place, namely the unchangeable past and the unknowable future. I lay there a little longer, just doing nothing, and doing it with every ounce of my being, for no reason other than because it was what I felt like doing. Nothing. It felt a little weird at first, but before long, I could feel every ounce of stress and strain leave my body, my mind and my spirit. I felt lighter than air.

Being a career woman and mother, heck, being a mother period, is hard, time-consuming work full of anxiety and worry over our abilities, stress over an ever-growing list of demands, and uncertainty over what lies ahead. We worry more than we should, and try to get more done than we need to, all because of the many roles we play, including breadwinner, cook, caretaker, guardian, warrior, mentor and boo-boo fixer.

But it all seems so unimportant when our own child reminds us of what really counts. Not our job performance or the current stock fluctuations. Not that promotion we missed out on, the mistake we made three weeks ago or the family reunion we have in two months. Not the three loads of laundry piled up in the hamper, the steaks that need marinating, or the e-mail that needs answering. Not how much money we make, or what kind of car we drive, or how big our house is. Not how we look or how clean our house is or what kind of clothes we wear.

What really counts is the present moment.

Fingers. Off-white textured paint. And ceiling fans.

Marie Jones

The Best Days of Our Lives

Newly divorced, with a seven-year-old son to support, I attempted recently to reenter the teaching profession I had left when Steven was born. As the job hunt stretched into weeks, however, I experienced a growing sense of panic. But one of the things I have learned in becoming suddenly single has been to reach out to good and gentle friends. One of them shocked me when he said I worried so much about the future that I had no time to enjoy the present.

"Go ahead and look for your job," he said. "But live in the now. Perhaps this time is a gift, one that may never be given again. Use it to discover who you are and what it is that is really important to you."

I began to see, just a little bit, what I had been doing to myself, what I have been doing all my life. Living in the future. Never really being present in my own here and now. What a thief I had been—stealing from myself. And I had absolutely no idea of how to change.

I searched my heart and memory for origins of the "work now, live later" ethic. And for the beginnings of the deeply held belief that if I was not actively productive in a way that was immediately visible—either in a paycheck, or a shiny floor or a possession—then I was somehow unworthy. Perhaps, I finally decided, the important thing is the awareness and the opportunity to become free, just a little bit.

That afternoon, I thought about Steven, and wondered how long it had been since I had taken time to be truly, fully, with him.

When Steven returned from school, I offered to play some of his games with him. He had tried to get me to play many times, but I always had something "more important" to do. He got out the games, and I noticed immediately that every one of them was somehow linked with achievement. How many points scored, words made and in the least amount of time. And don't forget to keep score. *So we are teaching it to them, too,* I thought.

I suggested to Steven that we might play without the scorecards. After his initial shock, and even reluctance, he agreed. Eventually, we even progressed to the point where we were able to make up our own words—though they were not in the dictionary—and to laugh at our own inventiveness. The experience left me hungry for more.

At Steven's bedtime, I said to him: "Honey, we haven't had much time together lately. You and I ought to just go off on an adventure. I just might show up at your school one morning, and steal you away for the day."

Steven's face registered surprise, then impish delight. "Oh, make it a Thursday, Mommy. We have book reports on Thursday, and I hate book reports."

"Teachers love book reports, Steven. It gives them a chance to sit down. I will make it a Thursday."

Two weeks later, I got to the school as California's December morning coolness was beginning to dissolve into warmth. When I entered the classroom, Steven eyed me calmly, but his teacher looked incredulous when informed, without explanation, that my son would be leaving for the day. I merely smiled and hoped the delicious sense of mischief in my heart was not evident in my eyes.

Looking sober and serious, Steven and I made our way safely into the parking lot, where we laughed until tears came streaming. Quickly, we made our getaway. I had packed everything that we might need—lunches, snacks, books, soft drinks, bathing suits, beach balls, warm jackets.

We turned off the Pacific Coast Highway, coming to a halt in front of gently rolling waves that sent white foam bursting on brilliant sunlit sand. Except for about fifty large seagulls and two men, a woman and a little girl, the beach was entirely ours. Steven changed into his swimming trunks and was in the water before I could even spread the towels and snuggle down with a book.

The little girl, attracted by Steven's beach ball, joined us in digging deep holes and tunnels in the sand. The child's father introduced himself and his party. They were Sioux Indians, he said. This was their first day in California and the very first time they had seen the ocean. They taught us the Sioux words for perfect day and beautiful children. Steven taught them the word Kool-Aid.

Then our visitors left. As I lay back on the sand and saw that little boy who is so special to me, really saw him, rushing out to meet the foaming waves, and heard his laughter and basked in his and in my own deep pleasure, my only regret was that I had not brought my movie camera. What I didn't know in that moment is that I will be able to run that scene over and over for as long as I live.

Later, we made footprints in the sand and wrote our names again and again, and laughed as the waves washed away all traces of our being there. We climbed rocks. We found a friendly dog and some fossils. We met a boy and a girl having a picnic lunch and asked them if they were playing hooky, too. They laughed; we all laughed.

The day seemed to flow from one good thing into another. When at last the breeze became cool, and the sun fell a little and our stomachs told us that it might be time to have another meal, Steven ran to me with his new treasures—seaweed, shells, bits of pretty rock—and said, "Mommy, do we have to go home?" There seemed to be a question beyond the words.

"No, Steven, let's drive down the beach to that restaurant with the big old booths in the windows, right smack on top of the waves."

As we were seated, with the surf pounding only a few feet below, we noticed a man running and jumping over the giant rocks that were covered with moss and looked to be slippery. He had only a few sandpipers, the wind and the sunset for companions.

From the next booth, we heard a man exclaim, "Look at that nut out there hopping on the rocks. And it's almost dark!"

Steven looked at me and smiled. After a while, he said softly, "I bet there are things some people just don't know about."

My son fell asleep in the back seat of our car on the way home. I could hear his soft snoring. When I carried him into his bedroom, he awakened and said, "Oh, Mommy, this has been the very best day of my life."

"Mine, too, Steven dear," I replied. "Mine, too."

Colleen Hartry

3

TEAMWORK

People have been known to achieve more as a result of working with others rather than against them.

Dr. Allan Fromme

Strangers No More

At six foot four inches, Richard was noticeable, even without his usual bright smile, as he ducked in the main office doorway. Relatively new to this large urban high school, I knew little of Richard, except that he was active and well liked by everyone including my boss, the directing principal.

Word was out that Richard had suffered a sudden heart attack and might have to limit activities for the rest of the year. Everyone knew it would be especially difficult for Richard if he could not participate as usual in the commencement of kids he'd helped bring to this point over the past four years.

I turned curiously from stuffing the mailboxes as I heard my boss greeting Richard, pale from surgery. Curiosity turned to alarm at his unusual lack of spirit when Richard confirmed his doctor had ordered immediate retirement. Although barely acquainted, I felt compelled to connect with him and called out "Richard, I'll be praying for you." Turning in the doorway he met my gaze. "Thanks," he drawled slowly, "but I feel like my life is over if I can't be with the students," and turned to leave the building.

I was stunned by his words, and shocked that he would

share such desperate thoughts with someone he barely knew. His words "my life is over" rang in my ears for weeks after, and as Thanksgiving vacation neared, my concern for Richard heightened. Uncomfortable to phone a "virtual stranger," I begged the school psychologist, and then my boss, to call, but both sympathetically returned the burden. It was the day before vacation when I finally accepted my boss's offer to "guard" my closed office door from interruption, as I dialed Richard's number.

A last-minute escape—to talk to his wife instead—failed when Richard himself answered the phone, responding with melancholy that his wife and girls were out picking up a few things for their trip to see family for Thanksgiving. Dumbly, I replied, "Okay. I will call back later." Disgusted with myself, my heart clenched in fear reviewing his emphasis on *they* are going rather than *we* are going. Frantically praying while redialing the number, a phrase from a verse where Jesus said, "When you give to a brother you give to me . . ." came to mind. Nodding my head in obedience, Richard's dull hello loosened a wall of emotion, releasing long-buried memories of my Dad's depression following a heart attack.

"Richard," I confessed, "I called a minute ago and asked to speak to your wife because I didn't know if you would speak with someone you barely know, but your reaction to your surgery reminded me of my Daddy and I would like to tell you about him if you would listen." His soft-spoken acceptance to "go ahead" led me back. His murmured words of understanding when I shared how my Dad loved his job and made it his life until a sudden heart attack weakened my "superhero" spurred me on. Recalling Dad telling me he felt like he'd never be whole again, Richard's "He felt that way, too?" held surprise and an invitation to continue. Memories came of how the family felt—helpless before the strange enemy of depression that literally locked Daddy away from his faith and beyond our reach.

My voice broke recalling our desperation to reach Dad, and as I wondered aloud if Richard's wife and daughters felt as we did—like failures—because they couldn't seem to get through to him as we couldn't get through to our dad, Richard's voice slowly came to life. "Why I never imagined they might feel that way," he said thoughtfully. "I know they love me and have been trying to help me".

Richard understood how my "pull-yourself-up-by-the-bootstraps" Dad was touched when our seven-year-old wrote John 3:16 on a card and carefully printed that he could trust God to love him even more than any of our family could because he gave his Son to do what even Grandpa could not do for himself. Once Dad found hope in God's message he was ready to listen to the doctor. A hopeful "Really?" came through when I told Richard the doctor's response that depression was a normal side effect for many people after heart surgery and "nothing to be ashamed of." That hopeful "really" encouraged me to ask Richard to make several promises—to join the family trip for Thanksgiving, to write down all that he read and saw that God had done for him and given him—and then to call the doctor and me when he got back. Richard's slow drawl responding that he supposed he could put off his plans for that evening, and his promise to "report in" after vacation gave me added assurance, as the call ended and my office door opened, that he would be under his family's watchful eye until he saw the doctor. A speculative "How'd it go?" from my boss turned to astonishment that I'd requested promises, then assurance that if Richard said he'd do something he would keep his word.

A silent prayer from a peaceful heart was only the beginning of a Thanksgiving I'll never forget. The following Tuesday morning the phone rang and a jubilant Richard, announced: "You were right, the doctor said I have a side effect from surgery and am starting a prescription today." He paused before adding that he'd already begun "the other prescription I gave him" and it had changed his life. I tearfully accepted his thanks thinking that was the end of the story, but there were two chapters left! The first was in the form of a card from his daughter, saying in part "We don't know all of what you shared with my Dad but that conversation changed his life. We have our Daddy back." To think I almost missed out on that blessing by being worried what someone would think of a stranger calling!

The second came the next morning when my boss reacted in surprise as a familiar shadow filled the doorway with a smiling Richard. His jocular "You see a new man before you," caused me to look up, and to smile shyly at a healthier and more peaceful looking man. Richard had come on a mission, however, and quickly revealed it as he pointed at me teasingly, while querying the principal "Did you know about her phone call?" Acknowledging the affirmative answer with a nod, Richard's glance held me breathless as he continued, "Well, what she didn't know," he paused effectively, "was that I had a gun ready that night and I had plans to use it. It took a stranger to call me and wake me up." The three of us were locked in a moment of startled silence and reverence for God's intervention through a reluctant messenger, when his words that lay closest to my heart even today came next, "but we are strangers no more."

Delores Christian Liesner

Leaving My Ego at the Door

Good leaders make people feel that they're at the very heart of things, not at the periphery. Everyone feels that he or she makes a difference to the success of the organization. When that happens people feel centered and that gives their work meaning.

Warren Bennis

My first professional position out of college was as an area (industrial) engineer, working at an automobile assembly division. I knew it would not be a glamorous position because, as an area engineer, I would be directly supporting the assembly areas where cars were manufactured. It was a factory, and it was everything you expect a factory to be: noisy, dirty, without temperature control. However, with all that in mind, I must say that I was a bit surprised by the hostile professional work environment into which I was thrust.

My job was to support the area in the plant called the "Cushion Room." This was the area where all of the car seats were manufactured, assembled and routed to be placed into the nearly completed cars. I will never forget my first day on the job. I was told to go out and introduce myself to the supervisor of the area. His name was James Lewis, and his name will be forever etched into my memory! As I went up to him to introduce myself, he came right up to my face and yelled, "Who are you, and why are you here?" I was so taken aback I could barely speak! When I finally stuttered out my name and what I was doing there, he then barked, "Who is your boss?" I told him and before I could say another word, he was on the phone to my boss complaining to him that he was *not* going to work with some young, female, college kid! But as his conversation with my boss continued, it was obvious that my boss supported me and that James was stuck with me.

As time went by, I tried everything I could to get him on my side. I was punctual and always did what I had promised. I spent time on the line trying to understand the challenges and obstacles he faced as a supervisor. I even brought him coffee and made a point to ask about his family, but nothing seemed to work. Everything I did or said was discounted and made fun of. I even talked to my boss about it, but he offered no advice other than to just keep on trying.

After a while, it became quite obvious that James wanted to discourage me and make me quit. There were days that I just hated to walk out to the line; it was almost unbearable. But what really surprised me about myself was that, even though I would sometimes cry all the way home from work, I realized that I was not going to let this man discourage me or control me and that I was not going to quit—unless it was on *my* terms.

As we neared the time of the year for retooling, I was asked to look at ways to make the Cushion Room production line smoother and more efficient. I started with the drawings and asked for advice from my colleagues. But it soon became evident that the person with the most knowledge about the subject was James. The day I went out to ask him for his opinion I was so nervous! I didn't know if I could take another putdown, but I persevered. I remember the moment so vividly. I went up to him to ask him if he had a few minutes to talk about the retooling. He made a snide joke and walked over to his office with me. With all the courage I could muster, I told him that I really wanted his opinion on the new layout . . . and then I waited.

Well, I wish I would've had a camera handy! His whole demeanor changed, and a big smile came across his face. He gently replied, "Do you know that I have worked here for thirty-four years, and no one has ever asked for my opinion?"

From that moment on, we were colleagues, working together to create this efficient, money-saving production area. With his input and guidance, we automated a very slow and dangerous manual seat-cover delivery operation, as well as streamlined the whole production process. Others in my office noticed that James was up in my office a lot and were curious as to what was happening. I just told them that we were retooling that Cushion Room, and that it was going to be amazing!

When all was said and done, the retooling was a major success on many levels. The Cushion Room became one of the most efficient operations in the whole plant. And James got all of the credit. Because of his knowledge of the operation, whenever we had to brief the plant manager, I encouraged James to get up there and talk about it. (This had never happened in the history of the facility—never had a line supervisor briefed the plant manager instead of the area engineer.) James was now looked upon as a local expert and was asked to assist in other re-tooling efforts. James was in his glory!

So what about me? And what is the moral of the story? Did my education and training lead me to approach James in just the right way? Was James on my side the whole time and was just waiting for the right moment to let me in on the secret? Did I use my female instincts and intuition? Or did I just get lucky? Well, maybe all of the above. But what I think happened was that I started acting and treating others as I wanted to be treated. I put my ego down and sincerely asked for help. And it made all the difference.

I have taken this early lesson into every other work environment I have been in. I always remember to ask for the opinions of the people doing the job, and I acknowledge their contributions. I give them public credit for the success. I understand that their success is my success. And, I work hard to leave my ego at the door. And it has paid off; in spades. And though I am not an executive at a Fortune 500 company, as an educator, I feel like I make positive differences every day, and I let others feel that they do, too. And to me, that is what success is all about.

Patricia Dillon Sobczak

The Back Corner Booth

The unexpected telephone call broke my concentration from a press release I was writing about modern dance.

"Can you meet me at Burger King for a cup of coffee?" asked a board member with a faux-casual sense of urgency. "Right now—and without letting anyone know you are meeting me."

Though a rookie to Big Business, I recognized this as a command performance. "Gee, I'm really busy right now" was not an acceptable answer. So I looked at Linda and the other staff in the performing arts center's small office and bravely waved, "I need a little walk to get my creative juices flowing. Be right back!"

On the brief walk to Burger King that humid midafternoon, I thought of how much I loved my job. Promoting entertainment was so perfect for me. Already, I envisioned it as a lifelong career. I really didn't want to get fired, but that's all I could imagine was about to occur.

I saw the caller immediately, but he was not alone. The scene greeting me was like a board meeting except for its odd location in the back corner booth of a fast-food restaurant. "Well, it looks like we have a quorum!" I chirped in a foolhardy attempt to lighten the moment.

"We know you have to get back to work, so we'll get right to the point," said the group's spokesman, obviously relying on his role as board chairman for authority. "We'd like to make you our new executive director."

"Wow, I'm truly amazed. . ." I began slowly, still reeling from the "I'm-going-to-be-fired-now-I'm-promoted" turn of events. "But what about Linda?"

If this were a soap opera, music would rise, actors would stare with exaggerated alarm at one another, just before a commercial begins. As it was, pairs of eyes were the only movement, save for the patron at a neighboring table dipping his French fries in ketchup. Board members slipped sideways glances at one another while facing me with frozen smiles.

After a long silence, comments came rapid-fire across the table:

"Linda has done a very good job, but she needs a change."

"Linda is very good, but you show real promise and we'd like to reward you."

"Linda has made some enemies."

Oh. So that's it, I thought. "Linda doesn't know that you want to replace her?"

It was Mr. Board President's turn again. "No," his voice was firmer now, "because we want a replacement named prior to making the announcement. You must realize this is a wonderful opportunity for you. You should be pleased to be considered at your young age."

Things must not have been going as planned, because here I was center stage at Burger King in front of an annoyed group eager for a quick affirmative. Although part of me did consider complying with the offer, I gathered up a resolve that later amazed me.

"You should be ashamed of yourselves," I began. "Many of you are good personal friends of Linda's, and all of you know that anyone in her position will make a few enemies over time. It comes with the territory whenever you raise money in a high-profile job. Everything I know about the arts comes from Linda anyway, so by promoting me you would end up getting another director just like Linda!"

Silence was filled only by the inaudible swoosh of my career going down the drain, but I was on a roll. "If you don't tell Linda about this in twenty-four hours, I will. And no, I won't make your job easier by agreeing to replace her."

It was a great exit line if this were a play, but the likely consequences of my brash convictions brought reality back as quickly as the summer heat that hit my face as I left the air conditioning.

Maybe it was a play after all, because the ending was straight from the pen of Neil Simon. After Mr. Original Caller advised Linda of the board's intentions, she showed her stuff by leaping into action. She rallied support from the highest levels, and within one week the board made its announcement:

The Performing Arts Center announces the creation of a Foundation to develop financial support for the arts. A new director will oversee operations of the Foundation, and a new director will lead operations of the Performing Arts Center.

Linda was named Foundation Director, and I was promoted to Performing Arts Center Director! The local newspapers ran a photo of Linda and me together, smiling. The "real story" never made the headlines.

Linda and I worked well together over the years. Even when we both went on to other positions in opposite parts of the country, we remained friends. Our careers continue to flourish—mine in the arts and Linda's in development. And through it all, Linda never tired of reminding me of the time I stood up for her, long ago, in the back corner booth.

Celeste Winters

The Best Sales Bonus

*It is not genius, nor glory, nor love that reflects
the greatness of the human soul; it is kindness.*

Henri-Dominique Lacordaire

One icy, winding road, and an early-morning commute, which included dropping off my daughter at her bus stop in time, had "accident" written all over it. Sure enough, as I approached the hill, accelerating a bit to overcome the drag, I was faced with the choice of running head-on into the garbage truck or swerving off the road. Choosing the latter earned me a collision with a telephone pole. My daughter and I were both very lucky. We were alive, no broken bones, just the bruised ego of having to report to my boss that I totaled the company car.

My boss, Dave, was an interesting man for whom I had a great deal of admiration. He was an artist by education, but managed to become one of the most talented sales and marketing vice presidents I had ever met. He grew up in New Jersey, but his career had taken him to California. Here, he associated with "Hollywood" types and generally lived what we called the "Big Life." From all indications of his lifestyle, Dave would find a kitchen to be a waste of space in a house, and reservations to a gourmet restaurant as the answer to all things relating to food. Parties at his house were always lavish, catered affairs. One could always count on Dave to be the life of the party and the center of lively conversation. In a word, he had FLAIR!

Despite all that, I knew that he was a fair and positive person. Yet I couldn't help but hesitate to report being the first salesperson to wreck a company car. As a single mother of three children, my commission-paid job was not only critical to our survival, but Dave's confidence in my ability to perform in my region was key to my keeping it.

The follow-up examination by my family physician revealed that the painful area left from the automobile accident was actually a palpable mass that would need to be assessed by an oncology surgeon. Like a second-year medical student studying pathology, I "knew" I had some life-threatening tumor. After a series of biopsies, blood tests and other medical probes, I was scheduled for surgery. I hoped that whatever they found would be treatable!

Arrangements were made for live-in help for the children, my will was written and recorded, and family was put on notice. The night before my scheduled surgery, the doorbell rang. Thinking that perhaps a neighbor was stopping by to offer last-minute assistance, I opened the door and was surprised to find standing on my porch, a half-frozen, shivering man, my boss, Dave. "What are you doing here?" I asked. "I'm here to take care of the kids of the best salesperson in the world," he answered, as he came through the door with his suitcase. "Where's the spare bedroom, and what time do the children need to have breakfast before I drive them to school?"

I will never forget the scene in my kitchen the next morning as I left for the hospital. It had been transformed!

The children were greeted with a white tablecloth, linen napkins, fine china and silverware as Dave, now wearing chef attire, served Cheerios from a soup tureen.

I knew that everything would be all right.

Beatrice E. Brown

A "Dish" with Integrity

When I was twenty-three I graduated from Bowling
Green State University with a degree in education. I was
aching to work in my field. Visions of standing before my
students in a cozy, poster-strewn classroom discussing the
nuances of Shakespeare and Sophocles plagued my
thoughts. Even the idea of grading piles of essays brought
a smile to my lips. However, the outlook was dim. Already,
many of my fellow classmates had taken jobs outside of
education because the market was flooded with eager new
teachers and jobs were impossible to find. I searched and
searched, taking time off from my minimum-wage job as a
hotel clerk to travel the East Coast in the hopes of finding
work. A semester passed, and summer was coming to a
close; I was beginning to lose hope when a job fair at my
alma mater boasted a host of Texas schools in search of
teachers. The unemployed flocked to the fair, passing out
numerous résumés and interviewing with many a smiling
face and Texas drawl. It was there that I interviewed for the
job that would introduce me to one of the most dynamic
women I have ever met.

Shortly after the fair I was offered a position teaching at
an alternative school. I was so anxious to procure work

that I did very little research about my new employer and knew only a little about what an "alternative school" in the state of Texas meant. In two weeks my husband and I quit our jobs, bought a new air-conditioned car and drove to Texas. What a risk! We had no idea where the school was and were going on the promise of a contract; we had no actual contract in hand.

On the first day of school a tall, powder-haired woman with a friendly pink smile and a firm handshake greeted me at the door. She introduced herself to me as Karla Dunn, and she was to be my new principal. It was her first year at the school as well, but not her first year as principal, and I instantly felt at ease in her presence. I did not know at the time how lucky I was to be in such a small school. There were twenty-five people on staff, and we all took turns telling a little about ourselves and getting to know one another. It was then that I learned that Karla had been a nun for eighteen years! She had left the convent and later married a man who had an affiliation with a Catholic school in Brazil where I had done my student teaching. She knew the school where I had trained, and it was a common ground for us in conversation.

Not everyone thought that Ms. Dunn was the best "man" for the job. The school where I worked was in Houston, Texas and was established to serve expelled and adjudicated students. Young as they were, many of the kids had been arrested for stealing, dealing or abusing drugs, or engaging in gang activity. Many of our students were in foster care or were parents themselves. We had a hodge-podge of races and opposing gangs that set the stage for a very volatile environment. Because she was an older single woman, and an ex-nun to boot, some of the teachers balked at her authority and the police officers, although compliant, sometimes raised a wary eyebrow. How could such a sweet and classy lady possibly work with such ruffians? Regardless, Ms. Dunn's message was unbending. No matter what the crime, no matter what the circumstances, these kids were still children and they deserved our respect, love and patience.

Despite the pressure, Ms. Dunn was never absent. Every morning when we arrived at school, whether in sheets of rain or numbing cold, there she stood greeting every child and employee with a hearty "Good morning!" and a smile. The students learned quickly to respond to her, and rarely did she have to chase a student down for a reply. She learned their names and took time to talk to them in the hallway. When there was trouble in the classroom she always supported her teachers, but encouraged us to empower ourselves. Her first question when we complained of trouble was, "Have you called the parents yet?" She knew that if we weren't interested in the lives or families of our students they could never be interested in anything we had to say.

And her wisdom was not limited to the students. Her office door was always open, and I drifted in on many occasions to spend a leisurely hour discussing my personal life. I was a new teacher, and had no idea how unusual this relationship with one's principal was; I was also oblivious to how incredibly busy she was and how much of her time I took. Ms. Dunn had a gift for encouragement and listening. She always made me believe I could do anything.

Her greatest gift to me was to make me understand what leadership meant. The staff was so small that daily meetings sometimes turned into "family quarrels" among siblings. Ms. Dunn mediated, listened and carried the weight of us all on her squared shoulders. She was strong in times of conflict but allowed us to feel that we had a say in decisions that were made. She had a gift for diplomacy and a tender heart. More than once I saw her bow her head, eyes filled with tears, and answer a hurt with a firm apology. She was a watcher from the outside, never privy to secrets, knowing she was criticized, but never wavering in her leadership. She had never given birth to a child, but she was a matriarch to us all.

The first year on campus was a hard one for me, as it is for all first-year teachers, and I nearly reconsidered my choice to be a teacher. My marriage was also in turmoil, and these things combined made for trying times. The second year Ms. Dunn wisely paired me with another young teacher who was experienced with troubled youth, and kept her door open to me. My visits became more frequent, but I was guarded in my conversation. My husband and I split, and I moved in with my partner teacher. Before long I began to date a coworker and I knew that in our close-knit school rumors were flying. I saw Ms. Dunn watching, and I could only guess what she thought of me. But her door remained open.

And then one day I decided to rent my own apartment. It was a big move for me and weighed heavily on my mind. I had many bills and had never lived alone before. Somehow, I ended up in Ms. Dunn's office. As always, she encouraged me to follow my heart. I searched for a place within my budget, and found a small but affordable one-bedroom with a pretty kitchen and a vaulted ceiling in the living room. I bought used furniture from coworkers and yard sales, and crunched numbers in my head. But it was Ms. Dunn's gift that touched me the most.

One day she invited me to her home for lunch, and when I arrived she brought me to the kitchen. Ms. Dunn, now known to me as "Karla," had set out a collection of matching beautiful blue-and-white dishes complete with teacups and serving plates—all in perfect condition. She sat me down at the table, motioned to the dishes and began a story.

"When I first left the convent and was just starting out a woman gave me these dishes because I was in need of them. She gave them to me with one stipulation," Karla began.

"What was that?" I asked.

"That whenever I came across another woman in need I would pass the dishes on to her. I have passed the dishes on before, and miraculously, God always makes sure they come back to me. These dishes are yours to help you get started, and when you get on your feet, and you no longer need them, I want you to wait for a woman who needs to get started, and pass them on to her. If they should come back into your hands, please continue the tradition."

"Agreed," I smiled. "Thank you so much for thinking of me."

It has been years since Karla gave me that gift, and sealed the gift of our friendship. Karla is still my dear mentor and beloved friend. I see her for lunch from time to time and she listens to my news, although she is more quickly tired from my visits. I still eat from the blue-and-white dishes, but it's time to purchase my own set. Often I wonder about the woman who will inherit these dishes from me. Perhaps in me she will see what I saw in Karla— a kind heart, a spirit that does not cast stones and a firm commitment to integrity. Karla's example is the true nourishment I get every time I eat a meal on these dishes.

Erin Kilby

The Monday Good-News Lunch Club

*The best way to cheer yourself up is to try to
cheer somebody else up.*

Mark Twain

I worked in the computer department of a major hospital in Seattle for a few years. I was the first one hired in
what would become a staff of forty-five. There were a lot
of changes going on in healthcare and tensions were
always a little high. The changes going on daily in the
technology area were enough to push a sane person over
the edge, but you combine the two and it seemed deadly.

We had a large cafeteria where most of our department
gathered at lunchtime. It was supposed to be a "break"
from work, but it turned out to be just a time where everyone unloaded and complained about all the stuff going on
in the hospital. I, however, wanted to talk about anything
but work, but it seemed no one else had a life. Except for
my friend Nannette.

She was the only bright spot in the whole bunch, as she
was hired as the recruiter to fill all the new positions. Even
though she had her reasons to complain, she also had a

life, so we got to talking. One day, she agreed with me that everyone else was just too depressing to be around, so we broke off from the group and sat at our own table. We just talked about good things and what was going "right." After lunch we both felt so much better, we decided we should do that again. Then the idea emerged, as we walked back to our office, that we should have a "Good-News Lunch Club," and if anyone from the department wanted to sit at our table, we would insist that they only talk about good news. We decided Mondays would be the best day, since everyone was always depressed to come back to work after the weekend.

The following Monday we sat at our table, and when a few people stopped by to ask if they could sit with us, we told them the rules. One walked away, and the other sat down. I acted as moderator and got them to say whatever it was that was good in their life. Nannette and I shared our good news and felt much better there than sitting with the others. The next day more people joined us, but we didn't say anything because it was Tuesday. By the following Monday we had several people come again to the table, then we laid down the law and told them about our "club." Most laughed and joined us anyway, but I enforced the rules and wouldn't allow any conversations that were negative. I went around the table and asked each one what good news they had to report. Some were silent, but most had something good to say.

Our table grew to be five or six tables all pushed together every Monday. We all ate silently while we went around the table and listened to each person report their "good news" for the week, and we all shared in their joy. We grew as a department and as a team. We welcomed all new employees and let them join our "Monday Good-News Lunch Club."

It's been a few years now since I left the hospital, but I

can still hear the voice of one coworker as she got up from the table on a Tuesday after everyone was complaining about work. "Boy, I wish this was Monday," she said, "so I could hear some good news."

Mickey Bambrick

"You seem to like your job. We want you to hate it here like the rest of us."

More Time for Mom (to Be)

Surround yourself with people who respect you and treat you well.

Claudia Black

Several years ago I had the privilege of working with a phenomenal group of people in a small marketing company in Phoenix. One of our team members was expecting her second child. Already the mother of an active preschool son, Susan was ever-cheerful but often exhausted by the end of the day.

I noted her increasing fatigue on a daily basis as her pregnancy progressed, and I pondered, *What can we do as a team to give her a baby gift she could really use—now?"*

At a team meeting we put our heads together to brainstorm some ideas. The usual baby shower was suggested, lunch out with the girls, etc. After listening to and recording all of the ideas on a dry-wipe board, I thought for a moment and said, "These are all really great suggestions, but what does Susan really need *now*?"

A bit of a stunned silence followed. I offered, "She seems tired. What if we were to give Susan the gift of *rest*?" I continued, "She seems to be holding up well, but she's simply exhausted coping with a house, an active son and a full-time job. What if each of the eight of us volunteered to pitch in one extra hour per week to take some of the job responsibilities off of her so she can rest?" The team immediately embraced the idea. The department supervisor gave it the immediate thumbs-up. He also agreed to donate an additional hour of his time per week.

From that time until the day before she delivered her beautiful daughter, Allie, Susan enjoyed taking off any eight hours per week she chose: an hour here or an hour there, a long lunch, time for a nap, or simply one day off per week.

A week after her daughter was born, Susan brought Allie in to the office and there were giggles and coos of delight all around. Each of us received a personally hand-written thank-you note from Susan.

The idea worked so well, it has since been incorporated in other departments of the company. Employees can choose to give one or more hourly increments of earned vacation, volunteer or sick time to coworkers who can benefit from this extraordinary gift when they need it most.

Today Susan and family are doing well.

Ellen Dietz

The Gift of Understanding

For many years, I have been a nurse. I have tended to the needs of my community members, friends, neighbors, relatives and strangers. I have loved and hated my job, sometimes within the same shift. Nursing can be exhilarating and uplifting. It can also be stressful and exhausting. Most of all, it can be lonely. The shift work, the work on holidays, the need for confidentiality, all of these can contribute to a sense of isolation, especially for a single person.

Holidays are the hardest time. I don't think that I could count, nor would I want to, the number of times that a coworker or supervisor has asked me to work a holiday for another, because, "You don't have a family." So I work Thanksgivings so that families can serve the holiday dinner in their home. I work Christmas Eves so that mothers can see their children in the Christmas pageant at church. I work the nights before Christmas so that fathers can assemble toys. I work Christmas Days so that parents can see the wonder in their children's eyes on Christmas morning.

These are difficult shifts to work. Many of the patients

hospitalized during this time will not see another holiday. They are there because they are too ill to go home. There are not many elective procedures scheduled during these times, and anyone who is able will hastily be discharged in time for the festivities. So nurses are usually left with the sickest and the saddest of patients. It is a time to minister to both the physical and emotional needs of your fellow man; it can be a time of great communion. After the shift is over, it can also be a time of great loneliness.

Going home to an empty house on Christmas morning can be a desolate thing.

This is what I faced the year that I received my most beloved Christmas gift. I was scheduled to work night shift on Christmas Eve, from 7:00 P.M. to 7:00 A.M. My family of origin lived several hours away and would be going to church, opening their gifts, having Christmas dinner. I would be working during most of these events and sleeping during the remainder. Eventually, when the celebration was nearly over, and I had attained some much-needed sleep, I would make the trip home.

It was a bitterly cold winter night when I arrived for work. The wind bit through my uniform and whipped at my face. The parking lot was nearly empty, as the hospital was down to a skeleton crew. I made my way through the lot, the corridors and to the elevator that would deliver me to my floor. Cursory glances at those around me revealed a subdued mood. But when the elevator doors opened on my floor, I could sense excitement. I thought maybe there were carolers on the unit, or that a favorite patient was going home to be with his family for one final Christmas. All of the nurses, coming on shift and going off shift, were milling around the desk at the nurses' station. This was rather unusual, because change of shift tends to be a very busy event, with not much time for idleness. After I clocked in, I made my way to the nurses' station to find out what was going on. When I rounded the corner, all of my coworkers were waiting for me with big smiles. Anticipation was hanging in the air, as heavy as the big red garland hanging from the pillars of the station. I knew something big was up, and that they were waiting for me to be a part of it. Just then, one of my coworkers stepped forward, and I realized that I was not just a part of it . . . I was it.

This kind and gentle person, whom I had not felt especially close to before that moment, had done a most amazing thing. She had celebrated an early Christmas Eve with her daughter so that I could have the shift off, and go home to be with my family. Another coworker had taken her shift, and two more had split that person's shift. My coworkers, my friends, my family; the line of demarcation was shifting irrevocably and the definitions were melding together at that moment. Happy tears filled my eyes as I was escorted back to the elevator and offered best wishes. By the time I reached the parking lot, I was crying in earnest. The tears froze to my cheeks as I reached the car.

There was hardly any traffic as I sped along the deserted roads toward home that night. Most anyone who was going somewhere was already there. The stars twinkled in the black sky, and I sang along in hearty voice to the Christmas carols playing on the radio. The air was frigid, and I was alone on long stretches of highway. But I was not alone in my heart, for it was filled with gratitude and wonder. My coworkers had given me the greatest Christmas gift I had ever received—their gift of friendship, understanding and insight into my world. Because of that gift, and the sweet memories of that night, I would never be alone on Christmas again.

Susan Stava

4

SPECIAL MOMENTS

Life is a blend of laughter and tears, a combination of rain and sunshine.

Norman Vincent Peale

Little Amigo

I'll never forget three-year-old Eduardo, my first pediatric patient as a nursing student. Diagnosed with herpes simplex virus type I, he had painful mouth lesions. Because he was refusing fluids, he was at risk for dehydration.

When I mentioned my assignment to another nurse, she laughed and said, "Good luck with that kid! His mother doesn't speak much English, and he understands only Spanish."

Eduardo eyed me warily from his mother's side as I introduced myself. Then, using pantomime to fill in the gaping holes in my high school Spanish, I explained that Eduardo must take in fluids and that I needed to take his temperature and look into his mouth. Eduardo shook his head no. Then I had an inspiration: I asked his mom to insert the thermometer probe under my armpit and take it out when it beeped. She did so, with Eduardo holding the probe base in his little hands and watching intently.

When I asked him if I could do the same to him, he slowly lifted his arm. I gently lowered his arm over the probe. Just as he began to resist, it beeped. I smiled and thanked him.

To encourage Eduardo to drink, I wrote his name in different colors all over a paper cup, adding stickers of dogs and a Ninja Turtle. Then I filled the cup with grape juice and handed it to him. He examined it closely, pointed happily to the Ninja Turtle sticker, and drank the juice. With each visit, Eduardo became more relaxed, even allowing me to shine my penlight into his mouth. On his last visit, Eduardo's mother approached me. "Eduardo make you a present," she smiled, and handed me a drawing—a very colorful nurse with a thermometer hanging out of her armpit!

Deana Ward

The Hammock

We were attending a big party at a beautiful home on Wisconsin's Lake Geneva when I saw it swaying slightly in the breeze: an inviting, big-enough-for-two hammock. I slipped in gently, relaxed a moment, then hurried back to the party.

Hurried. My whole life seemed hurried. Every minute of every day seemed pre-programmed. My whole body felt tense, yet I still hurried to work, then rushed home to take the children to baseball games, play practice and music lessons, then home to throw clothes into the washer. I hurried with my teenagers to the orthodontist, the dentist, then shopping so I could hurry home to fix supper. After dinner I'd even hurry through a storybook with my four-year-old so I could get down to my writing room to finish writing an article an editor wanted.

The speed with which life was engulfing me was giving me headaches. It seemed that every minute of every day was programmed. My back ached, my whole body felt tense, yet I still hurried to work, hurried home, raced to my evening class and flopped into bed at night, too exhausted to even think.

That hammock started haunting me. *Wouldn't it be nice . . . ?* I started to dream big dreams, but then I'd wonder if I could find time to relax in it if I bought one. Then one day, while waiting for my teens at the orthodontist, I saw an ad for a hammock just like the one we'd seen at the lake. On a healthy impulse, I ordered one.

When it arrived, my son Michael, age twelve, and I drilled holes in two backyard trees and mounted the screws and hooks that would support this new luxury. We did a fine job and the hammock looked marvelous and inviting.

Michael and I rewarded our efforts with an inaugural rest. Both of us plopped into the double-wide macramé rope hammock and chatted about what a great job we did. And we talked about other projects we might tackle together. A canvas swing in that tree over there? A small fence around the garden? We talked about school and then recaptured the excitement of the home run he'd hit the day before.

Then Andrew, age four, came bounding out of the house with unbridled enthusiasm for his first "ride." Michael gave up his spot and Andrew climbed aboard.

The two of us stared at the leaves above us. "Mommy," Andrew giggled, "look at that squirrel!" We watched it scurry from limb to limb.

Then silence for a few minutes. I closed my eyes. A breeze was rocking me toward slumber. But not Andrew. "You know, Mom, I think those clouds are moving. There's one up there that looks like Dumbo . . . See the trunk?"

"Uhhh, hummm," I answered almost unconsciously.

Andrew continued to chatter, but his little body hardly moved from the curves of my own as we snuggled in the hammock.

An hour later, I realized that I was, for the first time all summer, relaxing. Totally, completely relaxed. My headache was gone. Not only had the hammock provided a place to rest, it was the perfect place to talk to the children one-on-one. A place to open our hearts, to grow closer and to really listen.

That evening, Julia, age thirteen, spent an hour in the hammock reading. Next fifteen-year-old Jeanne plopped sideways in it to observe a colony of ants building a house directly underneath the hammock.

The next day when I returned from work, I walked right past the washing machine, grabbed a book I'd been trying to finish for over a year and headed for you-know-where.

It's funny how some rope, two wooden supports and a couple of good strong trees can change your life. Best prescription I ever took.

Patricia Lorenz

The Answer from Above

It had been one of those days, and you know what I mean. Since my husband traveled a lot, I was usually a single mom—so the balancing act between work and caring for my two young daughters was at times like spinning plates.

This day, I had taken off of work early in order to chauffer both of my kids to two separate soccer games. I picked them both up after school, (two different schools) dropped one off at her game, took the second one to the other game (halfway across town, of course), stayed for half an hour to cheer her on, traveled back across town to the first game to cheer for the other daughter at the first game, grabbed her and hurried back across town again in time to pick up the second daughter. Phew!

Then we went home and I made dinner. Both girls bickered with each other during the entire meal. Did the dishes (they couldn't help because they both had homework, sorry Mom!), found out the youngest daughter had a project due the next day that she had "forgotten" about? —caved to her pleading and tears—helped her finish the project, marched them into the bathroom, told them to take a bath together with no more arguing, put them to bed, read a story with them and turned out the lights.

Then I collapsed.

The best thing I could do for myself was to take a long, hot bath. I climbed into the bathtub that had so recently been occupied by my two battling babies. The steam drifted up and filled the room. As I sank into the warm water and closed my eyes, I whimpered to myself, *This isn't how I thought it would be. My kids don't even seem to appreciate anything I do. Is this all worth it?*

I opened my eyes and saw that on the mirror above the tub, the steam from the bath had revealed my answer:

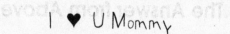

I smiled and sank back into the water. I knew it was more than worth it.

Patty Hansen

Respect and Pride

I do not come from a military family nor was there anyone in my family who had ever been a United States Marine and there definitely were not any females in my family who went into the service, let alone the marines. But somehow, in my upbringing, I developed this great sense of pride in my country, and the Marines were the only choice.

As a Marine, I was accustomed to many traditions and rituals, one of those being the daily ritual of "Morning Colors and Evening Colors." This is the raising and lowering of our National Colors, or the American flag. There is a set procedure for this. At 8:00 A.M. each morning, colors are sounded and the flag is raised. At sunset each night, the flag is retired. During the raising and lowering of the flag, all activity ceases. If you are outside, you stop what you are doing, face the direction of the flag, stand at attention, and if in uniform, salute, until the last note of the music is played. If you are in a car, you pull over to the side of the road and wait for the end of the music.

Fifteen minutes before the color guard is to raise or lower the flag, a warning will sound. This will allow you to get inside, get to your destination, or prepare yourself for the raising or lowering of the flag. During my ten years in the Marines, I saw many Marines run to get inside so that they would not "get caught in Colors." I always felt this was a sense of disrespect to the flag; however, I too, was guilty of rushing to get inside so as to not "get caught in Colors."

One particular drizzly day at Naval Air Station Whidbey Island, Washington, where I was stationed as an active-duty Marine sergeant, training the reserve marines in the United States Marine Corps, I was taking my two-year-old daughter to the doctor's office for a check-up. It was shortly before 8:00 A.M. and the warning was sounded for colors. We were in the parking lot walking towards the Naval Hospital. I heard the warning and said to my daughter, "Come on, Honey, we must hurry to get inside." After realizing what I said and what this would teach my daughter, I stopped and then asked her "Sweetie, would you like to watch them raise the flag?" "Yes, Mommy," she replied. So we walked to a bench close by and waited. While we waited, I taught her how to stand tall and proud and showed her how to put her hand over her heart, and not to remove it until the music stopped. I told her the importance of respect for the flag and the meaning of the flag. We waited. Just then the first note sounded. We both stood and faced the flag. She placed her hand over her heart and I saluted. We stood there, Marine, mother, and daughter and gave our flag the respect it so greatly deserved. We watched our comrades in arms raise the flag and then salute it himself. At the last note of music, we all cut our salute and proceeded on with our business.

The pride I felt that day was immeasurable. Still to this day, I burst with pride when I tell that story. I am proud to be an American and proud to have served my country and the only thing better than being a Marine is being a mom. After ten years in the Marines, I had to make a choice, full-time mom or full-time Marine. I still am raising my daughter with the pride of God, Country and Corps. I can only hope that as she grows and matures, that a little of my "Esprit de Corps" and love for our country will rub off. And what they say is true, "Once a Marine, always a Marine."

Semper fi.

Dianne C. Bradley

A First

I straightened my notebook and pen yet again, making sure the edge of the notebook lined up cleanly with my desk, the pen parallel to the notebook, uncapped and ready to write. But ready to write what . . . ? I glanced around in dismay at the bare conference room. My first day at my first job after graduate school and I was sitting in a conference room instead of an office. The walls were bare. No phone. No shelves. Just a round wooden table and four chairs. Oh, and me.

I glanced at my watch. Five minutes until I would walk down the hall and get my patient. My first real patient. After twelve years of regular school, four years of high school, four years of college and three years of graduate school, I was ready to begin my first day as a psychiatric physician's assistant. I slumped a little in my chair, gnawing on the end of a fingernail.

That morning, I had taken my thirteen-month-old to day care. While she was happy as a clam, racing into the room crowded with toys and games to sit down with "the gang" and eat breakfast, I was still wracked with doubt. *Was putting her in day care so I could finish PA school a good decision? Was starting a new job, even though it was part time, the right thing to do?* Even though I loved being a mom and while I had friends who were stay-at-home moms and I respected the incredible amount of work they did, there was a part of me that had always known I wanted to have a career.

But instead of appearing immediately after college, like a pot of gold at the end of the rainbow, my career had been elusive, involving jobs in sales, waitressing and reception before landing me in graduate school. As a young girl who dreamed of great wealth and fame, had a strong desire to make a difference in people's lives, and had graduated from an Ivy League school, I hadn't expected to be beginning my career at this point—in my early thirties with a husband, a mortgage, a thirteen-month-old and thousands of dollars of debt. But here I was. A trickle of ice had been forming in my stomach over the years, growing with every moment of frustration. Now, it had hardened into a large mass of ice, establishing how important this would be.

Christina, my first real patient, was not what I expected. She was petite and dressed in pressed cotton pants and a light blue sweater. She smiled easily at me as I led her to the conference room. I couldn't imagine what she could possibly be here for—she seemed much less nervous than I.

I tried not to cringe as we settled into the conference room chairs. Surely the bare room and lack of a phone, books or diplomas belied my inexperience! If Christina noticed, she didn't let on, and as she began to talk, a story unfolded which belied her composed appearance. For her entire life, she had struggled with violent mood swings, at some moments feeling full of energy and passion, at other moments, depressed and suicidal. Tears poured down her face as she described her anger, which sometimes grew so severe she would scream at her family or even throw things. She couldn't handle stress and would retreat to her room and be unable to cope. Her marriage was rocky due to her volatile moods and her kids were starting to avoid her. She had been treated by other doctors for the depression, but that had only increased her anxiety and irritability. Christina was at the point where she had lost yet another job and was considering leaving her family so that at least their lives could return to normal.

As I questioned her further, it became apparent to me that the young woman in front of me likely had a bipolar disorder, or what is commonly known as manic-depressive illness. People with this illness have periods of depression, but they can also have periods of increased energy, talkativeness, anger or irritability and difficulty concentrating. Despite being treated by several doctors over the years, she had never been diagnosed with or treated for a bipolar illness.

At the conclusion of my questioning, I hesitated. *How could I have noticed something that doctors had missed? First real patient, remember?* Christina was looking at me expectantly. Waiting. I squelched the tight feeling in my chest and tried to smile reassuringly. Cautiously, I brought up the diagnosis of bipolar disorder and what it meant. We went over the treatments. With a slightly shaky hand, I wrote out a prescription for medication and gave her the name of a good therapist.

Two weeks later, Christina returned to my conference room. As before, she looked well put together in fashionable dark blue jeans and a button-down shirt. We sat down and I spent a moment writing the date in the chart and reviewing the medications I had prescribed. Then came the dreaded moment. It was time to ask the question. I tried to appear calm. "How are things going since your first visit?" I waited for the tears.

Christina looked down for a moment, then her eyes met mine, several tears already welling up at the corners. "You've changed my life," she said simply. She sniffed and pressed a knuckle to her left eye. "I don't know what you gave me, but it was magical. I have been less depressed. I'm not angry anymore. I'm not snapping at my kids. We actually went hiking this weekend and even when a snake almost bit my son on the ankle, I was able to remain calm and handle it. My thoughts aren't racing a mile a minute. I had the first good night's sleep I can ever remember."

I felt a grin forming and tried not to show my amazement. My treatment plan had actually worked! This was not the same woman who had come to me in tears just a few weeks earlier.

"I don't know how I can ever thank you," she sniffed. "You've given me my family back. You've given me my hope back."

As I pressed a tissue into Christina's hands, I tried to hold back my own tears. There was an incredible shift in my stomach. The block of ice I had grown so accustomed to was starting to melt. I could feel the water trickling into my limbs, the cold in my gut replaced by warmth and comfort. Finally, it all clicked. All those years of struggling through jobs I hated, of wondering what my purpose was, of second-guessing my decisions, of dropping my daughter off at day care so I could finish school and start a job. They had led me here to this bare, ugly conference room. And I had changed a woman's life. A woman's entire future—and that of her family's. And she was only my first real patient!

Just think of how many more there were to come!

Rachel Byrne

"Everything?"

Paul White/National Enquirer.

Any Regrets?

We need to stop looking at work as simply a means of earning a living and start realizing it is one of the element ingredients of making a life.

Luci Swindoll

Seven years ago I was faced with the difficult choice of leaving my safe, comfortable career as a paralegal to take a job as a teacher's assistant in my children's elementary school. While ten years as a real-estate paralegal had proven to be reliable and prosperous, my husband and I decided that a change had to be made for the good of our family. We were both being stretched too thin, our sons were getting just "what was left of us" at the end of the day, and you can only eat so many meals from a fast-food bag!

After much discussion and prayer, some friends of mine at church opened a window of opportunity. Both of them just happened to be employed by the local elementary school and one of them, a teacher, needed an assistant. The other was a guidance counselor who helped me "get my foot in the door." A job as a teacher assistant is hard to come by in our area, so Scott and I felt that God was leading us in this direction. I would still be able to "bring home some of the bacon"—even if it was just bacon bits! And at the same time, have the same schedule as our children.

What amazes me, though, is two questions that still get asked of me.

The first question being, "Why?" Why would I go from a nice office, with adult conversation, doing what I had gone to school to do, while making a nice income? To work in the public school system, dealing with their perception of children (screaming, whining, cuts and bruises, upset stomachs and head lice), while only bringing home meager wages? My answer to the majority was then and still is today just this: "Where else can you help shape the lives of tomorrow, get hugs for a job well done, be home when your own children are home, and get paid for doing it?"

By the way, when I went to my parents seven years ago with this decision I was concerned. Here were two people who had spent their hard-earned money to put me through school so that I would have a good education and be able to be independent. Now I was asking them, "Is it okay with you if I toss my degree aside, and take a cut in pay, so that I can be home with my children more?" Their answer was "We didn't send you to school just to get a degree. We sent you to help you become a well-rounded person so that you could become a happy adult with options. Do what makes you happy!"

The other question that is often asked is "Do you have any regrets?" I have to weigh in my mind the following: On one side of the scale, I am sitting down with the checkbook sometimes juggling monthly bills. Waiting on payday to be able to make an "extra" purchase. And a "night out" may consist of only a rented video and ordering pizza. However, the other side of this situation is seeing a child's eyes light up when they can finally read that book or do that math problem. Being at home in the afternoons to help my own children with their homework. Having a sit-down dinner most every night with my family. Having two weeks in December with my family decorating, baking and making holiday preparations—not to mention making memories. Nice, leisurely summer days with my children, reading, playing ball and splashing in the pool with their laughter as my music. So my answer to "Do you have any regrets?" is a resounding "Absolutely not!"

Lisa Russell Motley

Performance Under the Stars

To fully enjoy life, to derive its greatest meaning and beauty, one needs to enter into it with not only the look of involvement and happiness, but the spirit of involvement, as well.

Luci Swindoll

They slouched in folding chairs in a semicircle, eyeing me suspiciously. Their ages ranged from fourteen to sixteen, and they were there because they loved drama. I was a new teacher, and I had absolutely no experience in directing drama. My background was in teaching, writing and literature.

No problem, I thought.

That was how I found myself in chaos late that fall, staging the musical *Godspell.* I spent countless nights at rehearsals coaxing my Jesus to sing louder and my Mary to tone down her body language.

My three-year-old, Breana, was the least of my worries. She was a sweet child, undemanding and easy to please. Usually I left her at home with my husband. But when he couldn't watch her, I'd throw her in the car and take her to rehearsals. She wandered about the stage, bottle in hand.

When I was wrapped up with responsibilities, I would pass Breana off to students. Her word for bottle was "baboo," and it was common to hear the pitiful cry of "Baboo!" from some corner of the drama room. The student nearest to her would then hunt it down.

As rehearsals for the play progressed, the integration of the acting with the choreography and the music became extremely time-consuming and intense. Breana seemed to accept my hectic schedule with characteristic charm. Once the play was over, I reasoned, I would give her back the time I was taking from her.

On the way home from one particularly good rehearsal, I asked lightheartedly, "Do you love Mommy?" She turned to me and said simply, "No." Wounded, I drove on in silence.

Opening night. We played to a sold-out crowd. My Jesus sang like a dove. The crucifixion scene had the audience in tears. At the last song, people were on their feet, wildly cheering for more.

The next night an even bigger crowd appeared, and we had to bring in more bleachers. Those who couldn't find a seat crowded shoulder to shoulder in the back.

Breana came both nights. The first night, she sat on her dad's lap—dutiful but fidgeting. As everyone complimented me on a job well done, she fell asleep.

The second night, she was bored. I sat her in a corner where she played quietly. Then she came over and pulled on my arm.

"Go outside," she whispered.

I looked in vain for her dad.

"Go outside," she whispered again.

I glanced down. Breana was looking especially pretty in a red dress with petticoats. Loose hair from her pigtails trailed softly down her neck in tendrils. I relented.

My cast could be without me for a few minutes.

There was a slight chill in the air. I let her pull me wherever she wished. We ended up outside the cafeteria, where there was a small amphitheater.

Breana pushed at my waist. "Sit, Mommy!" I did. She looked at me with sparkling eyes. "Watch me!"

Marching up on the stage, she put her arms straight out to her sides and began to twirl. Her red dress lifted up, revealing white tights that were bagging a little. I leaned forward and chuckled. She threw her head back and laughed gleefully as she spun.

Around and around she twirled like a plane out of control. I could hear the noise from the auditorium, but it began to subside as I focused on my daughter.

I remembered my countless hours at rehearsals. I remembered handing Breana off to others because I didn't have the time.

A rousing cheer came from the theater, but that was only background noise now. I was at the best performance—sitting under the stars, watching my three-year-old revel in her delight. She spun. She skipped. She finally bowed. And straight-backed on a wooden bench, I sat alone and clapped and clapped.

Rayleen Downes

5

OVERCOMING OBSTACLES

If the winds of fortune are temporarily blowing against you, remember that you can harness them and make them carry you toward your definite purpose, through the use of your imagination.

Napoleon Hill

The Other Side of the Glass Ceiling

Truth is the only safe ground to stand upon.

Elizabeth Cady Stanton

It was almost quitting time when my boss called me into his office. Feeling giddy about my vacation starting the next day, I asked the usual, "What's up?" Elation quickly vanished. It was obvious he was uncomfortable with the news he was about to deliver. He avoided looking my way and just stared out the window. All I could focus on was his crisp white shirt, necktie and navy pinstripe jacket, the uniform of company senior executives.

I reflected on all the years we worked together since starting as his program administrator. Memories flashed through my mind—the challenges, the obstacles, the revolving department heads, and finally the day he moved into the number-one position. I was there every step of the way being supportive, hard-working and loyal.

His voice quickly jolted me back to the present. There was no usual chit-chat or good-natured teasing. The topic of our conversation was the vacant position in our department, the one that was the next step on my personal career ladder. Very matter-of-factly he announced that he was filling the position with someone from the outside. An ad would start running during my vacation because—and these are the words that forever haunt me—"You are unpromotable!"

No word in the dictionary can describe the magnitude of that impact. What did I do wrong? My loyalty and support were unconditional. My work ethic was stronger than anyone's. Before joining the company I had put myself through college, earned assistantships for graduate school, and been successful in my previous jobs. Surely, these experiences had qualified me for increasing responsibilities and further career advancement.

A host of emotions took over—anger, confusion, frustration and most of all, sadness. Every missed birthday and anniversary celebration flashed through my mind. How naive and stupid to think dedication and hard work would advance my career with this company.

Without saying a word to anyone, I straightened the chaos on my desk and left the office. The parking lot greeted me with a downpour of rain. It wasn't enough to have this turning point permanently imprinted on my brain. Nature was giving me a living metaphor to make sure I didn't forget the dismal occasion.

On the drive home, I finished a mental update of my résumé. As I arrived, I glanced toward the sky. The rain had stopped and the parting clouds revealed the most magnificent rainbow ending almost at my door. Every color was clear and distinguishable with brilliant arcs layered upon each other. In an instant, I knew this was a sign that everything would be all right.

However, the next few months were unbearable. The "replacement" was hired, and my fate was sealed. Other than both of us being female, we had nothing in common. We were complete opposites in every way. She micromanaged,

I delegated. She worked alone, I built consensus. She took credit, I gave it. She flattered the boss, I offered positive counsel. In the end, her style fractured the glass ceiling, while mine couldn't crack that barrier.

Working for such polar opposites was even more difficult for the assistant we shared. Normally a strong person, she was reduced to tears one morning. Her mistake was correcting punctuation and spelling errors in a letter without asking permission. Instead of being complimented for her initiative, she became the recipient of a verbal assault mandating that she never change anything again, even if it was grammatically incorrect!

By the time this latest incident occurred, I had submitted my resignation and accepted another job. Since I was leaving, our assistant decided to ask for a departmental transfer. She knew she couldn't be successful under the current structure.

A position for which she was well-qualified was already open in another department. All it would take to complete the transfer was approval from her supervisor. Given the personality conflict there shouldn't have been a problem. But I hadn't counted on the glass ceiling effect again.

I was surprised to get a call from HR asking me to corroborate that our assistant was a management problem. In her short tenure, my colleague had already concluded that the assistant was a problem employee and would be an unfair burden to other departments, so no transfer would be forthcoming. I was shocked. As my assistant, she was competent, service-oriented and conscientious. Clearly her new boss's assessment contradicted my own experiences and the employee's record. I offered a highly positive recommendation but suspected this would have little bearing on the ultimate outcome.

My final day turned out very differently than anticipated. After the recommendation to HR my boss summoned me to his office. A lecture about not being a team player started before I could sit down. I had no right giving HR a contradictory report. It didn't matter that my working relationships brought out the best in people. According to him I had an obligation to give a consistent story even if—from my perspective—it was untrue. I couldn't believe my ears. Indignation rose inside of me. In frustration I finally asked for the exact words he wanted me to say to HR since I wasn't very good at telling lies. This exchange triggered a level of uncontrolled rage worse than any I had ever seen. Almost knocking the table over as he stood up, his final words to me were, "Why don't you just get the hell out of here right now and get on with your new life!"

And that's exactly what I did. As negative as it was, I can now look back on that experience with greater objectivity. My old boss was right. I wasn't promotable—not in that environment. To succeed I would have to become a different person with greatly compromised standards and values.

Time has tempered my original resentment. It was easy to blame the glass ceiling for my failures. But glass is transparent. You can see through it and decide if you really want what's on the other side. I've learned that companies are like gardens. Their growth potential varies as much as the gardeners tending them. Just as plants are chosen for their climatic compatibility, we must select employers with the same care. Some will cause us to wither, while others will help us grow and flourish.

My new role did just that. Each day presented fresh challenges and opportunities to work with great companies and influential corporate executives across the country. They not only listened to this once unpromotable administrator, they were paying her well, too.

Several years later, while finishing last-minute details for a business trip to Indonesia, my boss asked me to

respond to one more job applicant letter before leaving.
She knew I would normally delegate this to someone on
my staff so I was curious as to why she insisted that the
letter be answered by me personally. As I read through
the paragraphs of accomplishments looking for extraordinary qualities that would warrant her attention and mine,
I finally discovered the reason for the quirky grin on her
face. There at the bottom of the letter was my former
boss's signature. Seeing how little he had changed in com-
parison to my own growth since I left, one thought came
to mind. Breaking through the glass ceiling isn't all it's
cracked up to be.

Nancy Michel Bandy

"You might want to stop trying to break through that glass ceiling for a while, Ms. Gephart."

Reprinted by permission of Harley Schwadron.

Standing Firm

"It's nothing personal," Laura says as she leans back in her office chair.

I take a moment to study her face. Nothing personal, huh? I draw in a deep breath and say, "Well, it seems pretty personal to me."

At this point, I want nothing more than to get up and slam out of her office. But, I don't. We're in the middle of a discussion between her, our boss and me. Laura's protesting my application for a new position within the agency and wants to make sure our supervisor falls her way. I can't seem to stop my knees from shaking.

"I'm sorry you don't believe me," Laura says, "because I really mean it. I have nothing against you. I just feel that only those with college degrees should be considered for this position."

I level my eyes with hers and say, as calmly as I know how, "You know full well that a college degree is not required. If it were anyone from outside our agency applying for this position, you wouldn't bat an eye." What I don't comment on is that I'm aware this position pays close to what Laura makes, and I know that perturbs her.

Our boss shifts uncomfortably in his chair but doesn't say anything. Mr. Drake's a wonderful man who, unfortunately, doesn't want to take control of the situation. I've watched him stare down angry contractors and never break a sweat. But when it comes to his own employees, he'll do anything to avoid a confrontation. Which is pretty funny since he likes to accuse me of always taking the path of least resistance.

He does, to some degree, have a point. I can't deny I'm a doormat. But this time, I'm not giving in. I have every right to submit my application for this position. Not only that, but I have a responsibility to my children to do whatever I can to increase my salary.

"Listen," I say, "all we are even discussing here is submitting my application for consideration. I have no expectations beyond that. I know there's no guarantee that I'll win out over the other applicants." I look from Laura's face to Mr. Drake's. The message in her expression is unmistakable. She's not bending. Mr. Drake's eyes look weary, but I can see where he's headed. He looks at me.

"I'm sorry," he sighs. "I think we should just forget about it."

I'm stunned. I shouldn't be, though. Mr. Drake probably figures he'll have less conflict by agreeing with Laura. Her nature is to fight to the finish. Mine, generally, is to be the duck. Just let it all roll off.

This all occurs on a Friday afternoon, and my entire weekend is clouded with anger and frustration. Admittedly, much of that feeling is aimed at Laura and Mr. Drake. But most of it is directed at myself. I hate being the good little girl all the time. By Sunday evening, my mind is made up. I will not take this one lying down.

Bright and early Monday morning, I'm sitting across from Mr. Drake in his office. His sheepish expression shows how uncomfortable he is with the whole mess.

I get right to the point. "I have to tell you, I'm pretty disappointed in your decision last Friday. You know there's no harm in my being considered along with all of the other candidates."

"That's true," he says. "But I just don't want to be in the middle. I'll tell you what. You can file a grievance. I'll give you the forms, and we can turn them over to the director. I'll even drive you to his office to discuss it." Mr. Drake offers an embarrassed smile that makes it next to impossible for me to stay angry with him.

"Okay," I say. "Let's do it."

By the end of the week, we're sitting in the director's office. He leans back in his chair and asks a couple of simple questions. "Do you truly believe you can do this job?"

"Yes, I do."

"Are you prepared to undertake the physical demands of this job?"

"Absolutely."

"All right. I'll let you know something in a few days." He stands and motions us out of his office.

As we make our way to Mr. Drake's car, he says, "I think he'll accept your application."

"And how will you feel about it if he does?"

"Honestly?" Mr. Drake stopped and faced me. "I want him to accept it. You definitely should be considered for this position. But, as cowardly as it sounds, I don't want to be the one to go against Laura. She'll be happier, and everyone will get along much better, if she believes the decision didn't come from me."

I should be furious, but I'm not. Here is a man being nakedly candid about his shortcomings. How can I hold that against him? As my mom would say, "What will be, will be." I just have to be patient.

Within a few days, I learn that my application will indeed be included with the others. Within a couple of weeks, I'm offered the position. I accept.

Laura congratulates me and I offer her a genuine smile. But the smile is more for me than for her. I've conquered something much more intimidating than her bull-headedness. I've proven to myself that I can fight for something. And win.

Virginia Boshears

"You aren't actually being replaced by a woman. She's going to be doing her old job and yours."

She Believed in Herself—Not the Experts

Everybody is an expert in giving advice on how you cannot do somethinng. So forget about everybody. And then, when you encounter a hurdle—and I do that every week—view it as an opportunity, not the end of the world. Do whatever you need to do to get past it quickly. If you believe in your dream, you'll definitely get there.

Maria Elena Ibanez

When Maria Elena Ibanez was a teenager in Colombia, her father enrolled her in a course on programing mini-computers. Computers were becoming more common in Latin America, despite their $100,000 price tag and Maria Elena was instantly taken with this revolutionary technology. In 1973, she went to the United States to study computer science at the college level. After graduation, she had an idea.

Personal computers were selling in the U.S. for $8,000— a fraction of what Latin American businesses were paying for their mini-computers. *Why not set up distribution of PCs south of the border,* she thought, *where a fertile market was just waiting to be tapped?* She took her idea to the major computer companies in 1980, and asked for a chance to distribute their product in her home country.

"They told me to forget it," Maria Elena recalls. "The computer executives said Latin America is in the midst of economic crisis. Latin America is poor, they don't have money. They considered it too small a market for them to pursue."

Maria Elena saw it differently. She perceived opportunity where others saw limitations. "I figured, even if the market was only $10 million, it was still big enough for me, I could make money at it. And nobody else would go after it, because it's too small."

She was twenty-three years old, a woman, and had no sales or marketing experience, things the executives she encountered saw as three strikes against her. But she knew two things: Computers were cheap in the U.S.—and Latin America needed them. Hopeful and optimistic, she approached a banker and requested a line of credit. He wanted to see her business plan. Maria Elena had never heard of such a thing. The second banker asked for her marketing plan. She didn't know what that was, either. Then, she tried to go directly to the distributors. Most wouldn't meet with her, but two listened skeptically. She asked, "How much business are you currently doing in Latin America?" They responded, "None!" Maria Elena said, "I will sell $10,000 of your product a year in Latin America." Maria had to agree that all her orders would be prepaid. Altos Computers—with nothing to lose—gave her an exclusive distribution agreement for nine months.

Her next step was to call a travel agent. Maria Elena's instructions were simple: "Book me on a flight from Miami to Argentina, stopping in every major city I can without having to pay extra. That was my marketing plan. Ignorance can be bliss and sometimes it pays off. I didn't know what I was getting myself into."

With no experience, belief in her goal and common sense became her guides. She landed in Colombia, checked into a hotel, opened the Yellow Pages, and began calling computer dealers. "I figured, the bigger the ad, the bigger the company. So I chose the companies that had the biggest ads first."

The next day, fully scheduled with appointments, she hit the pavement running. In the 1980s a woman engineer was rare and many Latin American businessmen were not used to dealing with women—particularly a petite young blonde who looked about eighteen. She turned what might have been a disadvantage into an advantage by balancing her youthful enthusiasm with education and expertise. "They were fascinated by a young woman talking about the latest technology, things they didn't know. They responded very favorably because I had a tremendous product, the price was fantastic, and it allowed them to compete with the big guys."

A whirlwind three-week trip followed through Equador, Chile, Peru and Argentina. In each country, she used the same Yellow Pages approach to market her product. "I had projected sales of $10,000 a year and returned to the U.S., only three weeks later, with $100,000 worth of orders—prepaid, with cashier's checks in hand." For someone who was earning $6 an hour tutoring at the university computer lab, it seemed like millions.

Eventually, it would be millions—many millions. In the next five years, Maria Elena's sales grew to an astounding $15 million. In 1987, *Inc. Magazine* selected her company, International Micro Systems, as number 55 on its list of 500 fastest-growing businesses. In 1988, she sold the company and stayed on for another three years until sales reached $70 million.

Maria has since started a new company selling

computers to Africa. Once again the marketing experts told her Africa was too poor for personal computer products, especially if they were sold by a non-African female in a male-dominated culture. By now accustomed to negative responses, Maria Elena felt the experts were shortsighted. She believed in her own vision of the future. She flew to Nairobi, the capital of Kenya in 1991, armed only with a catalog of products and a map. She checked into a hotel and picked up the Yellow Pages. Two weeks later, she flew home with $150,000 in orders.

Working first out of her garage, then a small warehouse, she began shipping products, while more orders came in. In four months, she shipped $700,000 worth of orders. Her second year registered $2.4 million, a figure that doubled the following year, and again the next. With sales averaging $13 million each year through the early 1990s, International High Tech Marketing made *Inc.'s* 500 list. Maria Elena is the only person in the magazine's history to make the prestigious list with two separate companies built from zero capital.

Maria Elena Ibanez had good products to sell. But her success was built upon belief in herself and determination. There isn't a marketing plan in the world that can give you that.

Cynthia Kersey
Excerpted and adapted from Unstoppable

The Damn Cape

There can't be a crisis next week. My schedule is already full.

Henry Kissinger

When I was younger, before the reality of actually being a mom showed up with the birth of my first daughter, Madison, I had visionary ideas of the kind of mother I would be and the kind of environment I would raise my children in. Since Madison's birth about eleven years ago, I have long given up any illusions about a perfectly immaculate and tidy house with an alphabetized pantry, clothes hung in idyllic wardrobes, fresh flower arrangements on tabletops and Martha Stewart dinners. I gave up sophomoric ideals of calmly chaperoning my children to ballet, soccer, gymnastics and play group, not to mention all the volunteer work I would do at the PTA, the library and the Mommy-and-Me classes. I was going to make artistic little cookies and cupcakes, snowmen on paper plates with cotton balls, valentines from doilies and—of course—handmade Halloween costumes.

As we all know, life doesn't always turn out the way we

envision it. It doesn't mean that life is bad. In fact, more often than not, what we get is much better than we envision, but it is different. Instead of being an at-home mom, I work full-time and commute about four hours a day. With my schedule, it's impossible to do all the parenting things I used to envision. I wouldn't change the way things are, though. I love my job, and it's a "me" thing. However, I still feel it's important to do a lot of the other "mommy" things. My cookies aren't artistic, but I do make them. I don't cook like Martha Stewart, but I do make dinner on occasion. I have no idea what to do with paper plates, doilies or cotton balls, but I can draw a darn good butterfly tattoo with a gel pen.

Halloween is a big holiday for my kids, especially Madison, now eleven years old. Still, I have always felt bad that I never made her a costume. She's always had great costumes, but I mean really "make" one—you know, with fabric, patterns, string and needles. For Christmas last year, Madison received a sewing machine (she's much more domestic than I). This year, I decided I would make at least part of her costume. Madison wanted to be Lucilla, the emperor's sister from *Gladiator*. We found the dress and accessories without a problem, but then she decided she wanted a cape. That's when my life became hell.

When Madison said she wanted me to make her a cape, I was thrilled. I could make it, and it would be easy. Slap two pieces of material together, give it a tie and, *voilà*, you have a cape and a daughter who thinks you're "the bomb."

My first mistake was taking Madison with me to the fabric store and letting her pick the pattern and fabrics. I couldn't have possibly known that it was a mistake because I have never sewn a thing in my life and don't have a clue what a pattern does, how it works or what it means. However, after finding myself capable of threading the machine (albeit with the instruction manual) after a mere four hours, I felt like a pro.

Madison picked out what I thought was a lovely cape pattern. I didn't know what any of the number things meant on the package, so I just gave it to the nice lady at the really big cutting table and asked her to measure out the correct amounts of fabrics. Madison chose a cranberry velour for the outside of the cape and a cheery purple satin for the lining. When the nice lady at the really big cutting table measured out fourteen yards of fabric, I thought she was being generous so we could make a bedspread or tent or something with the leftovers.

I woke up early Sunday morning thinking I could surprise Madison by making the cape before church, which I was absolutely determined to get to. I pulled out the pattern. *Hmm. Lots of puzzle-like pieces. Must be what they call "pattern pieces."* They were numbered, which was good. Any moron can figure out that you put 1 with 2, 2 with 3, 3 with 4. I just hadn't counted on 9 with 10, 15 with 16. It took me two hours to cut out the "pattern pieces" and another two hours to pin them to the fabric. I was running short on time. I didn't want to miss church, but I couldn't leave what I'd started where I started it. I had to move furniture in the living room to lay all the fabric out, and I could just imagine the fun my three-year-old would have if she woke up and saw it just waiting for her to play on. I said a quick prayer, asked for God's forgiveness for missing church, and prayed there was a sewing saint to help me out. A little less than four hours later, I had the fabric cut and the first seam pinned together. I had no idea what the little black diamond things meant. I decided the pattern artist just put them there to make novices feel stupid. I ignored them. It was time to start sewing. By Sunday evening, I had the seams of the outside of the cape stitched neatly together. I figured I could wrap up the rest of the cape on Monday evening.

Monday evening, I raced home from work to get working on the cape. All I had to do was the lining and the hood and stitch everything together and hem it. Madison was so cute. She stayed in the room with me, trying to help as much as I would let her. She was so patient and smiled the whole time. I thought back to when I was her age. I would have been thinking about how pretty I would look in my costume and have fanciful imaginations about actually being the person I was portraying. I could tell from looking at Madison's face that she was in the same dreamlike state. At that moment I thought, *No matter how much work and time this takes, the look on Madison's face is worth it.* That's about when things started going downhill.

I stitched the lining together without a hitch. I was thrilled. I laid out the velour, then laid out the lining on top of it, certain that putting the two together would be a snap. Madison's face changed. "Mom, I think something's wrong with that." She was pointing to the lining. I didn't see it at first. And then my heart sank. I had sewn the eight panels of the lining right side up, wrong side up, right side up, wrong side up. I had to rip the whole thing apart and do it all over. I let out of stream of epithets that would make a sailor proud and ended with "damn cape."

Madison, bless her, said, "Mom, it's okay. Just leave it. It's just the lining. No one will see it." I gave her a hug. I think if Madison were anyone else, I would have left it, but I had seen the look on her face when she was thinking about how pretty she would look when she was dressed up, and I wanted it to be perfect for her. At least as perfect as I could make it. You see, Madison is a cancer survivor. She had cancer treatments, a bone marrow transplant and lots of complications suck up a majority of the last four years of her life. As far as I'm concerned, she has compromised enough. And I could do better than a badly sewn lining. That didn't mean my language cleaned up much, but I did manage to rip the lining apart and get it re-sewn correctly . . . I think. It was almost midnight. I put the damn cape away for Tuesday.

I raced home from work on Tuesday, determined to finish the damn cape. I laid out the velour and the lining on top of it. I started pinning the two sides together. I think I figured out why I was supposed to cut those little black darts. I think maybe that's what is used as a kind of guide to piece the pieces together. Maybe the pattern artist really wasn't an evil person with an intelligence complex. I would remember that next time. Had to make do for now.

I don't claim to know anything about fabric, but I have no doubt that the combination of velour and satin is about the most unfriendly combination you can encounter. The velour rolls up, you can't find a straight line, the satin slips around everywhere. In fact, I think it's an ideal way to torture hardened criminals. I don't know how many hours it took me to pin the thing together, but my repertoire of profanity developed at an envious rate, always ending in "damn cape." Madison just sat with me patiently. I think she was praying—if not for the damn cape, for me not to go to hell for all the swearing.

Finally pinned, it was late, and I knew I wasn't going to finish the cape, but I wanted to at least stitch the outside seams together. The fabric was so heavy and unwieldy, Madison had to help me. I slipped (okay, shoved) the first corner under the footer thing on the sewing machine and pressed the pedal. I had sewn about six inches (of 9,872) when the machine stopped. I stepped on the pedal again . . . and again . . . and again. Nothing. I tried flipping buttons and knobs. I tried plugs. I tried the fuse box. Nothing. I then took swearing to a whole new art form, crescendoing at levels that Pavarotti would never attain, ending yet again with "damn cape." I threw the cape on the counter and went to bed.

Wednesday morning, I e-mailed my dear friend, Jo, who is an incredible seamstress and knows things about machinery. She e-mailed me back, "DON'T PANIC. We can do it at my house Friday night." That didn't satisfy me. I called her at work. "IT'S TOO LATE! I'M ALREADY PANICKING!" She laughed at me. I swore at her and hung up.

Even though I was at work, my head was on the damn cape. And the sewing machine. I couldn't imagine that it was broken after less than a year. Singer was going to get an all-fired-up letter from me with a good resounding "what for"! I found myself in the copy center at work, moaning and whining about the sewing machine and the cape fiasco. Jose, our wonderful copy center person, was there. Jose is a quiet guy. He often knows a lot more about a lot of things than people think, but he never says anything. He had "a look." (I thought *if Jose knows more about that sewing machine than I do, I'll wear a tiara and call myself Diana.* I'll be shopping for my tiara this weekend.) As it turns out, Jose used to fix sewing machines. Go figure. He said the velour fuzz had probably gummed up the machine and told me what to look for. He said if that didn't work to bring it to work with me on Thursday and he would fix it.

I raced home from work on Wednesday and ran to the sewing machine. I pulled it apart and blew it all out. There sure was a lot of cranberry-colored stuff in there. I put the machine back together and gave it a test run. It worked! God bless Jose. In less than two hours I had the cape stitched together, complete with hood, and hemmed. It is a far cry from perfect and there's no threat that Armani is going to try to lure me, but it is complete and Madison is happy with it. It's huge. In fact, I think when Madison is done with it I'm going to use it as a car cover.

I like that I was able to make my daughter's costume, in spite of, or maybe because of, the frustrations. The joy on her face was priceless, as was the time we spent together making it. There were also a lot of wonderful lessons. I taught my daughter all the words she shouldn't use and their proper use. I learned that after thirty-seven years, I still don't have any patience, and God still isn't tired of trying to teach it to me. I learned that the little black diamonds are important and that not everyone is evil. I learned that the people you least expect it from can be your best resources. I learned that there is nothing more important, more rewarding, closer to heaven than being a mom . . . even if your name isn't Martha Stewart.

My house is now completely trashed. My three-year-old has been without a bath for four days and naked most of that time. There are at least a dozen loads of laundry that need to be cleaned. I don't remember when I checked the mailbox last. I should probably attend to these things now that the cape is finished. . . . Or I could just curl up with my babies under the damn cape.

Colleen Justus Eastman

Running for Office, Running for Life

Keep away from people who try to belittle your ambitions. Small people always do that, but the really great make you feel that you, too, can become great.

Mark Twain

November 7, 2000: At the Holiday Inn in Bismarck, North Dakota, Heidi Heitkamp, the Democratic candidate for governor, charges to the podium, her trademark mane of red hair moussed into submission. Heitkamp, forty-five, is big, beautiful and lit up from the inside. The election results aren't all in, but she appears jubilant.

"Isn't this a wild ride?" she shouts to the cheering crowd. As she speaks, she pummels the air with her right fist—the one sign that something about this campaign is different.

The fist is grotesquely swollen, each finger is a sausage, with no break between wrist and forearm. It's the telltale sign of lymphedema, the fluid retention that may occur after losing lymph nodes. And it is the only evidence that six weeks earlier, Heitkamp had her right breast and eighteen cancerous nodes removed—the only hint that she is fighting not just for her career, but for her life.

All that summer Heitkamp, the state's popular attorney general, and Republican John Hoeven had been in a statistical dead heat in the race for governor. Then Heitkamp saw her doctor about a lump under her arm. On September 15 she and her husband, family practitioner Darwin Lange, learned it was malignant.

Heitkamp didn't dwell on the negative. "I know this sounds corny, but when you come from a big family, you always worry about how something that happens to you will affect them," says Heitkamp, who has six siblings and two children (ages fifteen and eleven). "I felt this would be rougher for them to hear than it was for me. My personality type is, okay, you get three minutes to feel sorry for yourself, then you start dealing with it.

"Well," Heitkamp adds with a laugh, "maybe I would give myself a few more minutes."

But Heitkamp had something else to contemplate: 474,000 voters. She never considered keeping her cancer a secret. "People have a right to know about the health of elected officials," she says. But she wanted to wait—first, to find out the kind of cancer and second, to tell her family.

She didn't have that luxury: Someone leaked the news. Heitkamp gathered her family, who took it hard—"very hard," says her sister Holly. Then on September 20 at a press conference, she didn't hold back. "I mean, this is as much a surprise to me as it is to you guys," she said, her eyes filling up.

About a week later, after Heitkamp's surgery, she learned the cancer was Stage IIIA—it was advanced and had spread to her lymph nodes. Yes, she would need chemotherapy and radiation, but she could stick with the campaign. Besides, her family wouldn't let her do it otherwise. Her fifteen-year-old daughter, a swimmer, was direct. "Well, you're not going to get out now, are you? It's like quitting in the last leg of the 100 meter."

The press focused on her health. A candidate with breast cancer is news; one with advanced cancer—stop the presses!

North Dakota's *Forum and Tribune* ran stories putting the five-year survival rate for a Stage IIIA at fifty-six percent. Although they quoted experts saying Heitkamp's prospects were better, word was out: The woman who would be governor could have as little as a fifty-six per-cent chance of being alive a second term.

After reading what she took to be her death sentence, Heitkamp rushed to reassure her family. "My daughter's at a swim meet—how can I control what she's listening to? And I'm worried about my mother."

Her mother's reaction surprised her. "She said, 'How are you?'—not all grim and serious, but like, 'Hi! How the heck are ya?' And I said, 'Not bad for someone who's half-dead!' We couldn't stop laughing."

As it turned out, the outlook was not so grim. "I've received some good news," she told the public. "Doctors expect me to make a full recovery."

At any point, Heitkamp could have shaken fewer hands, cuddled fewer babies, stopped those 200-mile treks between Bismarck and Fargo. After her first chemo treat-ment, she needed her white-blood-cell count checked. If low, it meant she was susceptible to infection. Retreating into a back room of a Fargo clinic to have blood drawn, she looked pale and forlorn.

But when the results came, Heitkamp waved the paper at a campaign worker. "Look!" she said. "A normal count is about 4.5 to 11; I'm 4.9. The doctor told us if the count went to one, I'd have to avoid crowds and take precautions. But my white blood cells are reading favorably. We're ready to fight the rest of the campaign!"

Fight, as it turned out, was the operative word. During a radio show, outgoing Republican Governor Ed Schafer described his initial eighteen-hour days, then added, "I hope Heidi isn't going to get herself in a situation where physically it would be to her detriment to continue on in this job."

Then things got weird. A Bismarck man contacted the Heitkamp campaign to tell this story: A man identifying himself as a pollster had asked whom he was voting for. When he said Heitkamp, the pollster pressed on, "You know she's very sick, right?" Then the pollster cited possible side effects of cancer treatment—"hair falling out, lack of strength and so forth"—and concluded, "And you're still going to support Heidi Heitkamp?"

Hoeven's campaign denied involvement. Still, said his campaign manager, Carol Olson, there was no way to control thousands of supporters. And by November, Hoeven was leading by three percentage points, according to a poll. Even more significant, Heitkamp had dropped among women.

Election night, 11:00 P.M. Heitkamp can't ignore Hoeven's ten-point lead. Tearfully, the woman who would have been North Dakota's first female governor concedes, saying, "This is the proudest moment of my life."

Now spending time with her kids and volunteering, Heitkamp has a message for anyone who has a loved one with cancer: "I hope everyone gives her the ability to do her job and live her life. Because if the message is 'Go home, quit and if you can prove you're cancer-free, we'll let you back in the land of the living,' well, you start to believe it yourself."

Pausing, Heitkamp beams. "Every day is a contest," she says simply. "Gotta keep your eye on the prize."

Judith Newman

I've Gotta Be Me

When you know what you want and want it badly enough, you will find the ways to get it.

Jim Rohn

Twenty years ago I was a brand-new federal prosecutor in the U.S. Attorney's Office in California. One of my first cases involved the prosecution of a man who had been arrested by Drug Enforcement Administration (DEA) agents in a "reverse sting." Unlike a "sting" where the drug agents pretend to be buying drugs, these DEA agents were pretending to be cocaine sellers, and arrested Mr. Smith when he showed up with sixty thousand dollars cash to buy a kilo of cocaine.

Aware that I was a new prosecutor, Mr. Smith's attorney, an older experienced defense attorney, decided to take the case to trial, apparently assuming a "not guilty" verdict would be easy. Late one afternoon I began cross-examining Mr. Smith, who had the daunting task of trying to convince the jury that the sixty thousand dollars seized from him wasn't money from previous drug sales, and that he had a credible explanation for meeting DEA agents in a parking lot late at night. Like many new prosecutors, I had little experience cross-examining witnesses, and the result was that Mr. Smith was artfully evading my every question. My questions were technically correct but deadly dull. The jurors were bored and acquittal looked certain.

After court concluded for the day, the DEA agent who had arrested Mr. Smith dragged me back to my office, slammed the door, and began screaming at me. "You are going to lose this case! You've got to be like Ricky!" He kept insisting that if Ricky were cross-examining Mr. Smith, he would interrogate him in his own unique style that had brought many "kingpin" drug dealers to their knees.

I went home that night, devastated. *How could I be more like Ricky H?* I called a former law school classmate for advice on how I could magically transform myself into "Ricky" overnight. Her advice was simple: "You aren't Ricky, and don't even try to be! If you try to adopt his cutthroat, demolishing style, it will come off in front of the jury as phony and contrived, and you will lose the case for sure." I thought long and hard about her advice and decided she was right.

With newfound confidence that I could win the case "in my own way," I returned to court the next morning to complete Mr. Smith's cross-examination. By the time I got done, Mr. Smith's story and his credibility had been ripped to shreds. When I sat back down, my DEA agent leaned over and whispered "Great job!" The jury returned a guilty verdict in less than an hour.

Outside the courtroom Mr. Smith's attorney came over to me, shook my hand, and said, "That was fantastic. I didn't think you had it in you!" I learned that my success in the courtroom was not dependent on being like a man but would come from being myself.

Kristin S. Door

"You will meet a tall, dark, handsome man and
you will beat him out for a promotion at the office."

From The Wall Street Journal. *Permission, Cartoon Features Syndicate.*

The Red Bandana

Any working mother, unwittingly or not, has played the scramble game. It's that test of wills, endurance and patience where you come home from a long day at work, and are immediately met with "the crisis." For example, your child needs a costume for a school play or has to finish a science project she "forgot" about that's due tomorrow. The rules of the game are simple: Be as creative as possible using only objects found in your home (because by now all stores are closed) and finish before your child yells, "Mom, hurry, I'll be late!" It may sound easy enough to play, but there are always hidden obstacles: lack of sleep on the contestant's part, another child suddenly becomes sick or your husband informs you there is nothing in the house to make for dinner.

I've played the scramble game before, but I'm not good at it. I have great admiration for those mothers who can take tissue paper, some Scotch tape and a few pipe cleaners and—"voila"—their daughter now has wings for a fairy princess costume. MacGyver's got nothing on these supermoms. So instead, I go out of my way to avoid the game.

It was school musical time, and this year I had it all

under control. No scramble game for me. I had a plan. Fortunately, the costumes were simple: blue jeans, white T-shirts, and a blue bandana for my son and a red one for my daughter. We had all the components on hand except for the red bandana, which I went out and purchased one week prior to the musical. Five days before, all articles for their costumes were washed and folded neatly on top of each child's dresser, after which both kids were given specific instructions not to touch these items till Friday night. Yes, it would be smooth sailing from there.

Thursday night, I find my kids playing cowboy with our family dog who was now proudly wearing my daughter's new red bandana. I took a deep breath, then calmly instructed my daughter to remove the bandana and put it back on her dresser.

Friday morning, the day of the musical, we reviewed the game plan:

"Hanna, when you get home from school, help your father with dinner, then immediately afterwards, get dressed for the musical so there's no chance of spilling anything on your white shirt. Be sure and help your brother get dressed, too."

"I got it Mom!" she whined in her "We've been over this before, I know I know!" voice.

A quick kiss, and we were both out the door to start our day. As I walked to the van something suddenly caught my eye. Lying on the ground, in a mud puddle on the side of the driveway was a red bandana! My heart sank, but my adrenaline kicked in, and I quickly regrouped. Angry, I stomped inside the house and tossed the mud-soaked red bandana into the washer. I shouted to the sitter to please take the laundry out of the washer and put it into the dryer when it was done, and I stormed back out of the house now late for work. All day long, the sight of that red bandana and my daughter's lack of responsibility festered inside of me till I couldn't take it any longer. Promptly at 3:15 P.M. I called home. The culprit answered the phone.

"Hanna Florence," I said coldly, stopping one name shy of the full name triad that always meant business. "Where is your red bandana?" I asked, knowing the answer already.

"On my dresser with the rest of my costume," she replied confidently.

"WRONG! It's now in the dryer because I found it outside in a mud puddle, and I had to wash it this morning before work!" I continued on with the standard, "How could you be so irresponsible" lecture, and how she was "so grounded this weekend," that I barely noticed the sound of the dryer door opening as she looked for her red bandana.

"Mom," she interrupted me, "there's nothing in the dryer."

"Oh for Pete's sake! I told the sitter to put the clothes in the dryer when the washer was done! Look in the washer!" My anger was escalating as I anticipated another round of the scramble game: Did all the mud come out? Will it be dry in time? If not, will I have time after work to run to the store to purchase another red bandana?

A few moments passed, and she finally said, "Well, there is a red bandana in here, but it's not mine."

"Oh you know perfectly well it's yours! You had it on the dog yesterday, and I told you to put it back in your room. I suppose you must have 'forgot' and it fell off the dog while you were outside, and that's where I found it!" I rambled insanely, now drawing looks from coworkers trying to surmise the whole story from a one-ended conversation.

"But Mom," she insisted, "this one doesn't have the little rhinestones on it like mine. I'm up in my room now, and mine is on my dresser right where I left it."

I was shocked. *I'm such a horrible mother,* I thought to myself. I had accused my daughter without having all the facts. I muttered out a feeble, "I'm so sorry for yelling at you, Honey," as I breathed a sigh of relief. I asked her to put her father on the phone. I related the whole story to my husband, and we shared a short laugh before I reminded him to help our four-year-old into his costume after dinner.

"Um, he's already dressed," my husband replied sheepishly. "Now don't get mad, but . . ." his words trailed off slightly.

"Why, what's wrong, now?" I shouted to the chagrin of my eavesdropping peers.

"Oh, nothing really, it's just that he's had his costume on all day, and his jeans are a little dirty in the knees."

"What! How dirty? I do NOT believe this! Can no one in this entire family follow directions? Why do I bother? I specifically said—Oh, just forget it! I can't deal with this right now, I'll be home in an hour!"

An hour later I was muttering incoherently to myself as I bent over the sink frantically scrubbing the knees of the only clean pair of jeans my son had when I heard a tiny voice behind me say, "I'm sorry, Mama."

I looked down to see my four-year-old son, Hunter, with downcast eyes, his hands behind his back, dressed in a white shirt, blue bandana, and Scooby-Doo underwear. I was suddenly reminded of what being a good mom was all about—and it had nothing to do with clean jeans or red bandanas.

"Oh, Sweetie," I said bending down to hug him, "I know you're sorry, and it's all right now." I kissed him on the cheek, and he smiled a broad grin that instantly melted my heart. "Here, let's put these back on." As I smoothed down the cowlick in his blonde hair I added, "There, you look just perfect to me—my little cowboy!"

Later that evening, as I peered through the lens of my camcorder proudly recording my babies as they sang "God Bless America" with their classmates, I was reminded once again what a blessing children are. Kids are only kids for a short time. Before you know it, they are too old to be kissed in public and will routinely ignore you when they pass you on the street. You'll no longer be the one they run to when they are sad or hurt, and gone will be the days when they climb into your lap and wrap their tiny arms around your neck and snuggle under your chin. I may never be a "supermom" able to successfully juggle a career, a home and a family, but I'm learning to enjoy every precious moment I have with my children—even the difficult ones. For I know that all too soon they'll be grown up, leaving me with clean floors, tidy rooms and lonely memories of messier, happier days.

Jodi L. Severson

6

A MOTHER'S WORK

*T*he highest reward for a person's toil is not
what they get for it, but what they become
by it.

John Ruskin

THE FAMILY CIRCUS   By Bil Keane

"You used to WORK before you were married,
didn't you, Mommy?"

Reprinted with permission of Bil Keane.

Letters from My Daughter

It is not what you do for your children but what you have taught them to do for themselves that will make them successful human beings.

Ann Landers

When my daughter Julie was six years old, she wrote a letter to the Tooth Fairy and put it under her pillow with her tooth. I wrote back, telling her to be a good girl and always to brush her teeth carefully. Little did I know we were starting a tradition.

By the time Julie was in fourth grade, she had figured out that handwritten notes could do more than welcome the Tooth Fairy. Once, after a heated discussion we'd had about why she shouldn't buy a pair of clogs, Julie wrote me the following:

Dear Mom,

Here are the reasons I want clogs:

1. You wanted boots for a long time, and you finally got them.

2. If clogs hurt my feet that's my problem.

3. When Grandma gave us money for Christmas she said we could get whatever we wanted with it.
Love, Julie

I gave in—and Julie learned the power of the written word.

Over the next few years, Julie and I exchanged notes about boys, homework, phone calls and chores. Some notes were apologies after shouting matches. Others were just happy thoughts spilling onto paper. When Julie was in eighth grade, she responded to an affectionate note of mine.

Dear Mom,
Your letters make me feel great no matter what kind of mood I'm in. Sometimes they even make me cry because they touch me so deeply. I'm really glad we have the kind of relationship that we do, even though we have our arguments. I guess that's life with a teenager—or with a thirty-nine-year-old!
I love you. Julie

P.S. Writing my feelings down is much easier for me than trying to express them verbally.

Julie's postscripts explained why the note system worked so well for us. She was going through the traumas of adolescence, and I was having some problems of my own. Writing was the most effective way for us to communicate our feelings.

One day during the summer before Julie started high school, she left her razor on the tub where her five-year-old brother could have picked it up and cut himself. After I pointed out her carelessness, I asked Julie what she thought her punishment should be. She stomped off in a huff, but an hour later left a note on the kitchen counter.

Dear Mom,
   I'm sorry for being so thoughtless.
   For my punishment I will not:
   1. Go to the mall after school.
   2. Watch television in the afternoon.
   3. Snack before dinner.

She never left her razor on the tub again.

Two months later, on Julie's first day of high school, we had a fight about whether it was appropriate for her to wear eye makeup.

That evening I received a six-page handwritten letter from her.

Dear Mom,
   I'm sorry if I acted snotty this morning, but I really got mad. You didn't even give me a chance to say anything! If you would at least discuss things with me maybe it would be a little easier for us. Instead of telling me how awful my eyes look, you could help me to make them look better.

Page three contained all the logic my tormented teen could muster.

   1. I think I'm very responsible and can learn to put makeup on in ways that both you and I would like.
   2. I don't "cake it on" like some of my friends do—I read the directions on the package and advice in magazine articles on how to apply it.
   3. I'm growing up; I want to add to my looks and bring out my eyes.
   4. How about a three-week trial period to test my ability to wear it?

Needless to say, my daughter wore makeup—discreetly—from then on. Her whole face seemed to light up, not only from the touch of blush but from the sense of freedom she had pried out of her mother.

Not long after that, my husband and I separated. The next few months were chaotic. Besides trying to provide stability for my four children, I had to budget our funds and work longer hours. As my raw emotions caused my mothering skills to dwindle, Julie came to the rescue with a note.

Dear Mom,

I know you're going through a hard time and I wish I could make all your problems disappear. Unfortunately, I can only tell you how much I love you. We're all upset about the divorce, but you're still a great, helpful and loving mom.
Love, Julie

There were quite a few times that year when I took my frustrations out on the children. After one particularly nasty tirade, Julie dropped this message in my purse for me to read at work:

Dear Mom,

I know things are difficult for you right now, and we all understand. I think you should go out more often to distract yourself. We are all growing up and have our own interests and friends. We'll always be your kids, and you won't lose us.
I love you! Julie

A few weeks before her eighteenth birthday, I asked Julie what she wanted. "I'm working on it," she said.

I should have known that Julie was writing me the letter of her life. Here's what some of it said:

Soon I will be living on my own at college. I feel I have matured by following your rules with very few exceptions.

For my eighteenth birthday I would like to be treated and respected as a mature and responsible person. I'd like:

A later curfew or none at all.

*Permission to make and receive telephone calls after
10:00 P.M.*
The freedom to make my own decisions.
To be thought of as a close friend.

Now it was my turn to respond. I sat writing late into
the night.

Dearest Julie,
   *Adulthood isn't a sudden jolt of freedom to do whatever you
want. It is simply being responsible. If you believe you can
behave like an adult, I will treat you as one.*

I next addressed her birthday proposition list, asking
her to be considerate about curfews and phone calls. I
agreed that she should make decisions and said I would
offer advice only when requested.
   I ended with this:

   *Julie, I wish you a happy life filled with love and solid
decisions based on solid values. I hope you continue to
develop the many talents God has given you.*
Happy Birthday, my friend! Love, Mom

My daughter left home for college a few years later. I
missed her tremendously, but our tradition pulled us
through again. Her letters from college were wonderful!

Patricia Lorenz

"Read me the story about Jill and her associate going up the hill."

Pennies and Prayers

The three of us were gathered around our breakfast table. It was 7:00 A.M. on a Monday.

Our three-year-old son was perched on his booster chair, wearing cowboy pajamas, bunny-rabbit slippers and a corduroy robe. He looked up at us intently through oversized, sparkling blue eyes with long, fluttering lashes. Chewing his Cheerios, he started asking his usual questions.

"Is today a go-to-work day?"

"Yes, Sweetheart, it is."

"Can I go, too?"

"No, honey."

"Does Daddy have to go to work?"

"Yes, he does."

"Why does Daddy have to go to work?"

"Daddy has to go to work to make money. We need money to live in this apartment and buy food and milk and juice and cereal at the grocery store. We need money to buy other things, like our TV, these dishes and hamburgers and ice cream at McDonald's. We need money for all that. If Daddy doesn't go to work, we won't have any money."

This Monday morning was going to be very different from all the others, though. Today, I was going to have to leave for work, too. My husband, Alex, had just changed careers, and his compensation was now based solely on the promise of future commissions. We decided that I would begin working outside the home to help supplement our income until he got established. New questions from our son were sure to follow.

"But why do you have to go to work, Mommy?"

"Well, Vince, Mommy is going to work because we need . . . just a little extra money."

All of sudden, those big blue eyes of his lit up—as if finally he actually understood what we were trying to tell him. He jumped from his chair and took off running down the hall for his bedroom. We heard him open a drawer of his dresser, and then a clinking sound filled the air. The *chink-chink-chink* noise kept getting louder. It matched the cadence of running feet. Vince appeared, clutching his piggy bank to his chest.

Each time that grammas, grandpas, aunts and uncles or friends came over, they gave Vince money. He gripped every coin with his elfin fingers and carefully positioned each one to drop through the narrow slot. One at a time, they clinked into the top of his chubby, yellow, plastic pig. We thought this was a valuable tool to teach our son the concept of saving money. We explained to him that after there were many coins inside, it could be used for something very special. He counted the contents often and always referred to it as "my money."

He proudly raised his plump little piggy toward us. Still panting, with excitement in his voice and a big smile on his face, he said, "I'll give you all my money so you can stay home and we can all be together."

We couldn't speak. The lumps in our throats brought tears to our eyes. A sharp, cruel, arrow of guilt penetrated deep into my spirit. Could it ever be successfully removed? It felt like my heart had been wounded beyond repair. Could I ever forget the words my child just spoke? Would that look of anticipation in his eyes ever leave the camera of my mind? Had we made a mistake? Was the decision we made a bad one? Our desire was only to do what we thought best for our family.

That incident took place thirty-two years ago. In the years between then and now, we have learned how to seek God's guidance in our decisions and our finances. If at times, we felt we had made a mistake, we entrusted the outcome to God in faith.

That blue-eyed boy now flies 757 and 767 jet aircraft all over the world for a major airline. His profession has located him in a different state from where we live. Just recently we enjoyed a memorable seven-day visit at our son's home. A major topic of conversation during our stay was the possibility of our buying a condo as a second home in the area where he lives.

The three of us were sitting around his breakfast table. Sipping his coffee, Vince looked up at us with his sparkling eyes and said, "Listen Mom and Dad, don't worry about the money part of it. I've saved a lot over the years and I can pay your taxes and fees and whatever expenses you need help with. Just do it and we can all be together in the same place."

Some things never change. We have contacted a real estate agent and will fly back to look at property. Piggy banks are profitable partners. God's protective, loving hand can help overcome obstacles and mend a mother's heart until it is filled with overflowing gratitude, not guilt.

Peggy L. Bert

Night Shift

Kathy Smith, West Coast TV-news anchorwoman, claims that off-camera and without makeup she wouldn't be recognized. To avoid attracting attention in her Seattle neighborhood, she asked her children not to tell people what she did for a living.

One day, while her five-year-old son was getting a haircut, she overheard him reply to a question from the barber about her work: "I can't tell you what my mom does. All I know is she gets all dressed up and goes out at night."

Maggi White

"The lady of the house is out wheeling and dealing."

Embracing the Mommy Track

"Do you have children?" the job recruiter asked.

"Well, yes, I do," I said, pleased that he asked. I stirred, ready to dive into my purse for pictures.

"And do you have foolproof arrangements for caring for them?" he asked, staring at my resume.

"I do," I said, feeling surprised and defensive.

That summer, I was hired to do temporary on-site documentation for a large company. I took my place in a big room, riddled with cubicles that were filled by women. Since it was easy to overhear nearby phone conversations, I told my kids only to call when they really needed something. I had just hung up from a hushed and hurried conversation detailing one of those desperate needs, "She took the book I was reading and won't give it back," when I heard a coworker's voice rise.

"I told you to monitor that meeting," Joan said, sounding more distraught than usual. "Yes, well, we have an agreement and I'm counting on you to keep up your end of it."

She hung up the phone and sighed.

"Is everything all right?" I asked, peering into her cubicle.

"Oh, it's just my kids. I've developed a code for talking, so it sounds like business."

"You mean, all the conversations about event planning, catering, and meeting agendas, all those calls were your kids?"

Joan smiled and nodded. "They need a lot of attention when school first lets out."

I began listening more carefully to my coworkers. Denise inserted a Jello recipe into a deep conversation on allocation of scarce resources. And Alma was doing a masterful job of negotiating with a tough client, until I realized she was dealing with the toughest client of all: her thirteen-year-old. All across the room, women were doing their work, keeping to their production schedules and taking care of their kids.

At the end of every week, our supervisor brought us together, and each of us reported on number of pages produced and number of manuals completed. But the real accomplishments, number of fights prevented, number of scrapes and cuts nursed and soothed, number of chores monitored, were unspoken.

The next temporary job I interviewed for required a "detail-oriented, team player, able to multitask and meet tough deadlines." The job description sounded like my home life, although I was hoping for team members more articulate and sophisticated than my two kids.

When the boss asked me about previous experience, I said, "Well, I am a mom."

She did not return my smile. "We try not to get our personal lives involved here," she said.

I murmured something about my MBA and she nodded approvingly.

And so being a mom has seemed a liability in the business world, something to tuck in my corner pocket, something to "work around." I called those trips to the orthodontist "off-sites," those afternoons when I watched soccer games "prospecting meetings" and those days when a child was home sick "one-on-one's." I kept the mother part of me separate from the business woman part. Until a recent meeting.

A fundraising committee for a women's foundation brought twenty women together around a large table. The chairwoman asked us to introduce ourselves and a brief flow occurred: "lawyer, CEO, councilwoman, CPA." Then, my friend Kate spoke.

"I am the mother of three incredible children. On the side, I also spend fifty hours a week running a consulting company."

The silence spread like spilt milk. Everyone stared at Kate, perhaps wondering if she had seen too many fifties sitcoms. Who ever heard of businesswomen talking about their parenting status?

The chairwoman cleared her throat and nodded at me to introduce myself.

I had come to this committee to network, do good deeds and make valuable business connections. Admitting I was a writer was iffy enough. Yet something in me was tugging open. I felt a lump moving into my throat, tears hovering in my eyes. All those years of hiding my motherhood flared up.

"I am a mother and a writer. Both of these occupations are the most complex, wonderful and confusing things I've ever done," I said.

A few women nodded.

"My name is Susan and I don't have any children, but I have a dog that means the world to me. And by the way, I'm an investment banker," said the next woman.

"I want to reintroduce myself," the chairwoman said. "I never get to mention my kids in public."

At the end of the meeting, I thanked Kate for her bravery.

"I thought it was about time I talked about the people who are most important to me," she said.

And so, for those few moments, two crucial parts of my life were blended. "I am a mother" is one of the most heartfelt things I can reveal about myself. Those words hold a flood of dreams and adaptations, of heartaches and indescribable joys; they mean a commitment that goes to my very core.

For me, Kate started an important process. By defining ourselves as mothers, by declaring our love and pride in our children, we let others know who we are and what we value. And that, mother by mother, child by child, is one of the ways women transform the world.

Deborah Shouse

I'd Masquerade as a Mom
if I Could Sew the Costume

I've been unmasked by a simple Girl Scout patch. I'm not a good mom after all, just somebody covering for my lack of sewing and baking skills with a lot of secret trips to Wal-Mart. It started with a half-dozen triangle-shaped Try-It little badges my daughter, Mandy, received for successfully completing an activity in Brownies. The troop leader gave her the Baggie with her patches, had her recite the Girl Scout promise, then sent her back to me for final adhesion. My solution? A glue gun. A good glue gun is an invaluable thing in a non-crafty mom's arsenal. Forget Martha. I have a glue gun, and I know how to use it.

It didn't work. The patches refused to completely adhere. The edges started to peel and then one Tuesday, after a meeting, Mandy comes home with a blank vest. "Where are your patches?"

"They fell off during recess." She shrugs. "I couldn't find them." Off we trot to the Girl Scout supply store. On the way, I call the troop leader and get the names of the patches I need. There are hundreds of tiny bins with colorful badges around the store, each labeled and ranked

according to level. I glance at the area for Juniors and
Cadettes and groan. There are a lot of potential patches to
be had. With the replacements in hand, I head to the register. "How can I get these to stay on?" I ask the lady. "I
tried a glue gun, but it didn't work very well."

She cocks her head and looks . . . confused. "Glue gun?"

"Yeah. They just fell off. Are these iron-ons or something?" I flip them over and look for some kind of gluey
back.

"You sew them on."

"Sew?" I parrot. "As in a sewing machine?"

"Well, yeah."

"Oh." I haven't touched a sewing machine since home
economics. I made a shirt that ended up shorter on one
side than the other and a pillow that I accidentally sewed
shut before I stuffed it. To say I have even a modicum of
sewing talent would be stretching things. "You sure you
can't iron these on?"

"What would be the point?"

"To make it easier for moms like me."

The look in her eyes tells me what she thinks of mothers who don't sew. Apparently, we aren't the type to be
scout moms. "Don't you have a sewing machine?"

There's something from Kenmore collecting dust in my
attic, a gift from my husband, who thought it would help
us save money. I believe it has a needle on it and thread.
"I think so."

"Well, you'll have to sew them. That's the only way to
get them to stay on."

I can merge an Excel table into a Word file; I'm pretty
handy at operating my VCR, not to mention the seven-
function remote. Surely I can get a little patch to stay on
without resorting to a sewing machine. There has to be a
simpler way, I decide.

I head to Wal-Mart. The lady at the craft counter, an

older woman who looks exactly like someone's grand-mother, tells me to buy some really strong thread. "There's got to be a glue or something," I insist. She casts me a doubtful look but points me in the direction of fastening products. I return home with a bag full of things called Stitch Witchery and Tacky Glue. I try each in succession, but the patches are more stubborn than I am. I end up with glue all over the vest and the patches on the floor. After a long session of trial and error, I find that Stitch Witchery, an iron and a damp cloth sort of work. At least well enough for my daughter's next Brownie meeting. I send her off to school with her vest, and keep my fingers crossed.

When I pick her up a few hours later, she is sans two patches. I look at the other girls, all with neatly affixed patches. I ask a few moms how they got them to stay and they all say "sewing machine." In an age of technology, I have been undone by the simplest of tasks: sewing. If this were the nineteeth century, I'd have been sent to learn embroidery techniques instead of sent to college. But since I wasn't, I feel like the oddball out, and what's worse, my daughter is running around with a blotchy vest that screams, "My mother can't sew."

Immediately, I make a new vow. Now that school is out, I'm going to get myself down to the store and buy a new vest, and get replacements for every glue-smeared patch on her vest. Then I'm going to haul out that sewing machine, say a prayer and hope to goodness they come out straight and I don't sew my finger to the fabric. But before I do, I'll stop at Wal-Mart and see if they've developed any new miracle glue sticks yet. There's always hope. Even for moms like me.

Shirley Kawa-Jump

Coming to Mom's Rescue

The miracle is this—the more we share, the more we have.

Leonard Nimoy

It was one of the worst days of my life: The washing machine broke down, the telephone kept ringing, my head ached, and the mail carrier brought a bill I had no money to pay. Almost to the breaking point, I lifted my one-year-old into his highchair, leaned my head against the tray, and began to cry. Without a word, my son took his pacifier out of his mouth and stuck it in mine.

Clara Null

THE FAMILY CIRCUS®   By Bil Keane

"Can Jason stay over? His mother works."

Reprinted with permission of Bil Keane.

The Scooby Doo Band-Aid

That Monday started out all wrong.

First thing in the morning the sitter called. Her son had pink eye, so she wouldn't be able to watch my boys, ages two and four.

My "real job" was freelance writing and editing of business-to-business marketing communications (as opposed to my dream job of being a successful, published author of novels), and I had a catalog to work on.

Okay, I thought, *I'll get as much work done as I can with the kids here.* They could watch television for a couple of hours in the morning, and then I'd take the afternoon off and we'd go to the park.

As I hung up the phone, a power company truck pulled up in front of the house. I'd forgotten about the notice they'd left Friday saying the electricity would be off from 8:00 to 10:30 A.M. for maintenance.

That meant no computer, but I could work on the catalog by hand for a couple of hours. It also meant no TV, but we had a whole playroom full of toys.

"All right," I said to my sons, gathering my folders and pen. "Let's go to the playroom."

Now if the television had been functioning, a couple of hours spent playing with toys would have been perfectly fine. But since watching TV wasn't an option, that was all my four-year-old, Griffin, wanted to do.

When was the TV going to be working again, he whined nonstop for half an hour. He didn't want to play with any of his toys. They were all "boooring." So he decided to torture his two-year-old brother, Sean, instead.

Finally, amidst screaming, pummeling and more whining, I gave up, resigning myself to staying up until 2:00 A.M. to finish my work. I put my folders away, and we read stories and built a shopping mall out of wooden blocks.

About that time, I heard the mailman's truck, so I went out to get the mail. As soon as I opened the box, I recognized the self-addressed stamped envelope I'd sent along with sample chapters of my novel to a literary agent. I gulped and, with trembling fingers, tore it open.

Rejected. By the agent of my dreams. The one from New York who represented best-selling fiction authors and who had thrilled me three months earlier with his request to see my sample chapters.

Although my writing was "pretty good," he "just couldn't work up enough enthusiasm" for my novel to take it on. Perhaps other agents would feel differently, he wrote. If I was unable to find an agent, he suggested I submit the manuscript myself to smaller publishers or perhaps consider self-publishing.

Other writers had told me to expect rejection on the road to getting published. And I'd told myself not to get my hopes up, that the chance that this big New York agent would be interested in representing my novel was slim. But my reaction to the reality of the letter in my hands told me I'd allowed myself to dream more than I'd admitted.

Why had I ever thought I wanted to write novels? After all, I was successful and well compensated in my "real job." Maybe I just wasn't good enough. I didn't like being a failure. I was quitting.

Feeling demoralized, depressed, defeated and every other de- word I could think of, I walked back into the house.

Sean, my two-year-old, met me at the door. He needed a Scooby Doo Band-Aid, he informed me.

"Where?" I asked, looking for blood and wondering what his older brother had done to him now.

He pointed to his forehead. "Here."

I didn't see a mark. "What happened?"

"I got my feelings hurt," he said.

"Oh," I said, nodding. "Me, too."

I knelt and hugged him. Those little arms wrapping around my neck reminded me that life wasn't quite as bad as I'd thought.

We went to the medicine cabinet, and I stuck a Scooby Doo Band-Aid across Sean's forehead. After a moment's thought, I put one on my own forehead, too.

"All better now?" I asked.

"Uh-huh," my son said.

"Me, too."

And to my surprise, I did feel better.

I wore the Band-Aid for the rest of the day. I even wore it to bed that night. The next morning, I peeled it off, deciding I was ready to try again.

A writer friend told me she dances naked while burning rejection letters over the toilet. She said it helps her to deal with the negative emotions and move on. Whatever works, I say.

As for me, I'm going to continue writing novels and submitting to agents. I'm hoping for the best, but I'll keep a Scooby Doo Band-Aid on hand—just in case.

Lisa Wood Curry

7
MAKING A DIFFERENCE

We must not only give what we have; we must also give what we are.

Cardinal Mercier

Precious Cargo

When I put our daughter on the school bus that beautiful, sunny day last week, I couldn't have known the chain of events that would follow.

That day started like any other. As the bus pulled away from our driveway, I waved goodbye and headed back inside to begin my workday.

I could see that storm clouds were brewing in the distance—rolling in from Lake Erie. There was nothing unusual about that. While Western New Yorkers probably enjoy some of the most beautiful summers anywhere, we also prepare ourselves for some pretty rough winters. Most of us think the snow is beautiful, and easier to cope with than hurricanes, floods, tornados and mudslides. Snow is not an impediment—we carry on with our business without giving it much thought. Our local governments are well prepared for this type of weather . . . usually.

However, no one could have predicted what would happen. Although snow was in the forecast, no one expected anything of this magnitude. Not even the television weathermen, especially not this early in the season.

I got my first inkling of disaster midafternoon, when weather reports began to pour in and it became clear that Mother Nature was unleashing the land-locked version of "the perfect storm."

A quick phone call to the school district bus garage and the rumor was confirmed—our daughter's bus was just twenty miles to our north—where the ravaging storm was packing its most powerful punch. She was on her way home, but with thousands of motorists gridlocked and abandoning their vehicles on the road to seek shelter, could they make it? Their normal route home, on the highway, was impassable.

At that point, all of our prayers and hopes were with one person—Flo Russell, one of the most dedicated people we know—and the person behind the wheel of our daughter's bus. She, and her assistant Sue Shults, were charged with the safety of not only our daughter, but that of twins and another young special-needs boy. What would they do? How would they be able to protect them?

If there was anyone in this world whom we could entrust with that precious cargo it would be Flo. We've known her for five years, and her son frequently visits our home to play with our boys. She is friendly and outgoing, and we've been fortunate to have her as our daughter's driver for the last couple of years. While others might think of her as just a bus driver, the parents of those special-needs children know the truth—Flo has become a lifesaver in understanding and monitoring the condition of those kids on her bus. It's not easy and it's not simple.

The hours ticked by slowly. My husband and I made numerous phone calls to try and determine their location and relay our medical concerns. By early evening, our boys were repeatedly inquiring as to the whereabouts of their sister—three hours overdue.

Outwardly I was calm and reassuring, but I was beginning to feel fear gripping my throat. The storm had dumped over two feet of snow in a few short hours and a state of emergency was declared. The roads were impassable, phone lines were jammed and we all felt helpless. If the bus was trapped in that mess, there was virtually no way to evacuate those four kids. There was no way to help. They were only about twenty miles away, but they might as well have been on the other side of the planet.

Our daughter, Laura, is medically fragile. She has little vision, decreased hearing and cannot speak. For anyone unfamiliar with her it would be nearly impossible to anticipate or interpret her needs. She is fed through a "button" in her stomach and she needs special medication to control seizures. This situation was very serious.

Then, at 8:30 P.M. the phone rang—it was the district bus garage. Flo, in her infinite wisdom, had avoided the highways and had somehow managed to extract their bus from the gridlock and steer them to her sister's house. And, her sister was a nurse!

In five hours, they had only traveled a mile or two, but the kids were safe and warm, and medical care was available if needed. They would not be coming home that night.

After doling out drinks, food and blankets, Flo was on the phone with all of us. What medications and supplies were needed, she inquired. What special considerations did she need to know about? She gave me the phone number for the nearest pharmacy so I could make arrangements with our pediatrician to call in prescriptions.

With the kids now happily watching television and supervised by Sue, Flo stepped back out into the ferocious storm and slowly trudged through snow drifts to the pharmacy. Once there, she even requested that the pharmacist call the doctors back to ask for an additional dose or two of medications, because an early-morning attempt to travel home did not look promising—there was a driving ban.

Flo called us several more times that evening to report that medications had been given and all was well. She and Sue remained awake most of the night, watching over the children, and only slept for a couple of hours.

As the sun rose the next morning, Flo was again back on the phone communicating with parents, reassuring us that everyone was fine.

Their journey home resumed again at 10:30 that morning. Even in broad daylight, with a police-designed travel route, it took three and a half hours for the bus to make it to our homes—a distance of only twenty miles.

The bus rolled up our driveway with great fanfare—horn blaring and occupants cheering. Flo flipped open the bus doors and greeted me with a big smile and a hug. She had safely delivered her charges home once again.

We had many things to be thankful for on Thanksgiving—one of them was a little known bus driver from Orchard Park, New York, whom we consider a hero—Flo Russell.

Laurie Patterson
as appeared in A 6th Serving of
Chicken Soup for the Soul

The Odd-Shaped Vegetable

Don't sacrifice your life to work and ideals. The most important things in life are human relations. I found that out too late.

Katharine de Susannah Prichard, Australian author

The day had started as usual, busy and chaotic, and I was starting to feel exasperated when, for perhaps the hundredth time that morning, the voice over the intercom announced that I had a phone call.

"May I help you," I asked in a hurried tone, thinking of all I still had to do.

"My mother works 3-D puzzles," came the timid response. "Will you do a story on her?"

I hid my sigh behind a pause. I had been working for a community newspaper for about twelve years and found myself getting increasingly frustrated at what I referred to as the odd-shaped or large vegetable stories. A small town newspaper often has some unusual requests and, no matter how strange, each has to be handled diplomatically to avoid offending the paper's faithful readers. As I tried to form a tactful rejection, the woman continued.

"My mother has cancer," was the introduction to her story. In between sobs, she explained that her terminally ill mother had started working 3-D puzzles and the new-found hobby had become her source of therapy. The daughter, feeling helpless as she watched her mother's battle, wanted her mother to feel special and hoped that a story might offer that to the dying woman.

She talked about her mother and by the time she finished, we were both sobbing. I could not even begin to imagine the pain she was experiencing as she watched her mother slipping away. Feeling sympathetic, I made an appointment to interview her mother. A few days later as I drove along the country road to the interview I tried to think about the questions and anticipate the answers, but I was filled with trepidation at meeting the dying woman. I dreaded the sadness that I knew awaited. I felt bound to do the story but struggled for an angle. All I really knew was that a woman was dying and she worked puzzles. To write of her impending death seemed much too intimate to intrude upon and the puzzle angle did not offer enough substance to capture the reader's attention.

Still pondering my dilemma, I arrived at my destination and was ushered in to meet the subject of the story. I'm not sure what I expected to find when the introductions were made, but it was not the woman who was presented to me. Mrs. Jones was not crying, nor did she show any signs of sorrow. Courteously she invited me to sit, offered me a cool drink and thanked me for coming. Then she told me there was not anything special about her life to warrant a news-paper story, but she consented to please her children. Even facing the most dramatic fight of her life, she wanted to make things easier for her family and consented to an intrusion into her last days and into the very private way in which she was coping with her disease.

Seated across from me with her husband and a grandchild

close by, Mrs. Jones explained how she originally started working the puzzles because she needed something to keep her busy. Surprisingly she found that the hobby was therapeutic because the activity kept her mind occupied. Her life had always been busy and fulfilled as she reared her children, worked on the farm and dabbled in crafts. Her children were grown and the echoes of laughter that now filled the house were from the grandchildren she cherished. Her time was no longer spent knitting, sewing or cooking, so those hours were filled with the puzzles. She said there was nothing extraordinary about her or the puzzles she put together. Speaking in a voice void of self-pity, she said the hobby helped take her mind off the daily pain and her constant battle. By sharing her story, she hoped she might help others as they fought similar battles. Mrs. Jones explained that the puzzles allowed her to find peace at times when her thoughts might otherwise have been hard to bear, and gave her the ability to be strong to fight that daily battle with fear, doubt and weakness.

She didn't cry as she talked about her tragedy. Even though she knew that death was lingering closely in the shadows, she did not appear sorrowful or regretful. She spoke of her family and the joy they gave her. She beamed at a young granddaughter who wanted to brag on her grandmother's puzzle accomplishments. As she smiled at the child whom she would never see grow into a young woman, I saw the simplicity of life. This dying woman had never won a Pulitzer prize, nor flown to the moon. She had not touched the lives of multitudes, nor even saved the life of one. However, this quiet, dignified woman smiled contentedly as she talked about the love that had been bestowed upon her and did not lament the years she would never see. Even with limited time, her concern was to somehow help make the trip easier for her loved ones and for others who might travel the same road.

Several hours later as I climbed into my car my tears broke loose. During the drive to my office I thought of this woman I would never meet again and her story. The story became a labor of love as I tried to convey the message she wanted to send, while capturing in words her unselfish beauty. A few weeks later, Mrs. Jones's daughter stopped by my office to tell me her mother had passed away. She said the family would always treasure the story and, like her mother, they hoped that those last words would help others with their battles with cancer or other terminal illnesses. I may never know if the story touched the life of a reader or helped another deal with impending death, but my life was changed forever. The tears that fell then were not for Mrs. Jones or her loved ones, but for me. I realized that God blessed me by bringing that dying woman into my life for a few hours. Not only did I realize my many blessings, but also her courageous selflessness and humility helped me understand the little things that are important during life's journey.

I still work for a small community newspaper. Though I am now the news editor, I still write many of the stories each week and, almost daily, get calls about odd-shaped vegetables. Sometimes I feel the frustration building, but then I remember that if you listen with your heart, sometimes odd-shaped vegetables are inspirations in disguise. Mrs. Jones taught me to listen more closely so not to miss the stories that make differences on this road called life.

Rosalind Turner

What Do You Want to Do with the Rest of Your Life?

So many of our dreams at first seem impossible, then they seem improbable, and then, when we summon the will, they soon become inevitable.

Christopher Reeve

I will never forget my college guidance counselor, Cathy Martin. I met her when I transferred to Northwestern University as a sophomore.

Cathy invited me into her office and asked, "What do you want to do?"

I thought I was ready to respond boldly to the question. Proudly I announced, "I want to be in broadcasting."

Cathy seemed unimpressed by my declaration. She asked, "What, specifically, do you want to do in broadcasting?"

"I'll do anything."

"So will a lot of other people," she said sharply. "Broadcasting is a very competitive field. You need to know exactly what you want to do in order to succeed. You need to decide right here and now what it is you want to do."

I looked Cathy squarely in the eyes and stated with conviction, "I want to be a television news anchor and reporter."

She smiled. "Good! Now you know what you want to do. When you leave here, you tell everyone who you know what you want to do with your life—that you want to be a TV anchor and reporter. And on those days when you're feeling uncertain, you share that uncertainty with your family, with your friends, with me. But as to the rest of the world, you address them with certainty in all that you do."

I walked out of Cathy Martin's office. I had direction. I had a mission—to become a broadcast journalist extraordinaire. In December 1973, I graduated half a year early, to get a jump on the June graduates. Within several months, after countless rejections, I got that first job as a TV reporter. In fact, I was almost the first, as well as the youngest, female co-anchor in the United States at the time. I went on to become a coast-to-coast TV news reporter, anchor and talk show host.

When it came time for me to move on in my career, I thought back to how Cathy Martin motivated me to set a goal, to become all that I can be, to achieve my dream. I decided to take my broadcasting background and become a trainer and motivational speaker, sharing *my* secrets on how to make better presentations and enhance one's image, thus helping people to get the results they want by winning every audience. In essence, I became a coach. Once again, Cathy Martin's wisdom allowed me to achieve what I wanted to do. It all happened to me! Pushing through our fears and self-doubt can be a prolonged process or a simple decision. Cathy Martin taught me to decide—and to go for it.

Not long ago, a woman named Carol came to see me, seeking advice about the direction of her career. As I searched my mind for what would be most helpful to her at this important time in her life, Cathy Martin's words came flooding back.

"What do you want to do?" I asked her. Carol was ready to respond to the question. Proudly she told me, "I want to give talks to groups."

Acting unimpressed by her declaration, I asked, "What, specifically, do you want to speak about?"

"I'll speak on most anything uplifting."

"So will a lot of other people," I said sharply. "Speaking is a very competitive field. You need to know exactly what you want to speak about in order to succeed. You need to decide right here and now what it is you want to do."

Carol looked squarely in my eyes and stated with conviction, "I want to validate people's pain and make them feel better. I want people to love themselves and go for their dreams. I want to be a professional speaker giving talks on self-esteem."

I smiled. "Good," I said. "Now you know what you want to do. When you leave here, you tell everyone who you know what you want to do with your life—that you want to be a professional speaker who gives talks on self-esteem. And on those days when you're feeling uncertain, you share that uncertainty with your family, with your friends, with me. But as to the rest of the world, you address them with certainty in all that you do."

Carol left our meeting full of determination and confidence. Four years later, I learned she had become a sought-after professional speaker on self-esteem.

I can't help but wonder when she will pass on the invaluable advice my guidance counselor so generously shared with me so many years ago.

Linda Blackman, C.S.P.

One Hour a Week

What we love to do we find time to do.

John L. Spalding

William waits for me in front of Room 210, hands holding something behind his back, head tilted away as I approach. "I don't feel like reading today," he announces, avoiding eye contact. He is almost ten, handsome and polite, with dark brown eyes as big as pennies. And he's on to me. As the year has passed, he's figured out that I'm a pushover.

"How about one book?" I suggest, "In our favorite spot? Then we can play your game." Negotiations complete, he pulls the board game front and center, and we walk down five steps to a white window seat to begin reading *Frog and Toad Together*. Suddenly, he stops.

"Too many pages. I can't read that many pages."

"How about if you read one, then I read one. I'll start."

"No," says William. "I'll start."

And so it goes. Once a week for one hour, going on three years, William and I meet with the assigned task of improving his literacy. Mostly we goof around. On his high-energy days, we whip through Easy Readers. I celebrate every new word he masters with a cheerleader-like frenzy. "Wonderful! Great! You are a reader, William!" He fires back with enthusiasm of his own: "How many books can we read today? Ten? Twelve? Let's read eighteen!"

Sometimes we just play games—Trouble or Mancala. He plays to win, and does. Sometimes, we sneak into the school cafeteria, scouring it for a Popsicle or a bag of salty chips. Other days are a chore. He's distracted, annoyed even, watching his buddies swat each other's heads as they march down the hall to the Media Center while he's stuck with me. "William," I tease, "where are you?" On those days, I feel defeated. But I'm never sorry I came.

Once William came to school with a family crisis embedded in his face. As we sat together on the white bench, he shed his bravado and tucked wet eyes into my shoulder and I would have held him there forever. But he is, after all, nine years old. The storm passed quickly. He sat up, wiped his eyes and asked, "Can we play Trouble?"

A teacher I know stopped me in the hall one day to ask if I would be returning the following year. "Of course," I told her. "Well, good," she said. "William needs you." I wanted to correct her: *Actually, I need William.*

I am forty-three years old, with a full-time job I like and three neat kids who, so far, still like me. But sometimes I catch myself letting work problems distract me from them at home, when I open the mail instead of focusing on a detail of their day, or rush through their bedtime rituals so I can crawl into bed with a book.

Sixteen years into marriage, I'm a decent spouse. But the most romantic getaway we have these days is to the wholesale club to buy in bulk. At work, where I manage nine creative people, most days go well. But last week I missed a deadline and screwed up an administrative detail and got some facts wrong in a meeting and wondered why they ever hired me.

I have friends I adore who complete my world. But we can never seem to find time for lunch anymore, and one is battling depression and my words, meant to comfort, come out trite and patronizing. "Hang in there," I tell her. "It will get better." *Dear God.*

My world is safe and solid and good, except when the wheels come off unexpectedly and I feel as though I will drown in self-doubt. When I say something stupid, or feel envy, or bark at my kids because I'm tired, or forget to call my mother, or call my mother and feel ten years old again, or go to work with graham crackers ground into my shoulder and my sweater buttoned wrong.

But I have one hour.

One hour a week when I have no self-doubt. When I walk down a noisy elementary school hallway covered with children's art and my respite awaits me.

"When will you come back?" William asks.

"Next Wednesday, silly. I always come on Wednesday."

"I wish you could come on Mondays instead," he says. "Then I wouldn't have to wait so long for you."

One hour a week I am granted the greatest reward possible: The comfort of knowing that I am absolutely in the right place, doing the right thing.

My life will catch up to me soon enough. But for the moment, it will just have to wait.

Gail Rosenblum

To Return Tomorrow

We deceive ourselves when we fancy that only weakness needs support. Strength needs it far more.

Madame Swetchine
The Writings of Madame Swetchine

The phone rang on a dateless Friday night. John's family requested a visit from the hospice nurse. They said he wasn't able to make it to the bathroom, his weakness had increased. I assured them I would visit in about forty-five minutes, the time I needed to drive to their home. I was not John's primary nurse, but I had made a few visits. This sounded pretty routine. They needed support and an assessment. I would be home in a couple of hours.

John was in the room they had made for him on the first floor next to the kitchen. It was the hub of activity because he could see everywhere yet had privacy in his recliner, his bed for several months now. John was thirty-two years old in the final stages of testicular cancer.

"Hello, John," I greeted, making a visual assessment. I listened to his mother, and then proceeded toward the blue recliner with the footrest up. Gently I took his cool hand in mine. Dull eyes and a different lusterless voice greeted me back. Ashen skin with a fine transparency sat me down quickly to take vital signs. They concurred. John was near death, just as my years of experience told me when I entered the room.

Standing directly behind me was John's mother. "What is wrong, Susie?"

John was drifting, and I took her to the next room. Making eye contact, I said, "He is dying."

"You are wrong! He is not!" she screamed, then pivoted and leaped onto the day bed next to his chair. Leaning to his ear she said, "John, you can't leave me. I need you, John. Don't leave me." Tears streamed down her face as she stroked his head, "John."

I watched as John came back from the shadow of death's door unable to even lift his hand to hers. Their eyes met and he started in a garbled voice to recite Robert Frost's poem—"Whose woods these are . . ."

With each word he had a little bit more clarity as his spirit rose to the moment. When he completed the poem he looked into her eyes and told her it was time to leave, he was tired. "Mom, I love you, and I know we will meet again. I have fought very hard, but it is time for me to go. You will be okay."

"But I will miss our time together reciting poetry and scripture. John . . ."

"Mom, I love you." He drifted and never spoke again, although death didn't come for two more hours. Tears cascaded over both our cheeks. This was a moment I had never experienced in my long hospice career.

John's mother and I were the only ones to experience this resurrection of spirit to help a loved one come to grips with the final departure of her son.

Three days later a memorial service was held in an old

huge Presbyterian church close to the hospice office. The wooden pews were full from front to back with mourners. I sat alone. It was normal to attend funeral services, but this was unequaled. John's brother stood at the pulpit and read the entire poem "Stopping by Woods on a Snowy Evening" by Frost.

The tears that could not be repressed wet my clothes and embarrassed me. I was sobbing and I was the hospice nurse. Finally the service was over, and I returned to the office and sat in front of my boss, Carole.

"I am done in this career, Carole. I can't do it any more. There are no more tears. Today I cried for John, the experience I shared with John and his family, and all the other patients and families. I couldn't stop the tears."

Carole came around her desk and took my hands in hers. "You are grieving for many today. I think you will be okay but today you need to take care of yourself. Take the rest of the day off."

She gave me a solid hug and sent me home. I left the hospice office questioning if I could ever return to my present position. I found Carole's warmth and wisdom my healing salve. Rarely do employers see your needs and try so desperately to meet them.

Hospice has support groups for their staff, but it was giving me the time to heal that mattered most. In a few years I became a hospice director. This hospice experience was shared many times in telling the public what a difference hospice can make. John had given me a memory, and Carole had given me her wisdom.

Susan Burkholder

A Mother's Choice

*The history of all times, and of today, especially,
teaches that . . . women will be forgotten if they
forget to think about themselves.*

Louise Otto

Pregnancy is a very exciting time, and it can be quite
frightening because it is so unpredictable. When my husband and I found out that we were expecting our first
child, we were ecstatic! We were newly married, and I was
completing a teaching credential program while working
as a part-time substitute teacher. I could not have been
happier.

The pregnancy progressed well until the end of the first
trimester. The long hours that I'd put into work and
school were beginning to take a toll. I had to push myself
to keep up with the demands of my job, the program and
the pregnancy. Although I was exhausted when I came
home, I'd stay up until midnight to finish lesson plans,
grading assignments and study for my classes. Then I'd
wake up at 6 A.M. to begin all over again. I really thought
that I could handle the schedule.

One evening, I felt sharp twinges and a dull ache across my back while attending a seminar. I was nauseous and a trip to the bathroom confirmed my worst fear. I called the hospital and was informed that it was possible that I was beginning to have a miscarriage. The nurse told me to rest and call if the pain or the spotting got worse.

I saw my doctor soon after, and he told me that while my symptoms were common in first pregnancies, they were symptoms that concerned him given that the pregnancy was at the end of the first trimester. He checked to see if there was a fetal heartbeat. We had heard some noises before, but this would be the first time we'd hear the heartbeat—if it was there. The stethoscope was cold and I tried not to cry, but by the third try, we heard a faint beating that grew louder and stronger. I was elated and relieved. With some rest, my baby would come to term.

I again resumed my schedule, determined to meet this new challenge. But I again began to experience the same twinges and dull ache two weeks later. I knew that my body would no longer tolerate this schedule and create a new life without enough rest. I had to make a decision that would give the baby a chance.

I chose to withdraw from the credential program and finish my substitute teaching contract. My decision to withdraw from the program was met with frustration and anger from colleagues, friends and family. Nobody understood why I would jeopardize my teaching career. At that point, the miscarriage signs signaled a personal moral dilemma as well as a health issue. The question became, "Do I pursue my program and risk miscarriage, or do I adjust my schedule to pursue the pregnancy?"

Some colleagues voiced their opinion that I'd snapped under the pressure of working and completing a credential program. In their opinion, I was using my pregnancy to escape from the pressure of the program. Only two women supported and understood the spiritual dilemma that I faced: to exchange my present life for the life of my unborn son, or to continue, knowing that there would be future pregnancies. I admire the women who do continue because they have an incredible strength, but it was a strength I knew that I did not possess. I maintained my professional demeanor in the face of the criticisms and pursued the option that was physically and spiritually right for me.

I never realized that this decision would bother people so much. However, my choice flew against the trend for working women to sacrifice or deny their physical needs in order to appear professional and keep their jobs. I chose to pursue the pregnancy. I heard that tiny heartbeat. I had to listen to my body and not the tenor of the workplace. My husband understood. I chose to give our child a chance to live.

It has been six years since I made that choice, and I am grateful. Even though my career plans were temporarily delayed, our child was born healthy. I managed to finish the program that I had started and earn the teaching credentials that I had originally sought. It was not easy, but I'd look at him and know that I'd made the right choice. While I was finishing the program, he'd come over to hug me and tell me that he understood why I was so busy now. My husband and I realized how blessed we were to have a child like him.

Our son plays, reads, loves bugs and dinosaurs. He tells us how much be loves us and gives us great big bear hugs. He was born, and for that I am grateful. Always.

Renée Day

A Gift from the Woman in White

It is not how much we do, but how much love we put in the doing. It is not how much we give, but how much love we put in the giving.

Mother Teresa

Jim Castle was tired when he boarded his plane in Cincinnati that night in 1981. The forty-five-year-old management consultant had put on a weeklong series of business workshops, and now he sank gratefully into his seat ready for the flight home to Kansas City.

As more passengers entered, the plane hummed with conversation, mixed with the sound of bags being stowed. Then, suddenly, people fell silent. The quiet moved slowly up the aisle like an invisible wake behind a boat. Jim craned his head to see what was happening, and his mouth dropped open.

Walking up the aisle were two nuns clad in simple white habits bordered in blue. He recognized the familiar face of one at once, the wrinkled skin, the eyes warmly intent. This was a face he'd seen in newscasts and on the cover of *Time.* The two nuns halted, and Jim realized that his seat companion was going to be Mother Teresa.

As the last few passengers settled in, Mother Teresa and her companion pulled out rosaries. Each decade of the beads was a different color, Jim noticed. The decades represented various areas of the world, Mother Teresa told him later, and added, "I pray for the poor and dying on each continent."

The airplane taxied to the runway, and the two women began to pray, their voices a low murmur. Though Jim considered himself a ho-hum Catholic who went to church mostly out of habit, inexplicably he found himself joining in.

By the time they murmured the final prayer, the plane had reached cruising altitude.

Mother Teresa turned toward him. For the first time in his life, Jim understood what people meant when they spoke of a person possessing an aura. As she gazed at him, a sense of peace filled him; he could no more see it than he could see the wind, but he felt it just as surely as he felt a warm summer breeze. "Young man," she inquired, "do you say the rosary often?"

"No, not really," he admitted.

She took his hand, while her eyes probed his. Then she smiled. "Well, you will now." And she dropped her rosary into his palm.

An hour later Jim entered the Kansas City airport, where he was met by his wife, Ruth. "What in the world?" Ruth asked when she noticed the rosary in his hand. They kissed and Jim described his encounter. Driving home, he said, "I feel as if I met a true sister of God."

Nine months later Jim and Ruth visited Connie, a friend of theirs for several years. Connie confided that she'd been told she had ovarian cancer. "The doctors say it's a tough case," said Connie, "but I'm going to fight it. I won't give up."

Jim clasped her hand. Then, after reaching into his pocket, he gently twined Mother Teresa's rosary around her fingers. He told her the story and said, "Keep it with you, Connie. It may help." Although Connie wasn't Catholic, her hand closed willingly around the small plastic beads. "Thank you," she whispered. "I hope I can return it."

More than a year passed before Jim saw Connie again. This time, face glowing, she hurried toward him and handed him the rosary. "I carried it with me all year," she said. "I've had surgery and have been on chemotherapy, too. Last month the doctors did second-look surgery, and the tumor's gone. Completely!" Her eyes met Jim's. "I knew it was time to give the rosary back."

In the fall of 1987, Ruth's sister, Liz, fell into a deep depression after her divorce. She asked Jim if she could borrow the rosary, and when he sent it, she hung it over her bedpost in a small velvet bag.

"At night I held on to it, just physically held on. I was so lonely and afraid," she says. "Yet when I gripped that rosary, I felt as if I held a loving hand." Gradually, Liz pulled her life together, and she mailed the rosary back. "Someone else may need it," she said.

Then one night in 1988 a stranger telephoned Ruth. She'd heard about the rosary from a neighbor and asked if she could borrow it to take to the hospital where her mother lay in a coma. The family hoped the rosary might help their mother die peacefully.

A few days later, the woman returned the beads. "The nurses told me a coma patient can still hear," she said, "so I explained to my mother that I had Mother Teresa's rosary and that when I gave it to her, she could let go; it would be all right. Then I put the rosary in her hand. Right away, we saw her face relax! The lines smoothed out until she looked so peaceful, so young." The woman's voice caught. "A few minutes later she was gone." Fervently, she gripped Ruth's hands. "Thank you."

Is there special power in those humble beads? Or is the power of the human spirit simply renewed in each person who borrows the rosary? Jim only knows that requests continue to come, often unexpectedly. He always responds, though whenever he lends the rosary, he says, "When you're through needing it, send it back. Someone else may need it."

Jim's own life has changed, too, since his unexpected meeting on the airplane. When he realized Mother Teresa carries everything she owns in a small bag, he made an effort to simplify his own life. "I try to remember what really counts—not money or titles or possessions, but the way we love others," he says.

Barbara Bartocci

Old Deadeye Bean

*The whole art of teaching is only the art of
awakening the natural curiosity of young minds
for the purpose of satisfying it afterwards.*

Anatole France

My favorite teacher was Dorothy "Deadeye" Bean. She
was in her forties and taught American history to eighth-
graders in Grand Rapids, Michigan. The year was 1944.
Allied troops were battling their way across France,
Franklin D. Roosevelt was president, the Montgomery,
Alabama, bus boycott was more than a decade away, and
I was a twelve-year-old black newcomer to an all-white
school.

My mother, a widow from Harlem, had married a Grand
Rapids physician, and he had bought the best house he
could afford for his new family. We were not welcome in
our new neighborhood, however, and there was a lot of
angry talk among the adults.

Some of the kids, too, were quite nasty. They threw
stones at me, chased me home and spat on my bike seat
when I was in class. I was lonely, friendless, sometimes

frightened, and ashamed for being different.

But things began to change when I walked into Dorothy Bean's classroom. Whereas my other teachers were easing in their new black pupil by ignoring him for the first few weeks, Miss Bean went right at me. After our first assignment, she asked me the opening question.

I gulped and answered. It wasn't a brilliant answer, but it did show that I had read the assignment and that I could speak English. Later in the hour, when a classmate bungled an answer, Miss Bean asked me to correct it, and that established me as a smart person.

Thus, she began to give me human dimensions, though not perfect ones for an eighth-grader. Nevertheless, it was better to be an incipient teacher's pet than merely a dark, silent presence in the back of the room.

A few days later, Miss Bean asked my opinion about something Thomas Jefferson had done. I stared at her for a second. In those days, all my opinions were derivative. I was for Roosevelt because my parents were, and for the Yankees because my buddy from Harlem was a Yankee fan. Besides, I didn't have opinions about historical figures such as Jefferson. Like my high-school building, he just was.

"Well, should he have bought Louisiana or not?" Miss Bean persisted.

"I guess so," I replied tentatively.

"Why?" she shot back.

Why! *What kind of question was that,* I groused silently. But I ventured an answer. Day after day, Miss Bean kept doing that to me, and my answers became stronger and more confident. She was the first teacher to give me a sense that thinking was part of education and that I could form opinions that had some value.

Her greatest service to me came one day when my mind was wandering and I was idly playing with my pencil. She impulsively threw a gum eraser at me. It hit my hand and sent the pencil flying. She gasped, the class roared and I crept, mortified, after my pencil.

That was the icebreaker. Kids came up to me to laugh about "Old Deadeye Bean." The incident became a legend, and I, a part of it, became a person to talk to.

So that's how Dorothy Bean became Old Deadeye—and how I became just another kid in school.

Roger Wilkins

A New Perspective on Land Mines

A person without a sense of humor is like a wagon without springs, jolted by every pebble in the road.

Henry Ward Beecher

What a wild and reckless millennium summer of 2000 it was when I worked in the rebuilding effort after the Balkan War. The organization I worked with was very careful with their expatriate staff and tried very hard not to put us in danger. Sometimes the steps taken seemed to be almost careful to a fault, but "better to be safe than sorry" was their motto. Sometimes their warnings made us overly suspicious to the point of seeing enemies around every corner and land mines in every field.

Every morning, before we climbed into the white Land Rovers with our organization's logo on both sides, we waited for our field coordinator to return from the security meeting. The coordinator gave us a briefing before we headed out to the field to hold clinic in tiny buildings, called Ambulantas, scattered about the Kosovo country-side. If any areas were considered "hot," which meant a recent murder or riot occurred that day, our plans were changed.

This day's report was not unusual; in fact, it was fairly typical. In one town, a grenade was thrown into a crowd and, in retaliation, the crowd began stopping cars, pulling people out and beating them. We wouldn't go into that town today. Next, children in another nearby town found several live grenades and began playing with them. Fortunately, an adult saw this and took them away before anyone was hurt and reported them to the United Nations Police. The road that lead to Pristina was blocked that day, in protest to the increasing violence. Anyone needing to go to Pristina needed to take the longer route through Ferizji.

Before we departed, our leader reported one last thing. "There has been an increase in land mines found on the roads. Everyone should be on the alert for any objects in the road. If you see any, report them to the United Nations Police. DO NOT ATTEMPT TO REMOVE THEM YOURSELVES!"

With that report echoing in our ears, we headed down the bumpy road to Novoberde to hold clinic. It was a beautiful, sunny day. The sky was filled with puffy cumulous clouds contrasting against the deep blue sky. We were without a driver that day, which was unusual, but Rose, one of our doctors, had agreed to drive.

In the huge Land Rover, little five-foot Rose could barely see over the steering wheel. We joked about getting her a catalog to sit on. Everyone was in high spirits with the cacophony of laughter and chatter echoing throughout the vehicle as we bumped along the terrible, potholed road.

Suddenly, centered smack dab in the center of the right-hand lane, the very lane we were driving in, there it was—a land mine! It was a drab green, dome-shaped object, about ten inches in length and about seven inches across, with a slight curve to its three-inch high shape.

Those in the front seat saw it first as Rose simultaneously slammed on the brakes, sending us careening to the side of the road. Cries of protest from the women in the backseat, thrown forward by the sudden stop, were followed by dead silence throughout the car, as the eyes of the entire medical team focused on the object, only a few feet away from us.

During a long stretch of complete silence, each of us had our own private thoughts racing through our heads. Then ever so slowly, five protrusions extended from the mine— two along the longer sides and a single one on one of the shorter sides.

At the exact same moment, we all realized what it was and a riot of laughter broke out among us as the lowly turtle began to finish his slow trip across the road. We proceeded down the bumpy, pothole-filled road to Noveberde, laughing hysterically about "The MINE that grew legs!" It was just another day of work in Kosovo.

Nancy Harless

A Cat, Six Kittens and a Wheelchair

The older you get, the more you realize that kindness is synonymous with happiness.

Lionel Barrymore

I didn't care for Ike at first. Nobody did. Named after Ike Eisenhower, "Grumpy" suited him better. I suppose I'd be grumpy, too, if I sat in a wheelchair all day long.

As a community nurse on the Alaska Highway in northern British Columbia, I often encountered taciturn patients, but Ike took the cake. It was the dead of winter 1987. Snow swirled around, sneaking into my boots as I lurched through snow drifts toward the dilapidated pewter-gray shack on the outskirts of town. Ice crystals pierced my face like needles in the forty-degree-below-zero cold. The front door hung askew, a result of permafrost heaving the foundation. A large crack split the door frame. Wind whistled eerily through the house. Thick frost covered parts of the living room walls in spite of a pot-bellied stove puffing away in the corner. I could see Ike sitting at the kitchen table, a sour look on his bearded face.

How can anyone live like this? I wondered.

I had to treat him for bedsores on his heels caused when he carelessly threw his legs around like wooden posts.

I looked at the alligator head on the TV.

"Where'd you get that thing?" I shuddered.

"Aah, an Indian friend of mine came with me to Florida last year and we bagged it . . . not bad, eh?" He grunted, waving me off. Ike was like that, adventurous . . . unusual . . . didn't let a little thing like paraplegia stop him.

"Meow."

"Was that a cat?"

"Hmmm." Conversation was difficult with this taciturn man. He wanted his dressing to be done and for me to get out of there—a silent but direct attitude.

"How did you break your back, Ike?"

"Oh I was building a house for my family up at the 'half way' [a place further north in the wilderness] . . . it was supposed to be our dream house . . . had my boy with me . . . I was stupid really . . . sat on a rafter and fell off to the basement . . . broke my back . . . Jim took the truck . . . he was only twelve . . . and drove it to the neighbors twenty miles away . . . the closest . . . hardly a road except a dirt track. They got me out to Edmonton by Air Ambulance but there was no hope . . . so here I am . . . wife left me a year later."

Rehabilitation helped him cope as a paraplegic but no one helped him cope with being abandoned by his family. He disliked women, especially pesky snoopy community nurses.

"Meow." A plaintiff cry came from underneath the floorboards.

"Ike, that is a cat under your house—we've got to get her out."

"She's been there a couple days now—drives me nuts . . . ever since the blizzard blocked her escape hole. She can freeze under there for all I care!"

"You can't just let her freeze to death or starve . . . that's cruel."

"Why not? . . . no darn good to anyone . . . just a pest."

"Well, your dressing can wait. I'll see if I can dig her out."

"Yeah sure, you care more for a cat than for your patients."

The snow, like whipped cream, was piled high on the side of the house. I grabbed a shovel and started throwing the snow aside to reveal a hole to the crawl space. I peeked into the cavernous blackness. I could see green eyes peering out at me, but no way was she going to creep out.

"Well, she'll come out now when I'm gone." I finished his dressing.

"She's scared to death . . . she'll come out," Ike griped. "Then what?"

"Well, you can feed her for heaven's sake. I'll bring you some cheap cat food tomorrow."

Ike didn't answer but rolled his eyes toward the ceiling.

The next day I placed a huge bag of cheap cat food on the table in front of him.

He said little as I did his foot dressings. When I returned the day after that, during a Chinook warm spell, I found Ike with the back door open. A rusty tin pie plate sat on the back step overloaded with dry cat food. A very pregnant, beautiful, long-haired calico cat sat there munching away, quite content.

"Aha, so your heart isn't so hard after all."

"Well, she'll be having a bunch of kittens soon and what am I going to do with those?" He grinned sheepishly. He tried his best to be gruff but couldn't.

By spring Ike was the proud father of six kittens and a cat. Wild things they were, bouncing all about. They kept their distance, too, but approached gingerly to grab food from Ike's hands and scramble away.

"They'll only come so far, and they won't come for anyone else," he said proudly.

For the next three months Ike faithfully fed his menagerie and seemed softer, more pliable, less grumpy.

But all kittens grow up. One day, Ike declared he couldn't possibly keep all seven cats.

"I phoned a farmer friend, and she'll take the kittens if I can catch them. This is all your fault so you have to help me."

He handed me a pillow case in which to place the kittens. I leaped about, slithering on the icy stoop, arms akimbo. Ike laughed uproariously as the kittens scampered about, just out of my reach.

"I ought to get more pay for this," I grumbled.

Eventually with a lot of stealth, I got all kittens into the pillowcase, ready for transfer to the farm.

"What about Kitty?"

"Nah, I'll keep her and get her fixed . . . she's kinda attached to me by now."

"Sure." Kitty owned the place now.

As for Ike . . . well, he wasn't so bad after all. In fact I got kinda attached to him, too. Even though his coffee was lousy, I always had a cup with him as we laughed and talked about all kinds of things. As far as I know, Ike is still sleeping with his beloved Kitty. And the community nurse still visits and brings Kitty all kinds of treats. It's part of the job description, after all!

Arlene Alice Centerwall

Princess of the City

It had been a long day and the call that had just come in to our visiting nurse agency—a report on two abandoned children—would make it even longer. I had looked forward to getting off on time for once, but now that was out of the question. I hurried out into the darkening winter afternoon. It was bitterly cold. All day news reports had predicted snow.

When I arrived at the address, an apartment in a decaying tenement, I found two little girls huddled together to keep warm. A cold wind was blowing in through a window that was stuck open. As I struggled to close it, the shivering children clung to me. They looked about three and four years old. Both had dark curly hair and huge brown eyes that now were filled with tears. They were shabbily dressed in stained, ill-fitting jumpers. I wondered when they had last eaten a decent meal. When I checked the refrigerator, it was empty accept for a half-empty can of beer. On the kitchen floor lay a dead mouse. *Even a rodent couldn't survive in this place,* I thought.

Carefully I checked the children for bruises or any sign of injury. They were hungry and frightened, but unharmed, at least physically. I tried to console them as they cried pitifully for their mother.

"Where's Mommy?" they kept crying. Hurriedly I got them dressed and into some old jackets I had found in a jumbled heap at the bottom of a closet. They were a pathetic sight indeed, with their tear-stained faces, tangled hair and ragged clothing.

By the time I got the girls fed and placed in an emergency foster home, the lights were going on all over the city. The snow was starting to fall, and a harsh wind had risen. I hurried along the deserted streets feeling exhausted as I headed for home.

My apartment, hardly lavish, seemed like Shangri La after the grim tenement that was home to the little girls. Too tired to read or even watch TV, I thought about my job and how tiring and frustrating it was. Our office was always short-staffed; it was hard to get people to work among the poor in the inner-city. All day long, I walked the forbidding streets of blighted neighborhoods, then climbed dark staircases or braved ancient creaking elevators to visit my patients. Often the family problems seemed overwhelming—teenage pregnancies, drug addiction and chronic illnesses. All the problems were made worse by poverty.

As I sat alone in my apartment, I was haunted by the thought of the two children I had found today. What could the future hold for them? I felt overcome by sadness. I found myself thinking with envy of several of my friends who were married to successful businessmen and spent their days shopping, or amused themselves playing golf and tennis. At last I went to bed, only to toss and turn, troubled by dreams of crying children.

When I returned to work the next day, my assignment was even heavier than usual. How would I ever manage to see all the patients on my list? I took a deep breath to organize my thoughts. First, I had to visit the foster home where I had placed the children the night before. I worried that they would still be traumatized, unable to recover. I felt overwhelmed as I climbed the long flight of stairs to the foster mother's apartment.

But my weariness vanished when I saw the girls. Comfortably settled in the back bedroom of the cheerfully furnished apartment, they were playing "dress up" in the foster mother's old clothes. The four-year-old was resplendent in a flowing faded satin bathrobe she'd adorned with dime store jewelry. But her crowning glory was a blonde wig, perched atop her coal black hair.

"I'm a movie star," she told me, preening in front of the mirror.

"I'm calling her 'Princess,'" the foster mother said, laughing, as she hugged the three-year-old.

The snow outside had melted and sunlight poured in through the window. Brightly colored toys were scattered throughout the room. A teddy bear sat in a rocking chair and seemed to be regarding "Princess" with admiring eyes.

I could see that the foster mother was enchanted with the children. I felt my heart lift with hope. Who knew? Maybe a better future beckoned for the girls.

As I left, Princess waved good-bye to me, her bracelets jingling. She looked beautiful, hardly resembling the weeping, disheveled child of the night before.

I carried that image in my mind for the rest of the day. Such are the rewards that come to a working woman, never to be found on a golf course, or a tennis court, or in the most magnificent shopping mall.

Eileen Valinoti

United We Stand

When we quit thinking primarily about ourselves and our own self-preservation, we undergo a truly heroic transformation of consciousness.

Joseph Campbell

She stood staring at a television set with tears streaming down her face as we walked into the room. As we entered, she shut off the television and then we immediately became quiet. We had never seen our teacher so quiet or sullen. When the last person was in the door, we waited for her to speak.

"There's been a terrible tragedy in New York City this morning. Two planes have bombed the World Trade Center. It is suspected that terrorists have struck on our own United States' soil." Then she walked over to the television and turned the set on. As we watched in horror, we saw the first plane strike, and then the second. We saw people screaming and running from the site with blood and ash all over them. "Mrs. Skop" flipped through the channels to show us that the tragedy had pre-empted everything else on television. Then, she shut off the set and we began to discuss what this could mean for our country.

Mrs. Skophammer is one of the most positive teachers I know. She always has a smile on her face and a good joke or story to tell us. In her classroom we learn about the world from real-life situations, and she treats us as if we are older than we really are. On that particular day, we learned more from her than anyone could possibly imagine.

Mrs. Skop explained to us that her father had fought in World War II. He had seen unspeakable horrors in Europe. He'd been in on the liberation of a concentration camp and had photos of piles of dead people. In the weeks to come she would explain the parallels between the war he had fought in and the one we were engaged in right now.

After her initial crying, Mrs. Skop took action. She took the World Trade Center bombing and used it to teach about history, democracy, freedom, rights, the flag, patriotism and compassion for others. She vowed she would not let terrorists control what she did and where she went. She was going to live her life to the fullest. And because she was so positive, we were no longer as afraid. We understood that people have causes and you can't live your life being afraid to experience it.

Mrs. Skop had one group of students create linoleum printed note cards. She purchased envelopes, and the students packaged the cards and sold them. Then, six weeks after the bombings, Mrs. Skop hopped on a plane and took the relief money to New York City.

Mrs. Skop went directly to Ground Zero. She took lots of photos and brought them back to share with her classes. She explained the site in such vivid detail that we could smell the death in the air. But, along with the death, she helped us feel the hope that was all over New York

City. Memorials, people helping people, young children's cards of well wishing, and a country that now seemed to be uniting and caring about something other than material things and themselves were felt. Flags were flying all around and we could feel the United States pull together. United We Stand. Yes, Mrs. Skop was teaching all of us by example to take charge of our lives and know what we stand for.

Before the bombings, Mrs. Skop had always told us that it bothered her that at ballgames people didn't sing the national anthem or put their hands over their hearts. She said that it seemed that only she and a few other older people would sing. It also bothered her that during a parade, people along the route did not stand up to honor our flag or the veterans that carried it. Then, during the first football game after the bombings, the national anthem was played. People were singing, hats were removed and hands were placed over hearts. As I looked in her direction, even though she had vowed she was done crying, I saw a few tears slide down Mrs. Skop's face. And, in those tears I could see pride, patriotism, self-respect, democracy, freedom and history glistening. If teachers lead by example, this teacher sets a gleaming example for all.

As a teacher, Mrs. Skophammer, creates culture. She leads by example. She actively involves and challenges students and continuously expects winners.

Jenna Skophammer

Never Too Late

One of the most courageous things you can do is identify yourself, know who you are, what you believe in, and where you want to go.

Sheila Murray Bethel

It was an unusually busy day for the hospital staff on the sixth floor. Ten new patients were admitted and Nurse Susan spent the morning and afternoon checking them in. Her friend Sharron, an aide, prepared ten rooms for the patients and made sure they were comfortable. After they were finished she grabbed Sharron and said, "We deserve a break. Let's go eat."

Sitting across from each other in the noisy cafeteria, Susan noticed Sharron absently wiping the moisture off the outside of her glass with her thumbs. Her face reflected a weariness that came from more than just a busy day.

"You're pretty quiet. Are you tired, or is something wrong?" Susan asked.

Sharron hesitated. However, seeing the sincere concern in her friend's face, she confessed, "I can't do this the rest

of my life, Susan. I have to find a higher-paying job to provide for my family. We barely get by. If it weren't for my
parents keeping my kids, well, we wouldn't make it."

Susan noticed the bruises on Sharron's wrists peeking
out from under her jacket.

"What about your husband?"

"We can't count on him. He can't seem to hold a job.
He's got . . . problems."

"Sharron, you're so good with patients, and you love
working here. Why don't you go to school and become a
nurse? There's financial help available, and I'm sure your
parents would agree to keep the kids while you are in
class."

"It's too late for me, Susan; I'm too old for school. I've
always wanted to be a nurse, that's why I took this job as
an aide; at least I get to care for patients."

"How old are you?" Susan asked.

"Let's just say I'm thirty-something."

Susan pointed at the bruises on Sharron's wrists. "I'm
familiar with 'problems' like these. Honey, it's never too
late to become what you've dreamed of. Let me tell you
how I know."

Susan began sharing a part of her life few knew about.
It was something she normally didn't talk about, only
when it helped someone else.

"I first married when I was thirteen years old and in the
eighth grade."

Sharron gasped.

"My husband was twenty-two. I had no idea he was
violently abusive. We were married six years and I had
three sons. One night my husband beat me so savagely he
knocked out all my front teeth. I grabbed the boys and left.

"At the divorce settlement, the judge gave our sons to
my husband because I was only nineteen and he felt I
couldn't provide for them. The shock of him taking my

babies left me gasping for air. To make things worse, my ex took the boys and moved, cutting all contact I had with them.

"Just like the judge predicted, I struggled to make ends meet. I found work as a waitress, working for tips only. Many days my meals consisted of milk and crackers. The most difficult thing was the emptiness in my soul. I lived in a tiny one-room apartment and the loneliness would overwhelm me. I longed to play with my babies and hear them laugh."

She paused. Even after four decades, the memory was still painful. Sharron's eyes filled with tears as she reached out to comfort Susan. Now it didn't matter if the bruises showed.

Susan continued, "I soon discovered that waitresses with grim faces didn't get tips, so I hid behind a smiling mask and pressed on. I remarried and had a daughter. She became my reason for living, until she went to college. Then I was back where I started, not knowing what to do with myself—until the day my mother had surgery. I watched the nurses care for her and thought: I can do that. The problem was, I only had an eighth-grade education. Going back to high school seemed like a huge mountain to conquer. I decided to take small steps toward my goal. The first step was to get my GED. My daughter used to laugh at how our roles reversed. Now I was burning the midnight oil and asking *her* questions."

Susan paused and looked directly in Sharron's eyes. "I received my diploma when I was forty-six years old."

Tears streamed down Sharron's cheeks. Here was someone offering the key that might unlock the door in her dark life.

"The next step was to enroll in nursing school. For two long years I studied, cried and tried to quit. But my family wouldn't let me. I remember calling my daughter and yelling, 'Do you realize how many bones are in the human body, and I have to know them all! I can't do this, I'm forty-six years old!' But I did. Sharron, I can't tell you how wonderful it felt when I received my cap and pin."

Sharron's lunch was cold, and the ice had melted in her tea by the time Susan finished talking. Reaching across the table and taking Sharron's hands, Susan said, "You don't have to put up with abuse. Don't be a victim—take charge. You will be an excellent nurse. We will climb this mountain together."

Sharron wiped her mascara-stained face with her napkin. "I had no idea you suffered so much pain. You seem like someone who has always had it together."

"I guess I've developed an appreciation for the hardships of my life," Susan answered. "If I use them to help others, then I really haven't lost a thing. Sharron, promise me that you will go to school and become a nurse. Then help others by sharing your experiences."

Sharron promised. In a few years she became a registered nurse and worked alongside her friend until Susan retired. Sharron never forgot her colleague or the rest of her promise.

Now Sharron sits across the table taking the hands of those who are bruised in body and soul, telling them, "It's never too late. We will climb this mountain together."

Linda Apple

8

LIVING YOUR DREAM

Nothing much happens without a dream. For something really great to happen, it takes a really great dream.

Robert Greenleaf

Reprinted by permission of Harley Schwadron.

Against All Odds

When you get in a tight place and everything goes against you, till it seems as though you could not hang on a minute longer, never give up then, for that is just the place and time that the tide will turn.

Harriet Beecher Stowe

As she rushed up the hill toward the brownstone building in the bitter cold of a December morning, Bonnie Bentley Cewe prayed she would not let herself down.

The long gash just above her hairline barely had healed, the puncture wounds on her hand still showed, her leg ached inside the brace. She fought to keep her concentration as she took her seat in the drafty room. She wished the chairs weren't attached to the long table. They barely swiveled on their posts, and she felt cramped.

For six years, she had immersed herself in books, college courses and term papers to prepare for the next five hours. It had taken every ounce of determination to get this far; if she failed now, she wasn't sure she had it in her to try again.

Surrounded by dozens of people sniffling, coughing and blowing their noses, Bonnie looked at the other law school hopefuls, wondering whether they all had taken the preparation class for the law school admission test.

She had meant to.

At the end of the 1960s, when she dropped out of her junior year of high school, Bonnie had little doubt she would never look back.

She had lost interest in school. She quit, and in a few years was married with two sons. For a while, she dressed windows and set up displays for a department store and modeled; later, she helped her husband with the books for his home improvement business.

After years of a stormy marriage, Bonnie sought a divorce. She didn't want her sons to grow up thinking that kind of relationship was normal.

Three days before Christmas in 1983, she walked out of her marriage and into an apartment she could barely afford, but where she and her sons, then three and four, could start over. She used money relatives had given her for the boys for Christmas to pay the first month's rent.

Christmas morning, the three gathered in the kitchen to eat their Cream of Wheat. They ate it standing up. One of the boys asked why they were eating on their feet, and the other said, "Because there are no chairs." The simplicity of the answer threw the boys into convulsions of laughter.

It was a hard Christmas, unlike any they had ever had.

Bonnie was twenty-eight years old. A high school dropout. A single mother on welfare.

She could see herself fifteen years in the future, ringing up groceries at a supermarket, for her boys who would be teenagers with no chance for college. The thought scared her.

She would have to go back to school.

Her first stop was to go to an open house at an event

with a name that fit Bonnie's state of mind: "You Can" day.

At first, Bonnie planned to take the last route to college—prepare herself for an exam to get her high school equivalency diploma. But a teacher at the program persuaded her to attend the full-time night high school program. Night classes, homework and studying would better prepare her for what she knew she would work toward: law school.

In the divorce, she had lost her house, which had been in her in-laws' name as a safeguard in case her husband's business failed. She was worse off financially than she had expected, and she felt helpless and victimized by the legal system.

But adult high school classes were a long way from law school, and about a dozen years had passed since Bonnie was a student. Now, as she walked past the locker that she had used as a teenager, she had to fight her feelings of failure.

But when she finished the year, her grades were nearly perfect.

Her sons, Daniel and Nicholas, joined the hundreds of guests at the adult education commencement exercises in the spring of 1985. When Bonnie walked to the high school stage in cap and gown to receive her diploma, Daniel and Nicholas stood up in the middle of the seated crowd and clapped their hands together so proudly, so ecstatically, that their mother would never forget it.

Now, as the proctor handed out the LSAT exam and booklets in the drafty room, Bonnie still wondered how a thirty-four-year-old single mother could compete with the young pre-law students in the seats around her.

They probably didn't worry about money, she thought. *Their parents probably put them through college, placed credit cards in their wallets, bought them cars.* In her wallet, behind her college identification card, were her week's worth of food stamps.

Who am I kidding? she thought as she looked around the room.

When she opened the test booklet, the words on the page blurred. Her thoughts raced. She fought the old fear of failure.

Earning her high school diploma gave Bonnie a year-long taste of how crammed her life would be and how little money she would have if she went on to college. It would be another seven years of scrambling to make ends meet, another seven years of juggling studies and child-rearing and her job as a bartender.

She plunged on.

If she went part time to Albertus Magnus College in New Haven, where she was accepted after earning her diploma, and went part time to law school after that, she was looking at fifteen years of school.

Fifteen years.

She couldn't say it with a straight face. She would have to do it full time.

She worked as many nights as she could, sometimes six or seven a week, as a bartender because her ex-husband rarely sent her child support.

Albertus Magnus accepted her on the basis of her grades in the high school program. School officials were impressed by how passionately she believed in herself.

Even in those first interviews, she spoke of law school.

The head of the business department, Sister Charles Marie Brantl and a finance professor, the Rev. Charles Shannon, raised their eyebrows as they listened. It wasn't her desire they doubted, but her ability to go far with the burdens she had to carry.

It had taken Bonnie so long to be walking across a college campus, she wouldn't cheat herself of any opportunities. A finance major, she took high-level courses, sometimes with one or two other students. She joined several business clubs. She studied theater.

But sometimes the burden of trying to do everything at once overwhelmed her. One night, before final exams, she walked through the piles of clothes and toys carpeting the floor of the boys' room to put some clean clothes away. She stepped on something and heard it break. Her calm broke with it, and she angrily fled to her room in tears, slamming the door to her bedroom in her fury.

An hour or so later, she heard a tap on her door. When she opened it, her boys were standing there. Close your eyes, they said, as they marched her to their bedroom. They had done something special for her, she knew. *Boy, they really know what I'm going through,* she thought.

She opened her eyes to a surprise, but not the one she was expecting. They had not cleared the room, but merely a passage through the mess, a tunnel just wide enough for her to pass. She looked at them cross-eyed. The three fell on the floor, laughing until tears streamed down their faces.

There were other people who helped, relatives, friends. Her parents cared for her sons often. Her sons' soccer coach took the boys to after-school sports practices and games. And Bonnie couldn't afford to be embarrassed when she asked other mothers for rides or babysitting.

For six years, her boss at the restaurant, Dan Alix, overlooked her studying between drink orders, the books lying open on the bar. More than once, he worked the bar for her so she could be part of the audience at her sons' school plays or be home when they were sick.

Sometimes friends asked her why she didn't leave the restaurant for one of the better-paying restaurant jobs in various hotels in New Haven. She shook her head—bosses such as Alix were hard to come by.

Coworkers and customers at the restaurant let her know they were floored by the years she intended to put in. In some ways they let her know they didn't think her dream was possible, in other ways they encouraged her.

For a theater class, Bonnie had to do a skit. She needed an audience, but she had had little time to make friends. The day of the skit, as she walked onto the stage for her monologue, she looked down at the theater seats. Two waitresses from work were sitting there, her small but precious audience.

Working at the restaurant was barely enough to cover the bills, let alone pay for college.

She took out student loans, trying not to be conscious of the risk totals. She would owe so much, tens of thousands of dollars.

Albertus Magnus gave her financial aid, her high class standing won her scholarships.

When Gertrude M. Moshier and members of the Wallingford Business and Professional Women's Club first heard about Bonnie, they wanted to help. As Bonnie won their respect with her perseverance, Moshier came to believe "she was the most deserving person the group had ever seen."

That group, and the Wallingford Junior Women's Club, pick a different student for their scholarships each year. After they discovered Bonnie, she became a woman they kept believing in, and awarding scholarships to, throughout her time at Albertus Magnus.

There were other groups that gave her money; $500 here, $200 there, checks that added up to thousands of dollars in tuition that Bonnie would not have to pay back.

For all of them, she became a cause celebre, a symbol of what women who took control of their lives could accomplish.

She made the honors society, keeping up a 3.8 cumulative grade-point average—the equivalent of straight As—for four years.

Until this moment, in the drafty room, Bonnie somehow always had been able to pull it off. But she could lose it all in the next few hours. She refocused on the test in front of her. An essay. She read the instructions.

The question asked her to choose between two potential athletic award candidates and make a case for selecting one young women over the other. To one of the young women, winning came easily. To the other, success was a struggle, a struggle she overcame with hard work and persistence.

In her essay, Bonnie passionately argued the merits of the second young woman, the one who wasn't naturally gifted.

She was arguing for herself.

Early one hot summer morning in 1989, three months before she was to take her LSAT exam, Bonnie was sleeping in her apartment. A silent figure pushed up an unlocked screen to her living room and made his way to her bedroom.

Her room was dark, except for the dim glow of a nightlight. The man climbed on top of her in her bed. She recognized the voice; it was her neighbors' seventeen-year-old nephew, who had recently arrived to stay with his relatives. He had befriended her boys, played basketball with them.

He whispered that if she made noise, that if she resisted, he would kill her sons. Then he raped her.

She was frightened, frozen; her mind raced. He was big, strong, violent. She wouldn't be able to protect her children. She was as quiet as she could be. She prayed her sons would not awaken.

The man dragged her from the apartment and forced her to drive her tiny red Ford Escort, a used one she had gleefully bought with a loan three weeks earlier after years of worrying that one old car or another might break down.

Twice, he made her pull the car over so that he could beat her. After the second time, he forced her into the luggage compartment of the car. As it began moving again, she lay there, trying to envision escape scenes from films she had seen.

She carefully unscrewed the pliable cover above her, a small particleboard section that raised when the hatchback was opened. To keep it from rattling, she held it in place until the car slowed down.

She was certain he would kill her the next time the car stopped. *It can't be over*, she thought. *We have so much look forward to.*

She thought about her boys. She decided then that she would fight back.

When the car slowed, she picked up the jack, and, with whatever energy she had left, shot through the compartment. She slammed the jack against the side of her attacker's head. The car skidded through a row of guardrails, knocked down a highway exit sign and somersaulted down a twenty-foot drop.

She woke up hours later, her body straddling the front and back seats. Her forehead was split open. She wasn't sure whether it happened in the accident or whether her attacker used the jack to get even. He was gone.

Blood was everywhere. It matted her hair, covered her clothes. She got up and slowly stumbled up the rocky ledge to the highway. A gasoline station was ahead. She had to get to a telephone, tell someone the boys were in danger.

Somehow she reached the station and banged on the door for help. Two attendants, frightened by her appearance, told her they wouldn't protect her. They told her to go away, to the McDonald's restaurant a little farther up in the highway rest area. She shook her head and stood there, begging.

The attendants relented, but were so frightened that her

attacker might return that they made her squat under the counter of the station. Her first thoughts were of her boys: *What if the attacker went back for them?* She was frantic. The attendants called 911.

Waiting for the rescue squad, she used the station telephone to call her ex-husband and ask him to get their sons.

The boys were awakened by their father and the police banging on the apartment's windows. Before they answered the door, they went to their mother's room. They saw her bed covers in a heap at the side of the bed, and they thought she was dead.

For four days, Bonnie was in the hospital, where she was treated for her head injury, her leg injury and scores of cuts, bruises and other wounds. Crisis counselors tried to help her with the psychological wounds.

Afterward, she went to stay with her parents and the boys went with their father. She needed the boys, wanted to be with them, but her mother couldn't care for them. She had just had major surgery herself.

Bonnie lost sleep knowing he was out there, on the run. She gave up her apartment so he couldn't find her, explaining to her landlord what had happened. But he took her to court for the lost rent, many months' worth and won. She found a new apartment, but would have to pay her old landlord $5 a week until the debt was covered.

The teenager charged with raping her had escaped from a prison for minors in Maine, where he had been sent for raping a woman. Weeks after he ran from Milford, he was accused of raping another woman in Georgia. In 1994, the perpetrator was convicted of kidnapping, assaulting and raping Bonnie, and was sentenced to twenty-five years in prison, to be served after he serves his Georgia sentence.

Six days after Bonnie was attacked, her senior year began at Albertus Magnus.

Intent on finishing school, she concealed her head wounds with creative hairdressing. Her leg in a brace, her head bandaged, she drove to class.

When she pulled into the school parking lot, it was empty. Determined to return, but with her emotions reeling, she had arrived a day early.

The next day, she went back again. Her dream would be her savior. She couldn't let it slip away.

Her boys' coming home, about a month after the rape, boosted her spirits. And her boss, Dan Alix, amazed her when he sent her paychecks regularly even though she couldn't work. She was on the books as a part-time employee at the time and he didn't owe her any money. But he ignored her status. He was going to help.

Bonnie had planned to take a preparation course to get ready for the law school entrance exams. But now she was out of money and emotionally battered. She couldn't do it.

Every time she tried to study for the LSAT and her regular classes, she had flashbacks. He could have killed her, left her boys motherless, even killed them.

The night before the law school entrance exam, her parents watched her two children so she could study. She sat at her worn kitchen table. She took a sample test made up of three forty-five-minute sections and then worked on a writing exercise. Her thoughts were jumbled. She was terrified about the next day. But she scored well on the test she gave herself.

About midnight, when she finally lay down, she cried herself to sleep.

She had worked so hard, overcome so much already. The man, "that creep," could take this from her, too, if she couldn't force the images away.

Bonnie turned the page of the test and took a deep breath. The next three sections were multiple choice. The questions bounced around in her mind, rebounding off the sides of her brain and then coming back like a boomerang. Sections on logical and analytical thinking—brain teasers.

Next came lengthy reading passages, followed by a string of questions, to prove her ability to understand what she had read.

She turned to the last page of the test. She was done.

Nothing could ease the anxiety during the eight weeks it took for her score to arrive in the mail.

Some of her mail still was being sent to her parents' house, where she had stayed for a while after the rape. The envelope was delivered there one day in February.

Bonnie was in her apartment, and asked her mother to open the envelope while she waited on the telephone. Her mother searched for the score box, Bonnie waiting, impatient.

Finally her mother found it. Above average. Strong enough to get her into a law school, but not into the one she wanted.

In the spring, Bonnie graduated from Albertus Magnus College with highest honors. After the ceremony, she wished that she could have her friends over, buy a bottle of wine to celebrate. She didn't have enough money.

About the same time, she was invited back to her high school to attend the adult education graduation. When the scholarships were being announced, they called her name, again and again. This time the money was for law school. She hustled up to the podium in a cropped jacket and short skirt, frosted blond hair flying. She kept her chin down, trying to hide her emotion.

Today, Bonnie is a practicing attorney, having graduated from the Quinnipiac University School of Law in

1993. Once, she had dreamed of doing so well on the LSAT that she would get accepted at Yale Law School. That's okay, Bonnie says. She'll just teach there someday.

Amy Ash Nixon

"I love being a partner, Mr. Jenkins!
There's just one problem."

Reprinted by permission of Dave Carpenter.

The Power of Perseverance

If you can dream it, you can do it.

Walt Disney

It was a long four years. Even after I had actually graduated, the nightmares began to haunt me. The university would call to say I hadn't truly graduated. There had been a mistake and there was just one more class I needed to take. I was always so relieved to wake up and realize that it had only been a bad dream. In reality, I had completed every course needed for my degree, and I was a full-fledged college graduate!

Now, the rest of my life loomed ahead of me. Sometimes a bachelor's degree prepares you for a specific occupation—you train to be an accountant, you graduate and get a position in an accounting firm. Often, however, your stint in college only prepares you to make further decisions regarding your future. You're pretty sure what you don't want to do!

During my senior year of college, I had toyed with the idea of changing my major. At that point, I had finally discovered what captured my heart. But, wanting to finally be finished with school was a stronger pull. So, I took a few courses in physiology and exercise science, but not enough to receive a degree in physical therapy. That would require advanced schooling, beyond my bachelor's degree—and I just wasn't ready to tackle that. Having completed my B.S. degree, I didn't have any intentions of furthering my education.

So, I did the safe thing and got an office job—the very thing I was sure that I didn't want to do! I detested the office politics, the suits I had to wear and the downtown environment that I had to drive to every day. I knew this was not where I belonged.

But God knew what path my career was to follow. A position opened up at the most exclusive health club in our city, so I applied. This was my kind of environment—an active, vibrant kind of place—completely at the opposite end of the spectrum from the office environment where I found myself. The position required that I work Saturday nights and Sunday mornings. *Perfect,* I thought! *I could keep my office job Monday through Friday and work at my dream job on the weekends.* This arrangement lasted several months until, eventually, a full-time position opened up and I was able to resign from my office job.

Over the next few years, I worked my way up the ladder, gaining experience in several different departments. I found my niche as the Director of Member Services— catering to our clientele and providing them with numerous cutting-edge programs. I would have stayed at that job forever—it seemed to be the pinnacle of all my dreams fulfilled. Here were fellow employees who had a passion for the same things that I did—health and fitness. Yet again, God had other plans for my life.

Within two years, a newer, bigger, better and more state-of-the-art health club facility was built—just five miles down the road. Despite all our best efforts, we lost many members to that club. And, in turn, the owner lost thousands of dollars. One by one we were each laid off.

After trying unsuccessfully to land another similar position elsewhere, I knew what I had to do. Go back to school!

Working on my master's degree in exercise science and sports medicine was different from getting my bachelor's degree. Now I was surrounded by other students excited about the same things I was. We spent hours discussing kinesiology and biomechanics—it was fun! I had truly found my passion and school was something I looked forward to, instead of just something to get through as quickly as possible. My goal was to turn my passion for fitness into a long-term career.

Soon after my graduate schooling, my husband and I moved to a small mountain community. I was hired right away to teach classes at the only health club in town. I was rapidly promoted to director of their weight-loss program. I was able to put much of my graduate school training to use as I conducted fitness tests and counseled clients on nutrition and fitness principles as a personal trainer. I found my education to be so relevant to what I was doing that I continued to seek out as much knowledge as I could. I received several certifications specific to my industry, and my credibility with the clientele grew. I loved this job, but was always ready to take on new challenges.

As my reputation within our community continued to grow, my dream began to grow, as well. I began to envision my own business. I pictured myself loading up my truck with fitness equipment and traveling from client to client—arriving at their doorstep to provide a personalized and private workout that would help them on their way to better health and physical fitness. The personal training industry as a whole was still in its infancy at this point, so this idea seemed ridiculously far-fetched, at best.

Yet, along my career path I had become friends with another instructor in the fitness industry who eventually went on to become a "trainer to the stars." I knew that she could give me some beneficial tips. We met several times, and I gained valuable insight from her experiences. As I reconsidered my dream, it still seemed fairly unrealistic.

One day a friend of a friend called to say that she had heard I was working as a personal trainer at the local health club. She was looking for a trainer, but preferred the privacy of her home. Would I be interested? *Would I? Absolutely!* Fortunately, I had done all my homework. I knew how much to charge. I knew what paperwork I needed to have her complete and sign. I had already obtained liability insurance and had all the necessary equipment. I was ready to take on my dream and make it a reality!

From there, my business blossomed through word of mouth. I had client after client scheduled throughout the day. And everything was just as I envisioned it to be. I had my own successful business, and I was doing exactly what I wanted to do—help others to improve their lives.

A few years later, when my husband and I moved to a new town, I was able to quickly rebuild my business with new clients, using testimonials from my former clients. I had so many positive referrals from my initial group of clients, that I again had more clients than I could schedule into my day.

Sixteen years ago, I never thought I would achieve what I have—that the vision that had gradually taken shape over several years would actually become a reality. But with hard work, persistence and never letting my dream die, God fulfilled every plan he had outlined for my life!

Denise Schupp

She Gave New Shape to the Shoe Business—Then She Added the Soul

"I believe the reason that we were able to do this was because we saw a need in the market, had incredible passion, and were committed to making it happen. Our enthusiasm was totally infectious and we found people that wanted to help us."

Sheri Poe

Why not?

That's what Sheri Poe kept asking herself when she and her friends came out of exercise class with backaches and sore feet because their shoes were all wrong. Sheri did some research and discovered that women's athletic shoes were only scaled-down versions of men's shoes, although the female foot is shaped differently. She and her husband, Martin Birrittella, had been looking for the right business to start and thought, why not. Why not start a company that manufactures athletic shoes specifically designed for a woman's foot. Shoes that fit.

People were more than willing to tell them why not. For

one thing, they had no capital and no experience in the industry. Experts said it was sheer lunacy to think anyone could compete against Nike and Reebok, mega companies that had the athletic shoe market all laced up. Besides, neither of them had a college degree. Sheri's education had been cut short after she'd been raped in her freshman year. The traumatic event was followed by years of bulimia, hepatitis and other health problems stemming from her attack. Her dedication to fitness helped her through the healing process. Having conquered the biggest obstacle—recovering from such a degrading physical assault—Sheri knew she could meet the challenge of creating the perfect fitness shoe for women.

First, she did her own footwork. Posing as a graduate student, she spent months interviewing hundreds of customers and shoe salesclerks. Her research confirmed a real need for women's athletic shoes.

For seed money, Sheri and her husband took a third mortgage on their modest home and borrowed from friends, family and anyone else who shared their enthusiasm for the project. Then they went to venture capitalists for serious financing. "The reactions were always the same," said Sheri. "They said it was insane to think we could break into this market having no experience within this industry and to create a new brand in such a competitive field. They suggested we take the idea to Nike or Reebok and forget about doing it ourselves."

"We started Rykä because we knew the demand was great and no one was addressing the need. We dreamed of one day seeing our shoes on aerobic instructors, in retail stores, and having a booth at a big convention right next to Nike and Reebok. It was a picture so exhilarating that any negativity I heard didn't even matter."

Still, it wasn't easy. Their dream required an enormous financial investment and venture capitalists suggested the best way to raise the money was to take their new company public. After several months, they found an investment banker that thought the idea of "shoes made by women for women" was a hot one, and loaned them $250,000 and a letter of intent to go public in the spring of 1988. They were finally on their way.

They say timing is everything, but time didn't seem to be on Sheri and Martin's side. Just as they were about to go public, the stock market crashed. "I was in shock," Sheri recalls. "How were we supposed to pull off an initial public offering right after a crash?" They expected a call from their banker asking for the money back. Instead he called the next day to say there was still a tremendous amount of interest in their company and they were going to move forward with the IPO.

Rykä Inc. went public five months later. They raised $4 million in stock without having shipped a single shoe. The future looked bright indeed. Their undying passion and commitment made it happen. They would need that commitment.

The first pair of specially ordered shoes arrived and Sheri put them on. Her heart sank. The shoes were nothing like the ones they had designed! The manufacturer had mistakenly used the wrong foot form, and had made a smaller version of a man's shoe. The whole point of their enterprise had been lost, and thousands of the shoes had already shipped to retailers nationwide.

Sheri acted quickly. She contacted key retailers and buyers and explained the production problem. The shoes were returned and she had them remade according to their original specifications.

They were back in business but they had missed an entire season of selling. This was a major setback. Sheri knew she had better get the word out about her new product—and fast. With limited funds, she designed a program for the women who could be walking billboards for her product—aerobic instructors. She offered her shoes to them at a discount, then challenged the instructors to put her shoes to the test. After wearing them, the aerobic instructors immediately experienced a difference. They spread the word about Rykä shoes and a grassroots movement developed.

It was time to expand her reach even further and another "Why not?" occurred to Sheri. In 1987, women executives in the athletic footwear industry were virtually unheard of. She wanted to capitalize on her uniqueness and since Rykä could not afford a national advertising campaign, she came up with an alternative plan—she took her story to the media. She hired an inexpensive PR firm and sent out a box of shoes with a letter to the editor of key magazines and newspapers telling the Rykä story. Her strategy worked and within a year, Sheri was featured in *Entrepreneurial Woman, Working Woman* and in dozens of articles appearing in sporting goods trade publications and other women's magazines.

One notable woman to whom Sheri sent her package was Oprah Winfrey. Every few months she sent boxes of shoes and T-shirts to Oprah and her staff, hoping to get their attention. The phone rang one day and it was Oprah's producer inviting Sheri to be on Oprah's show. "I was so shocked," Sheri recalls, "that I turned white and could barely breathe." The producer said Sheri had not originally been on Oprah's list, but during a staff meeting, they were considering various female entrepreneurs for an upcoming show, and Oprah's eyes caught the boxes of Rykä shoes stacked in a corner of the room. "I know," she said, "what about our Rykä woman?"

Sheri's appearance on the show was the chance to show off her innovative footwear to a nationwide audience of millions of women viewers. Within weeks, all of Rykä's shoes sold out, with no stock to replace them. What should have been a business bonanza became a setback that took Rykä three months to recover from, as she reorganized her company to satisfy the demand.

Years later came another unexpected break in the form of England's Princess Diana. Reading about Princess Di's public confession of her battle with bulimia, Sheri acted on impulse and wrote the princess a letter to express sympathy and share her own story. She wrote not as a fan, or a shoe manufacturer, but as a fellow survivor. To ensure that the letter reached Diana's desk, Sheri inquired of her distributor in the United Kingdom to find out the name of Princess Diana's trainer. The trainer loved the shoes and agreed to deliver the note and a pair of shoes to the Princess. That letter yielded unexpected rewards. In every photograph Sheri saw of Diana during the next three months, the Princess was wearing Rykä's.

Women around the world also saw those Rykä's, and began buying them in increasing numbers. In 1994 sales reached an all-time high of $15 million. Yet for all her success, Sheri felt the real soul of the company was missing. "We are a company that sells products solely to women. I felt a need to contribute on a corporate level to women's well-being. I had always felt that if my company became profitable, I wanted to make a difference."

Realizing that domestic violence had become the leading cause of injury to women, she founded Rykä ROSE— Regaining One's Self-Esteem—a separate, nonprofit foundation that funds shelters, education programs and rape crisis centers. Additionally, each pair of Rykä shoes carries a tag offering women tips on how to be safe and what to do if attacked.

Sheri Poe gave the sporting goods industry a wake-up call about the importance of the women's market. Since then, the women's athletic footwear industry has grown into a five billion dollar industry. Rykä, now merged with Global Sports Inc., continues to sell shoes designed especially for women's feet. Sheri remains founder and spokesperson for Rykä and is now pursuing another entrepreneurial passion, developing children's products.

Thanks to Sheri Poe's passion and determination, women can now work out in shoes that fit their needs. Even more importantly, the sales of those shoes meant that thousands of abused women are safer and more confident.

Why not?

Cynthia Kersey
Excerpted and adapted from Unstoppable

From Under the Boot Heel

There is nothing like a dream to create the future.

Victor Hugo

In my twenty years as a paramedic, I have been charged with performing duties that require enormous amounts of bravery. I was about to learn a new kind.

Several years ago, I sat in a dilapidated office housed in a condemned hospital building in the center of a nondescript town in south Texas. I lit a cigarette (this was back in the days when one could smoke in a building) and watched a large cockroach climb up the wall in front of my desk. I began my 457th day of acute self-pity.

Tim, an EMT coworker, strolled in and flicked the ugly bug onto the floor, slamming down on it with the heavy heel of a patrol boot. Even with that pounding, the bug wouldn't die. *Sort of like me,* I thought. *Stomped on unmercifully, and I keep coming back for more.*

In the year since my divorce, there had been few happy days. My entire existence seemed to depend solely on my life-saving duties. Responding to an emergency was the only time I knew my heart was beating. My thoughts turned once more to the core of my problem. *If only I could find a nice man . . .*

I suddenly felt ill. *What was I thinking? Am I to waste my entire life waiting for Prince Charming?* He certainly had not been around during the first thirty-seven years.

I stood up and walked past Tim and out to the street. Standing on the curb, I surveyed my surroundings. *Oh my God!* I said to myself while continuing my slow turn. *There is nothing to see here, no view, no green trees or water, no spiky mountains. Not even a hill. Why am I here?* The question was the internal combustion I needed. I smiled and felt hope welling up within me. Standing there on the curb of Center Street, dressed in my uniform, I laughed until tears streaked my face.

That night I pulled out a yellow legal pad. On it I wrote: "WHAT I WANT." Under the heading, I listed eight items: 1. To live in a beautiful place with a 360-degree view; 2. To make a good salary; 3. To once again own a red sports car; 4. to never see a cockroach again; 5. to have a wonderful job teaching EMTs and paramedics; 6. To be proud of myself; 7. To never, ever need a man again, except for plumbing repairs; 8. To spend my next forty years in peace and happiness. I worked until the wee hours of the morning, polishing my resume, and then I sent copies to Emergency Medical Services offices in four northwestern states.

Over fifty people attended my going-away party, and each of them asked the same question. "Wendy, how can you just pack up and go to Alaska without knowing anyone there?" Some of the women said, "I could never go off to the wilderness all alone." One man informed me that there were seven men to one woman in Alaska. "You're going to get a husband, right?"

Yeah, right.

The truth is, I had chosen to enjoy my own company for a while. Something I had never really done.

In one week, I would become the Emergency Medical Services Coordinator for Southeast Alaska. The job required travel by boat and float plane to outlying areas—the frontier of Alaska. I was to spend time in these isolated communities teaching classes on emergency services. I never knew such a career existed, and it was as if I had designed the position myself.

As I looked around at all the doubting faces that day, I felt absolutely no fear—just joy. Two suitcases and four boxes of training materials were all I had packed. I purged myself of all belongings.

As I said my good-byes, I realized it took no bravery to pack up and move to Alaska. The bravery had occurred when I made my list and resolved to fulfill it. I recognized that I could control my own destiny. The weakness was in waiting for change instead of creating it.

Who do I need? Me. Who do I depend on? Me. Who do I love? Me. Who makes me happy? Me. Selfish, you say? Darned right. And there are no cockroaches in Alaska.

Wendy Natkong

Life—It's All Good

I have always viewed employment as more than just work to earn money. My belief is that you should work to live, not live to work. Your job should not completely define the person you are, but since it will be the activity you spend most of your time at, you should find meaning and enjoyment in your work.

I lost sight of my perspective in exchange for respectability, prestige and the lure of a good paycheck. Having joined the workforce with a degree in sociology and a background in physical education, I initially jumped into a position as a recreation counselor with "at risk" adolescents in a residential facility. It was hard, draining work, but rewarding and meaningful. I felt similarly about my next position as the Teen Talk/Crisis Line director at a suicide prevention and crisis center. I enjoyed making a connection and "being there" for the teenagers, but the emotional involvement and constant availability wore me out physically at an early age. My decision to return to school to pursue a graduate degree in journalism was based on my dream to write and perform communications work for a nonprofit organization whose mission I could support wholeheartedly.

Instead, I found myself at IBM, first as an intern, then five years later as a Web site manager and corporate communications writer/editor. While my position at IBM afforded me the realization of dreams such as travel to exotic destinations and a large home on acreage in the Rocky Mountains, it did nothing to inspire me or feed my soul that I felt was in the process of slowly shriveling. So, on the verge of the breakup in my ten-year marriage and the recovery from a major mental meltdown and depression, I opted to take a severance package and "find myself."

Two weeks later, a flyer advertising for white water raft guide certification training caught my eye as I found myself alone at the library on a Saturday night. The rest, as it is said, is history.

At age thirty-four, I discovered a new calling. I became the one female raft and rockclimbing guide for a company known as "Rock-N-Row." My cushy corporate life with a secure paycheck became a distant memory as I spent my days outside in the sun, wind, heat, cold and snow. I learned to row, to read the water, to steer the paddle boat and call commands with authority, to rescue "swimmers," to tie appropriate knots, to belay safely and entertain the adventurous folk who came to play.

My sense of self, severely undermined in the years preceding the divorce, became stronger, and my self-esteem grew as each day passed with new experiences— successes and disappointments. I learned not to take life so seriously, and to be able to laugh at myself. My physical self benefited from the outdoor challenges and I liked the person I was freeing myself to be. The new man in my life—my best friend—appreciated my inner and outer qualities, and we enjoy skiing, rock climbing, hiking, and even skydiving on occasion.

To emerge from the soft, safe, corporate computer world

into the sometimes brutal realities of outdoor life was a wake-up call. Two near-death experiences—one as a result from a flip in a Class IV rapid at high water and the other from a rock shelf breaking loose above me as I belayed a climber—taught me that if I planned to take risks, they should be calculated. I carried my motto of "No Fear" into my professional and personal life and learned to trust in me—my decisions, my emotions, the person I am. The winter before my dramatic life changes was one of discontent, yet the time since has been one of affirming life and reawakening my soul. I can honestly say, no matter the situation, "It's all good." For what is the alternative?

Patty Lataille

Discovery Toys

If I were asked to give what I consider the single most useful bit of advice for all humanity, it would be this: Expect trouble as an inevitable part of life, and when it comes, hold your head high. Look it squarely in the eye, and say, "I will be bigger than you. You cannot defeat me."

Ann Landers

Twenty-five years ago, twenty-nine-year-old Lane Nemeth went toy shopping for her newborn daughter. She wanted simple, sturdy toys, like the ones at the Concord, California, day-care center where she worked. But the local stores carried what she considered plastic junk.

The more annoyed she got, the more she became convinced she could do better. She knew what kids liked and what mothers wanted. Friends gently pointed out the obvious—nothing in her background qualified her to run her own business.

But Nemeth's father and husband thought she was on to something. They suggested the Tupperware approach:

Sell toys at home-based demonstration parties.

Nemeth bought toys from her day-care center's suppliers and asked friends to hold toy parties. Encouraged by their modest success, she borrowed $5,000 from her grandmother to purchase select merchandise from Israel. Discovery Toys was born.

Nemeth converted her garage into a warehouse. Since she couldn't afford a staff, she offered three friends a title—"educational consultant"—and gave them a percentage of every sale they made.

Her enthusiasm was infectious. In the first year she grossed $20,000—enough to risk quitting her job. With a little more money borrowed from her family, she leased a small warehouse in Concord in August 1978 and set herself the goal of selling $100,000 worth of toys by the end of the year.

Business was so good that most of her inventory was depleted by October. She would not be able to fulfill her Christmas orders. "It was horrifying," she says. "I'd get an order for forty toys and only be able to send two."

The following year Nemeth was determined never to be caught short of toys again. She leased a larger warehouse and crammed it with toys. Sales broke $1 million. But at year's end she still had excess inventory and was $100,000 in debt. No bank would lend her more money, so she borrowed from a finance company at 27 percent interest.

Six months later, in even bigger financial trouble, Nemeth got a call from a venture capitalist in San Francisco. The man had gone to a Discovery Toys demonstration and had been so impressed that he offered to bail Nemeth out. She sold him 20 percent of the company.

Business picked up, and she expanded her operation again. But increased debts drove her to the brink of bankruptcy.

For the first time, Nemeth considered giving up. "I

always thought of Discovery Toys as my other child," she says. "So I said to myself, 'If this were my daughter, and she were seriously ill, what would I do?' When I looked at it that way, it became clear."

Nemeth cut her payroll and found a bank to help. By 1985 Discovery Toys reached $37 million in sales. In 1989 it sold $100-million worth of games, books, toys and audio tapes through a nationwide part-time sales force of 48,000.

Nemeth's most important lesson? "Mistakes are fine. Just don't make the same one twice."

Doug Garr

[EDITORS' NOTE: *Discovery Toys made $39.8 million in sales in 2002.*]

Tuning In

*R*ealistic people with practical aims are rarely
as realistic or practical in the long run of life as
the dreamers who pursue their dreams.

Hans Selye

I never thought I'd be a working woman, in the sense of
working in a career. I thought I would be an at-home
mother, raising my children the way my mother did. Some
of my fondest memories are of rushing through the front
door after school and flying up the stairs, two at a time, to
tell Mom about my school day over freshly baked cookies
and milk. This is what I saw for my own future someday.

Yet after only a short marriage and before children had
expanded our family of two, I became a widow at the age
of twenty-five. Within months of my husband's passing,
my young mother died of cancer of the colon. Life as I
knew it had ended, and I found myself thrust into a new
world that required a career.

Setting the course for a new identity, I decided to move
over two thousand miles from my little Pennsylvania
town for a fresh start in Southern California. I was at

National University in San Diego one weekend, taking a career development seminar to determine what I would like to do every day, when a woman who was also attending approached me. "Have you ever thought about sales?" she asked. While sales to me screamed polyester suits and door-to-door insurance salesmen, I stayed open to her suggestion that I contact her husband, who had just opened a computer store. This was 1980 and just before *Time* magazine named the personal computer as Man as of the Year. I carved my new identity in the rapidly changing world of computers, and within a couple of years, was recruited by AT&T to head up their National Data Sales Organization. I had discovered a lucrative career with stability and a future. Yet, inside, I felt a nudge. A feeling unfulfilled.

Each Mother's Day since my mother's passing I had baked apple dumplings as a celebration of our time together, and baked more cookies than I could give away at Christmastime in remembrance of my mother's custom of doing so. Baking was a way to continue family tradition—a way to stay close to my mother. Baking was my way to nurture.

Southern California sunshine breeds healthy exercise routines, and I joined the large health-conscious population with visits to the gym during lunch breaks and short runs before or after work. The mileage increased until eventually the daily runs turned into training preparation to run organized marathons. I would get up at 5:30 A.M. and run ten miles before I headed to my office located in downtown San Diego to begin my workday. Many times I would participate in an early morning meeting that included greasy donuts, and I'd think, *What I wouldn't give for a good home-baked muffin instead.* As my dissatisfaction with working in a corporate culture rose, so did my desire to create work that fed my soul as well as my bank account.

Running was like a form of meditation when, at a certain point, my mind released rampant to-do lists, my breathing became even and synchronized with the up-and-down motion of my legs, and in between these spaces spontaneous and unexpected thoughts would surface. In the cool mist of an early morning run, a thought came through the fog loud and clear: *You can build a business on muffins.*

January 1, 1987 was the beginning of a new year and a new business of my own called "Lil' Miss Muffins." With me as its owner and spokesperson, I saw myself as the healthy Mrs. Fields. I had taken all of my savings and then some, and left the secure job and life I had created, betting it all on a dream. I had no training to own and operate a bakery, but I hadn't had any background in selling computers and had done very well. This is what I kept reminding myself as I hired minimum-wage staff who would be so different to manage than my corporate salespeople had been; and started my day in tennis shoes on concrete floors, mixing large tubs of muffin batter—so different from my stylish pumps worn with suits in business boardroom meetings.

My staff of three and I baked thirteen different kinds of muffins each day that included favorites like blueberry, apple cinnamon and honey bran, in addition to the "flavor of the day." Our customers were the same companies that I had sold thousands of dollars of computer equipment to: law firms, banks, utility companies. Not only did I get to eat my fresh-baked muffin each morning, so did others in San Diego! As the business grew, so did our product line and staff. Within a year's time, we baked cookies, croissants, brownies and more, and expanded our sales to two off-site sales locations in Balboa Park. Another year later, two more additional locations included juice bars in local gyms. We were five locations and fifty-five employees strong. Lil' Miss Muffins was becoming a household name. Yet, I had created a business that operated twenty-four hours—baking by night, and operating five locations by day, and had lost any life outside of muffins. I was running very little now—just a few miles first thing before the workday began, and there was no balance. I had purchased a home closer to my business to eliminate the half-hour commute that had provided any personal time, albeit small, and now I literally slept and worked—eating muffins along the way. While the dream of creating something wholesome and healthy had been realized, I had forgotten to nurture myself along the way. Running the business had become like running a marathon—when you hit the wall and keep on going to the end, no matter how it feels. I began to question what end did I desire for my business? How did I really feel about my life? Was this the life I wanted to create for myself?

Balance now became my goal. As a working woman and business owner, everyday occurrences like buying groceries, doing the laundry, keeping my barely occupied house clean were like unclimbed mountains in the scale of my day. Returning to a gentler more joyful life where I could enjoy all parts became a "one step at a time" process with no more "running forward in constant motion." I started to tap into that same intuition that had guided me across country, into a lucrative career, and then to the exhilarating experience of starting and owning a business. I knew that I had all the answers inside to guide me—I just needed to tune in.

The same nurturing person inside me, who wanted to offer "milk and cookies" to the world, needed to take time to enjoy some myself. Little by little, I handed off more duties and daily tasks to my employees. I retrained staff to acknowledge I had a job, and it wasn't helping them each with theirs. I set better guidelines and standards for them, so that I could improve the standard of living for us all.

The business flourished and so did I. Intuition once again nudged me in a new direction. I felt ready to experience other things in my life, and to make the space for a simpler life. Turning inside and tuning in to an inner voice, I decided to sell all but one location. As soon as I put out that message to the universe, and compiled the appropriate financial and equipment list, a friend I hadn't seen for several years came into the main location inquiring if I would be willing to talk to her brother-in-law about starting a small deli. He and his wife were in town, visiting from the Bay area, and would love to get together with me over coffee. I said, "Kate, I can do better than that. This business is for sale!" Just that easily, and one meeting later with a wonderful and enthusiastic young couple, the business was sold.

In the following months I learned to fly an airplane and received my private pilot's license—a lifelong dream; and I have continued to create work from my heart, listening for when it is time to build, when it is time to nurture and when it is time to let go. We all have the answers inside if we take time long enough to stop working, and tune in.

Susan L. Gilbert

Take Two Lemons and Make Lemonade

All men who have achieved great things have been great dreamers.

Orison Swett Marden

Our house invariably had an aroma of "home." Scents like the mouthwatering zest of frying onions at dinnertime, and crisp vanilla spice that wafted through the rooms during the day. But after six months wading through the loneliness of widowhood, I realized I didn't like the whiff of sad staleness now permeating the house.

I'd drifted through those last months as though half of me was missing. Not strange, I suppose, after forty years of marriage to the same man. But a day arrived when I realized I had to decide what the rest of my life would be like. Did I want to wander the empty rooms being half a person, or did I want to get out and see if I couldn't become whole again? And if I did want to repair my psyche, how would I go about achieving this metamorphosis?

My children and grandchildren helped me decide.

"You love to write, Mom," they chorused. "Write a book."

Write a book? I thought. *At my age?*

But how many times had I told my children to live their dream? It was strange, however, to realize I might be able to live my old dream; a vision swallowed up for so many years with housework, husband and children. Not that I would change a minute of it; that was my life and I loved it.

But it wasn't my destiny anymore, and, as the homily goes, the sooner I realized it the better. Time has a way of slip-sliding through your life and before you know it, your children are married and have children of their own.

Let's face it, if life is made up of seasons I've got autumn challenging me, I thought.

Did I want to find out what else life could possibly contain for me, or wind up a shriveled, bitter old person? That question made me shudder. I'd always been an active optimist. Over the years when my children jumped from sports to dance and back again, I'd volunteered for everything from Girl Scouts, through mentoring youngsters, to vice president or secretary of the many clubs and organizations I'd joined. Then, for eighteen years I'd run my own business, a candy and gift shop. Later I'd handled events and promotions for a local bookstore.

I had what is now referred to as "life experiences." So, did I want to start another business? Volunteer somewhere? When my husband was alive, I'd published a few articles in various magazines. However, my children were correct; I'd always wanted to write a book.

Before I had a chance to dwell in other areas, a new world opened up. An editor, hearing about my desire to link my love of children with my love of Houston, approached me through a mutual friend. Would I write about Houston and what children could see and do in my city? Interesting—I'd tossed a desire into the universe and an answer had drifted down. Without any warning, I had my chance to write that book. From then on, my life took off in another direction.

I spoke with a good friend and we tossed around ideas. Before I knew it, we were on our way. We'd write a special book. Forget the lists, we'd base our book on the core curriculum here in Houston. We researched, interviewed and photographed our way though museums, parks, science exhibits and the many hidden treasures to be found in our city.

When the book was published, I glowed with pride and my children stifled "I-told-you-sos." But I was even more thrilled when a national bookstore chain named us "Authors of the Month" in our area, and a major literary group asked us to be featured authors for their annual literacy event. Before we knew it, we had a second contract, and my world and work continued to expand.

At the same time, trying for a social life and further development of my "right brain," I went to Sedona, Arizona, for an Elderhostel art sampler. While watercolor wasn't my thing, I loved working with colored pencils. Back in town, I joined an Artist's Way group facilitated by my coauthor and began colored pencil painting. Once again the universe sent help in the form of a supportive and synergistic group of people who are not only talented, but share their love of art and joy of living. At the urging of one of the artists in the group, I agreed to enter a local art show. To my great surprise, I won three ribbons and sold a painting.

I could have stayed at home and felt sorry for myself. Thank goodness I didn't. Oh, don't get me wrong; I did stay at home, but it wasn't to moan about my loss, but rather to work at fulfilling my life's dream. While doing so, I was also filling my life with something meaningful.

I've always known we have many choices in this world. The trick is to select correctly; don't opt to drain life, choose to fulfill life.

As I write this, I'm pursuing both my writing and

art careers. And loving every minute of it.

Yes, the fall season of life is a challenge. But I realize that when those lemons start falling from the trees in summer, it's wise to collect them. Autumn, especially here in Houston, is still hot. What better than to mix some lemonade with ice tea and sip while working on the latest project?

Action, the joy of living life, throws winter far into the future.

Elaine L. Galit

Not So Dumb

Your vision will become clear only when you look into your heart.
Who looks outside, dreams.
Who looks inside, awakens.

Carl G. Jung

Lisa Kudrow has created one of television's most memorable "dumb blondes." But the thirty-eight-year-old actress, who plays Phoebe on the NBC comedy *Friends,* earned a bachelor's degree at Vassar College and is known to be logical, analytical and intuitive.

Although she had acted in grade and middle school, Kudrow didn't consider show business as a career. "I thought all actors were idiots whose lives didn't work," she says. "If I became an actor, I was afraid people wouldn't take me seriously."

What Kudrow was also afraid of was making a mistake. But the pull towards acting was strong, and by 1990 she had joined an improv group. Still, she avoided taking risks. Auditions were infrequent. And her social life was even bleaker than her career. "It was the fear of being wrong that held me back," she says. "I finally learned that you can make a mistake, and the world doesn't come to an end." Kudrow won her role on *Friends* in 1994 and went on to star in such films as 1997's *Romy and Michele's High School Reunion*. She got married in '95 and had a baby in '98, playing a pregnant Phoebe on her show.

"People ask if I'm worried that I'll only play Phoebes and Micheles," she says. "What if that's all that happens? Do I care if people think I'm an idiot? I cared too much about that when I was younger. Now I listen to myself."

Gail Buchalter

"Uh, oh, Regina has her lawyer with her . . ."

No Spring Chicken

Those who dream by day are cognizant of many things that escape those who dream only by night.

Edgar Allan Poe

At forty-eight and single, I was no spring chicken. Working as a registered nurse in a busy Montreal hospital, I burned out after seven years in a particular job and was looking for a change. However, retirement seemed to loom ahead, causing me to think more carefully about any further moves. I was just as keen as anyone else for a good pension.

One day, I phoned a dear friend in Fort St. John, a northern Lilliputian town on the Alaska Highway and happened to tell her my woes.

"Why not move up here and get a job? The place is booming, and they're always looking for nurses."

"If I move there, I'll quit nursing and do something else!" I said.

"Sure, come and stay with me," Ann encouraged.

The thought of giving up all those retirement benefits

and a secure job made my knees turn to jelly at my age. I'd done it often before . . . but now, I didn't know. Was I getting too cautious with aging? Should I chance it or should I tough it out and finish another fifteen years of a frenetic hospital pace? I shuddered, knowing I'd likely keel over before collecting any pension.

I knew that if I was going to make the move, I should do it sooner rather than later. I wrote and obtained my British Columbia registered nurse's license, just in case. After thinking about it a couple of more months, I decided on the move. I didn't have a job, something I'd never done. And I seriously considered simply abandoning my nursing career.

The dead of winter 1998. A wind-chill factor of sixty below zero. I stepped off the plane and icy entrails of wind whipped up my skirt. Shivering, I clenched my teeth and knifed through the gusts pressing against me like an over-inflated balloon. My high-heeled leather boots clacked on the black ice on the tarmac. I'd forgotten that this was a tiny airport and we had to walk outside to the airport door.

Monarch butterflies danced to Western music in my stomach. What had I done? This latest adventure might be the end of me. All my life, adventure beckoned me to resign perfectly great jobs in management and teaching in hospitals to follow dreams. Now though, I wondered whether this latest escapade would be too much. Why couldn't I be like everyone else, satisfied with routine? Sigh!

Ann met me and whisked me off to her home.

"Put your résumé in at the Peace River Health Unit, Arlene."

"You know, Ann, I'm going to think about it awhile longer and see if I want to give up nursing altogether."

Within a couple of weeks, I had a job as a chambermaid

at a motel on the Alaska Highway. It was a different kind of job, but I enjoyed it. However, after three months I decided to submit my application at the Health Unit as Ann suggested.

I drove home. The phone rang as soon as I opened the door.

"I've just received your application for a position in Community Nursing in Extended Care. I was about to hire someone else, but I'm interested in interviewing you."

I was amazed.

"Well, I'm thinking of giving up nursing altogether," I equivocated.

"Oh, don't do that, with a résumé like you have! It would be such a waste and you might like community nursing. Do come in for an interview," Joan pressed.

"I'll think about it and call you back in a month," I replied.

I don't know why or where I got the audacity to say this, but I've always believed that if a job is meant for you, that no one else can have it. Later, Joan told me that she was astonished that I would turn down a job like this when many of the nurses in the area wanted this plum position.

I had no intention of calling her back. I hung up and prayed about it. "Lord, if you want me to have this job, you have Joan call me back in a month." A simple but heartfelt prayer.

One month later, the phone rang.

"Arlene, what have you decided? Can you come in for an interview today?"

I knew then that this job was mine. She hired me.

My first day, I was to be orientated by a nurse named Diane. I arrived a little early and a little scared. I'd always worked in hospitals and this was entirely different. Would I measure up?

"Hi, you must be Arlene. I see you came from Montreal. Were you born there?"

"No, I was born in a little hick town in northern Quebec; you wouldn't know it."

"Try me."

"Rouyn Noranda," I said.

"I was born there," she exclaimed.

"You're kidding. When did you leave there?" I could hardly believe that I was meeting a person from my hometown, three thousand five hundred miles away. What a strange and small world!

"Oh, we left when I was eight and moved to Watson Lake in the Yukon," she laughed. "Small world isn't it?"

"I had an aunt in Watson Lake by the name of Lucky Arsenault."

"You're not going to believe this," Diane stared at me in awe. "Lucky's daughter Nicole was my best friend all through high school!"

I almost wept. Surely this was no coincidence. My cousin was her best friend, and I was meeting her like this in a tiny health unit. Suddenly I knew this was the place I was to be for now. I grinned from ear to ear, knowing that my leap of faith was another leap into a new adventure.

And that's what it turned out to be, the best job I ever had. When I retired later I was still no spring chicken, but I left with an amazing number of stories just like this one, and all because I followed a dream.

Arlene Alice Centerwall

A Long Hot Summer

There are numerous reasons why a middle-aged woman who has been away from the workforce rearing her children decides to go back to work. The obvious might be for money, but that was not my reason.

After my children departed for college, perhaps I was just bored, or possibly I was suffering from the empty-nest syndrome, but in actuality I think I decided to return to work because I was just plain, *hot*. Colorado was experiencing an extremely hot, dry summer and my home lacked air-conditioning. It was *hot*, and I was *hot*. I determined a cool air-conditioned office was where I belonged! Years ago my first job was that of a bookkeeper—it was then that I worked for money. While my children were growing up I worked part time in the school system as a teacher's aide.

This time around I wanted to do something different, something new and exciting, and the money wasn't too important, as my husband made a very comfortable living for us. But what should I do? What sort of job should I look for? I knew I needed to be cautious as to what I became involved with. I am not a "quitter" and therefore I hoped to avoid becoming obligated to an employer in a job that might turn out to be a mistake for me.

While I agonized over what to do, I was reminded of a past incident where I needed to replace my original engagement ring as the gold was wearing thin. My husband and I shopped and shopped for one, everywhere we went, even when we were on vacation. Finally this nonstop searching prompted my poor husband to ask, "Just what kind of ring do you want, what exactly are we looking for?"

My reply was, "I honestly don't know, but when I see the correct setting, I will know it." That was the way I felt about the new career I wished to pursue; I didn't have a clue as to what I wanted to do, but knew there was a perfect fit for me, if I would just be patient.

Fortunately, that summer while attending my twenty-fifth high school class reunion, I overheard a former classmate describing what she did for a living. She was a travel agent, and she and her husband had just returned from a trip to Hawaii where they acted as chaperones for a group of travelers. WOW, that sounded like fun, considerably more fun and exciting than being a bookkeeper. Apparently this profession also had some great travel benefits. I innocently pondered the idea of becoming a travel agent. After all, how difficult could it be to write airline tickets and plan vacations? I reasoned if my friend could do it, I probably could, too, and after all, "I love to travel." I later learned uttering the phrase, "I love to travel", is a sure-fire way to prevent you from being hired when applying for a job in the travel industry. That phrase is definitely a no-no!

BINGO! It was as if fireworks lit up the night sky! Right then and there I knew without a doubt, I had found the perfect fit; I wanted to be a travel agent. Little did I realize travel agents are a specialized group of individuals whose work is both stressful and demanding. Theirs is a profession requiring special education, training and experience to become proficient. There is definitely more to it than meets the eye. There is unquestionably more to it than just generating airline tickets.

I began scanning the "help wanted" ads in my local newspaper and quickly discovered agencies were interested in hiring "experienced only travel agents, or airline personnel." I was neither. However, one agency located near my home (how lucky can you get) had an entry-level position available that involved answering the phone, typing itineraries and packaging tickets. The owner made it very clear this position would never lead to an agent position or agent training, but offered me an interview if I was interested. I was definitely interested! I interviewed and was hired. Bravo, at least I had my foot in the door.

After working on the packaging desk for nine months, I approached the agency owner, and again expressed my desire to become a travel agent. Fortunately, she made an exception and broke her "no experience no training" rules by enrolling me in a United Airlines computer training course. Thus, I realized my dream and became a full-fledged agent.

My confidence and self-worth increased with each error-free reservation and each satisfied customer. I was having a ball! I learned as much as possible about the foreign destinations I booked and got to know my clients well, so their special needs could always be met. I loved my work and took pride in it. I am proud to say, never once did I take the marvelous travel benefits I was receiving for granted. I did keep track of them, however, and received a great deal of satisfaction the year the value of my benefits exceeded my yearly salary. Now that is what I call a job! Way back when I began this career, I could not imagine myself working full time, but just as quickly couldn't visualize myself not working full time, for I was having the time of my life!

What a positive impact those middle-age "hot flashes" had on my life. Ultimately, I became a top-producing corporate international sales agent before my early retirement seventeen years later. I also experienced a world of travel, some shared with family and friends. Most importantly, I proved to myself I could do what I made up my mind to do, no matter how difficult or foreign the task. Yes indeed, life is beautiful and life can begin at forty-plus years of age.

Carolee Ware

First-Year Working Woman

"Are you Joan Clayton?" a man's voice asked on the phone that early morning.

In late August, many teachers find greener pastures, and this superintendent had to have a replacement immediately.

Having graduated the previous May with a master's degree and honors in education, I thought I had arrived. I had applied everywhere within driving distance. There were no vacancies. *All of that money my husband spent to get me through college just wasted,* I thought.

"Well, get yourself over here," the superintendent was saying. "We need an interview."

"I just washed my hair and it's in big ugly rollers." What is wrong with me? Why did I say that? I wanted the job!

"Well, take those rollers out. We like our teachers to look pretty."

I snatched my master's diploma as I went out the door. Since it was a hot summer morning, I drove the thirty minutes with all the windows down, hoping my long hair would dry. I stopped one block shy of the superintendent's office and took the rollers out. My hair fell down, limp, wet and looking like a straggled hound.

I made the best of it, introduced myself and shared my philosophy of teaching. After all, he was meeting the world's best teacher and every student would learn. Boy! Did I ever have stars in my eyes. *World. You just wait. You haven't seen this working woman yet!*

"You be here bright and early Monday morning for the first faculty meeting before the children arrive." The superintendent shook my hand and I thanked him with great enthusiasm.

"Yahoo!" I shouted when I got in the car. I couldn't wait to get home to tell my husband.

I arrived an hour early on that first Monday morning, eager to get my wonderful expertise rolling.

I had never seen so many children in one room . . . and still they came. By 10:30, surely every child had arrived. I counted the children, all thirty-nine of them. My well-thought-out and marvelously well-written lesson plans somehow didn't fit these third-graders.

"Now class, we are going to write about what we did this summer." I gave the writing papers to a student to pass out and right away he dropped them. I had both outside doors open because of the heat and no air conditioning. The breeze from outside blew the papers all over the room and thirty-nine children turned into ants, except ants don't talk!

When I finally got everyone settled and busy writing their story, I had another big surprise! Quite suddenly, for no rhyme or reason, Ben stood up in his chair desk, flapped his arms like a rooster and yelled at the top of his voice: "Err . . . err . . . err . . . err!"

They didn't tell me about this in college, kept going through my mind. My principal, seeing I had minor trouble (yeah . . . right) with discipline, brought me some little brochures. The titles read "Tips on Discipline." One of the tips suggested: "When lining up the children, let all the children with blue eyes line up first, or all the children with brown eyes, etc."

The longest school week ever finally came to an end for this working woman. I breathed a sigh of relief when the three o'clock bell rang. Completely exhausted and worn to a frazzle, I went to the exit door and announced:

"All the children with two eyes may line up first!" Immediately a stampede occurred. I dodged just in time. As the last student went out the door, he exclaimed: "Teacher, you get sillier by the day!"

In my second week of teaching, I lost what common sense remained. I thought a quick way of checking math papers included a long line of children waiting at my desk for their turn. This fiasco turned into a zoo, too. Did I actually think thirty-nine kids were going to wait quietly in line? The last little girl in line handed me a blank paper and asked: "Teacher, do we put our name on our paper?"

I was still hanging in there at Christmastime, but I panicked when told I would be presenting the Christmas program for the grade-school parents. I decided to have the children do a rhythm-band number. It went pretty well, I thought. When the performance ended, I instructed the children to pass their instruments down to me, cautioning how careful and quiet they must be, and they turned into little angels. As we quietly exited the gym, the children followed right behind me. My arms, being full of bells, tambourines and noisemakers gave way and all the instruments toppled to the floor with the thunderous sound of an earthquake. The zoo was back! Children came from everywhere, grabbing this and that, shouting "I got it! No, that's mine. I saw it first! Get out of my way!" The parents hid their faces, trying not to laugh. About this time, I would have made a great candidate for an aspirin commercial. Whatever happened to the world's-best-teacher-working-woman?

Back in our room, one oversized plump boy popped up and down in his seat. I asked what he was doing. He replied: "I'm popping them mustard packs I got at the show last night. Don't it smell good?"

When May rolled around, I felt both happy and sad. Happy that in spite of all my "boo-boos," these children had won my heart. I found myself planning for next year. A lot of new ideas and strategies beckoned me.

The students' achievement scores during my first year as a working woman were extraordinarily good. My students had learned in spite of me, but I had learned more than anyone!

My first year as a working woman, despite the many "boo-boos," turned into a thirty-one year teaching career, and I wouldn't have missed it for the world!

Joan Clayton

"Opportunity? Opportunity who?"

Reprinted by permission of Donna Barstow.

A Memoir of a Friend

I first met Lamar Dodd nearly fifteen years ago, one spring evening in Athens, Georgia. Ancient oak trees overhung the winding path to the Georgia Museum of Art, a century-old building of antique brick and narrow windows. The night air, I recall, was as smooth and cool as running water, and I was dressed in a light silk suit, I was shivering as much from social jitters as the temperature.

The museum was hosting a special exhibition of Dodd's paintings and everyone of importance in our small university community was going to be there. Lamar Dodd was a legend in Athens, where he had created one of the most renowned university art departments in the country. But to me, he was more than an eminent educator, he was a man who had dared to live his dream.

Having worked for years at the University of Georgia, where the routine and the bureaucracy stifled me, I had reached the top of the glass ceiling. Either I remained where I was without hope for growth or I moved on to pursue goals of my own. But I was full of self-doubt and afraid to make a move.

As my husband and I crossed the museum's gray marble floors, which glistened like polished ice, I nervously watched men in white dinner jackets and woman in chiffon and lace holding long-stemmed glasses and chatting familiarly in the crowded corridors and vestibules. Among those confident achievers, I felt woefully out of place. The heels of my shoes clicked a little too loudly as we steered toward the center of the main exhibition room where Lamar Dodd stood, surrounded by a large group of admirers.

He was not a big man, five feet nine or ten, but he commanded attention. Fluffy snow-white hair crowned his head, and he leaned on a gold-topped cane like a king on a ceremonial scepter. My husband navigated us to the front of the crowd to present me to the artist. I was immediately struck by the brilliance of Dodd's light-blue eyes, the color of a hazy summer sky—but more than the color struck me. We talked for only a few minutes before I noticed the way Lamar focused all his attention on me while he spoke. Something in his bold manner made me feel strong and included.

I went on to view the canvases commissioned by NASA to commemorate the exploration of space. They were large works filled with dominant graphic lines and splashed with brilliant color. The artist's concepts and powerful movements were as audacious and venturesome as the exploits they celebrated.

After that night at the museum, I didn't expect to see Dodd again. But a week later he telephoned. A major psychiatric corporation had commissioned him to create a painting that depicted the healing of the psyche. Lamar asked my husband to be an informal consultant for the project, and he invited us both to his home studio to see his initial sketches and to talk about the work.

So one Sunday afternoon, we drove past towering magnolias, Georgia pines and a magnificent gingko tree near the entrance to Dodd's curved driveway. The artist and his wife, Mary, lived in an old part of Athens full of rambling front yards and brick homes covered in ivy. Lamar's house was hidden from the street, but the yard had been landscaped by someone with an artist's eye.

Lamar met us at the door, wearing Nikes and an Izod shirt, his thick white hair stuck out in the back as if he'd slept on it at an odd angle. As I walked inside, I was greeted with the smell of lacquer and turpentine.

Lamar guided us toward his studio which sat just a few feet from the front door. On the way we passedprecious artifacts and fossils that he kept encased in glass. Inside Lamar's studio a huge picture window faced the entrance, allowing sunlight to penetrate the room and perhaps capture the wandering gaze of the artist. Outside I saw flowering azaleas and rows of blooming jonquils and tulips. The view itself was a painting.

In the center of the room stood a huge easel, holding one of the largest canvases I'd ever seen. Pallettes of paint and jars, brushes and other sundry bottles rested on a small table with wheels to the right of the easel. Hundreds of canvases were tucked in cubbies behind the easel, and still more filled empty spaces in the room. Piles of sketches and small watercolors covered the top of an architect's table. Paintings dotted the walls (including a self-portrait). An antique clock stood on the far right wall. Here was evidence of a person full of energy, bursting to create.

Lamar directed us to sit in one of the odd assortment of chairs, each looking equally uncomfortable. Once seated, he told us he wanted to portray the emergence of the soul from illness through struggle to health. He and my husband discussed the images that might best capture Lamar's vision.

"And what do you think, my dear?" Lamar asked me.

He so naturally included me in their discussion. I soon found myself talking about my dream to start a business for myself which would allow me to teach and to write, two things I loved most.

"You're frightened," he said matter-of-factly, as if he'd just told me it had begun raining outside.

I protested.

"It's fear. I know the symptoms," he said.

"That's hard for me to imagine," I told him.

"Why? In some ways I've been frightened all my life, but courage may be no more than cussed stubbornness, and I have plenty of that Southern virtue. It means getting up each day and doing what you have to do, going on when circumstances get you down, pushing ahead when others hold you back."

It was still hard for me to believe that this man's charmed life involved much struggle.

"When I graduated from high school," Lamar said, "my mother and uncle sent me to Georgia Tech to study architecture. But my heart wasn't in it. Perhaps I was like you. I was trying to please others, not myself. I went home after less than a year, and I felt like a failure. It was as if someone had turned off the switch. I couldn't paint, couldn't read, couldn't visit. I stayed in my room."

"How did you break out?"

"I got an offer to teach art in a small school in Alabama. Teaching young people and seeing their joy in creating saved me. I threw off the doubts and fears and plunged into painting."

And the rest is history, I thought. Apparently, however, the rest was not history. Lamar later went to study in New York City where his teachers were not always positive about his work. His life was full of the same kind of irritations and doubts that plague us all. Still, he had managed to overcome the barriers.

At the end of our afternoon, we heard the sound of whispering and the rolling of wheels. A nurse appeared with a small woman in a wheelchair. The woman's thin hair was neatly combed, and she was freshly groomed, but her eyes were dull. She sat hunched in her chair. Her shoulders seemed as delicate and as fine as bird's wings. Even though the room was warm, she wore a light blue sweater buttoned to her throat. I guessed this woman to be Lamar's wife, who I knew was suffering from Alzheimer's disease.

"This is Mary," Lamar said, crossing to her chair and laying a hand on her shoulder. She did not look up. He chatted on, including Mary in the conversation as if she understood, but she never raised her head or responded.

On that day, as I glimpsed the deep sadness on Lamar's face while he interacted with his wife, I finally had to question my illusion that those who create were blessed with a charmed life.

Lamar Dodd and I became friends. I went to see him many Sunday afternoons, and he encouraged me to take the dare I was setting for myself. I drank on his strength, but I still deposited the monthly checks into my account and made no attempt to begin the business I dreamed of.

Lamar unleashed a series of brilliant water colors, bursting with reds, yellows, greens, purples—each more magnificent than the previous. The scenes emerging from the canvas came from long-past memories of the bursts of sunflowers he had seen on his trips to Cortona, Italy, and of shoreline visits resplendent with lobster cages and fisherman off the coast of Maine. Lamar's enthusiasm overflowed, and his brush stood ready to produce more. His imagination and ability to create seemed endless.

Then Lamar had a stroke.

For weeks I feared seeing him again. His right hand, the hand with which he painted, was paralyzed, and along with it, I was sure, his courage crushed.

I drove up the magnolia-lined drive and parked outside. After a short pause in my car to prepare myself for what lay ahead, I walked up the concrete path to his door.

Following my knock, I heard painfully slow, sluggish footsteps approaching. When he opened the screen and I saw the well-known crop of white hair, it was as though time stood still. His eyes were cloudier, but I spotted the familiar gleam I'd seen the first day I met him.

"Such a pleasure, my dear." His voice was deeper but still clear. He leaned on the gold-topped cane, his right hand resting on the head, immobile. He led me into the small sitting room adjacent to his studio. One of his brilliant, sunburst scenes from the space series adorned the wall over his fireplace, a cruel reminder from years past.

I blinked and tried not to show my emotions. We talked about many things, except the appalling subject at hand—his devastating transformation. And gradually, like the Southern gentlemen he was, he turned the conversation to me—my concerns and ambitions. He was always gently encouraging.

In a while it was time to go. Still struggling with my emotions, I asked to use the restroom. There I leaned my head against the cool mirror and cried for him, for his loss, for his future, for his pain. Then I dried my eyes, reapplied some makeup, and went out to bid Lamar farewell.

But he had disappeared. I heard a noise in his studio. He had shuffled over to his easel and was standing before it in intense concentration. Sitting on the large frame was a magnificent oil painting of an island jutting out of a turbulent blue-green sea. The pink sky of the background looked as if a majestic sunset had just begun. There was a softness about the work that I had not seen in his other landscapes.

My heart broke for him. How sad it must be to contemplate the work you can no longer do. I watched in silence from the hallway, barely able to breathe, much less say good-bye.

Then something remarkable happened. Lamar picked up a large paintbrush in his left hand and inched forward toward the huge canvas. I watched while he placed the brush in his lifeless right hand. With extreme effort he trapped the brush between his two front fingers and rested the shaft against his palm. Then with his left hand guiding and with agonizing care, he pushed the brush across the surface, leaving a perfect line of color.

After a few moments, he slowly put down the brush and turned to see me watching. Tears were making my newly applied makeup run again. I went over to him and took his paralyzing right hand in mine.

I kissed his cheek and quietly found my way out.

My life changed after that visit to his home. I went after my dream. Like Lamar, I faced the challenge of leaving everything behind to chase something unknown. Like Lamar in his early days, I wondered if I could be successful. I hope, like Lamar, who continues to paint at eighty-six, I will overcome the obstacles that life will place before me and push forward.

Joan Curtis

[AUTHOR'S NOTE: *Lamar Dodd passed away in 1996.*]

The Creation of a Caring Corporation

If you want to start a successful business:

• Don't choose an industry that's already dominated by several large companies.
• Don't plan on selling products without an advertising campaign.
• Don't mix politics with sales.

Any Harvard business graduate will tell you that. And that's exactly why someone from Harvard Business School is the last person Anita Roddick plans to hire.

Anita broke just about every rule in the book when she started The Body Shop to sell naturally-based cosmetics, and she's still breaking them today. There are consequences for Anita's irreverence, of course. In her case, they read like this: The Body Shop now has more than 1,500 stores throughout the world, is worth over $500 million, and has influenced the products and marketing of all its chief competitors. Those are just the business consequences. The company is also a powerfully effective vehicle for social and environmental awareness and change which, as far as Roddick is concerned, is the most important consequence of all.

From the moment in 1976 when she first conceived the idea of opening a naturally based cosmetics shop, Anita was thinking in a most un-businesslike manner. Most entrepreneurs set out to establish a company with growth potential that will hopefully make them wealthy someday. Anita was just looking for a way to feed herself and her two children, while her husband, also a maverick, was away on a two-year adventure, riding a horse from Argentina to New York.

Her first challenge was to find a cosmetics manufacturer to produce her products. No one that she approached had ever heard of jojoba oil or aloe vera gel. They thought cocoa butter had something to do with chocolate. Anita had discovered a market just about to explode: the young female consumer who would prefer her cosmetics guilt-free and environmentally responsible. When manufacturers failed to have the same foresight, Anita found a small herbalist who could do the work.

Since Anita was not the typical entrepreneur, she saw no drawbacks in starting her company with almost no capital. To save money, she bottled her cosmetics in the same inexpensive plastic containers hospitals use for urine samples, encouraging the customers to bring them back for refills. Because she couldn't afford to have labels printed, she and some friends hand printed every one. It couldn't have turned out better if she'd planned it that way. The product now had the same natural, earthy image of the ingredients themselves.

Anita opened her first branch of The Body Shop in her hometown of Brighton, England, where the proprietors around her were taking bets on how long she would last. Less amused were the owners of local funeral parlors who insisted she change the shop's name. No one, they complained, would hire a funeral director located near a place called "The Body Shop." She stuck to her guns and the name stayed.

The store was only minimally successful. Nevertheless, Anita decided to move right ahead with a second one. The bank questioning her wisdom, refused a loan. So she found a friend of a friend willing to lend her $6,400 in exchange for 50% ownership. Today he's worth $140 million. Signing over half of her business was the only real mistake Anita ever made. But it wasn't the only decision that *looked* like a mistake. Here are three more:

- She never advertised—even when she opened shops in America. People told her it was suicide to enter a new market without massive advertising support.
- She doesn't sell in any outlet other than The Body Shop stores. (Some Asian stores are situated within department stores.)
- She resolved early on that her shops would be a catalyst for change, not just in the business world, but the world at large.

These decisions turned out to be some of the most inspired "mistakes" in the history of business. Without advertising, Anita's nonconformist ideas have inspired hundreds of articles and interviews generating valuable publicity. Her first shop in New York was packed from the day it opened. At one point, a thirty-five-year-old woman on roller skates threw up her arms and shouted: "Hallelujah! You're here at last." So much for advertising.

Anita doesn't need the department stores either. There is a new branch of The Body Shop opening somewhere in the world every two and a half days. Occasionally she has had some trouble getting into a local mall. But having a past that was filled with challenges, she was accustomed to coming up with creative solutions. In one instance, she organized every mail order customer within a 110-mile radius to write letters to the management of a mall that had turned her down. Within a few months, a branch of The Body Shop was going in.

Finally, this ludicrous idea of putting ideals ahead of profit. From the start, Anita wanted not just to change the faces of her customers, but to change the entire face of business. She envisioned a company that was socially responsible and compassionate. "I see the human spirit playing a big role in business. The work does not have to be drudgery and the sole focus does not have to be on making money. It can be a human enterprise that people feel genuinely good about."

Some of the raw materials for her products are harvested by groups of people in underdeveloped regions, thus providing them with the means for generating an income. The Body Shop has launched campaigns to save the whales, ban testing on animals in the cosmetic industry, help the homeless, and protect the rain forests. All with the help of a strong brand and loyal customer following.

Employees can be involved in almost all these efforts. They're paid a half day a month for community volunteer time and some went to Romania to help rebuild orphanages. Customers are encouraged to register to vote in the shop, recycle their plastic cosmetic containers, and bring their own shopping bags to save paper and plastic waste. For all these reasons, some have suggested Anita's company should really be called "The Body and Soul Shop." Customers emerge not only looking good, but feeling good.

"Business as usual" isn't part of Anita Roddick's make up. But as far as she's concerned, that is what has made all the difference.

Cynthia Kersey
Excerpted and adapted from Unstoppable

A License to Follow One's Dream

People are never more insecure than when they become obsessed with their fears at the expense of their dreams.

Norman Cousins

In April of 1998 my son was accepted to a very expensive college, and I knew I needed to find employment to help with expenses. At that same time my brother was experiencing health problems that were forcing him to make a very important decision of his own. His dilemma was whether or not to close the family feed business that my grandfather had started in 1924. "Grampa," as we called him, was a legend in our town, and since his death in 1991, at the age of ninety-eight, his grandson (my brother) had not only kept the business open but had relocated it downtown. He had brought it up to date in some areas yet kept just enough of Grampa's style to give it an "old-fashioned" feel. However, with gradual changes in his circumstances and health, my brother was faced with the decision of closing it down.

Our mother, who had helped run the store since the

seventies, didn't want the business responsibility even though she hated the thought of not having the store in her life. The extended family of over one hundred people also felt a wave of sadness, but at the same time no one was really in a position to take it over. One day, a few of us were sitting around the store as the inevitable end drew near. My brother nonchalantly said to me, "You know, you were always good with numbers, do you want the store?"

Immediately, I exclaimed, "Not me! I don't want to be married to the Feed Store." That statement stemmed from all the memories I had of my grampa devoting most of his time to the business and then watching my brother do the same. Nevertheless, that night I couldn't sleep. I tossed and turned, restlessly contemplating the possibility. I finally got to sleep knowing that the next day, the Thursday before Good Friday, I had to go to the bank regarding a very important financial transaction in another area of my life.

The next morning as I drove to the bank I was totally preoccupied with this new entrepreneurial decision. When I arrived, I decided to table my thoughts on owning the Feed Store and turned my attentions to my upcoming banking transactions. Upon meeting with my consultant, I realized I had forgotten some additional paperwork to complete the business at hand. Again I got behind the wheel to retrieve these documents. Once on the road, my mind wistfully reexamined the future of my grandfather's business. It had always been my favorite place. Fond memories of the smell of the feed in the barn, the feel of the tiny mustard seed running through my fingers and the sounds of the baby chicks in their warm cozy incubators kept running through my head. These sentimental visions danced in my subconscious as I drove along. Coming out of my daydream, I noticed the traffic light up ahead had turned from green to yellow and as I slowed to stop I glanced at the license plate on the car in front of me. The first part of it read "RISK IT." Being the type of person who is always looking for spiritual "signs" to facilitate decisions, I jokingly spoke out loud, "You're not speaking to me through license plates, are you?" The light methodically changed from red to green and we all proceeded forward.

On my way back to the bank, traffic was once again routinely halted by a red light. Once again I glanced at the cars patiently waiting. My heart skipped a beat when there to my left, just ahead of me, was that same car with that same license plate! I could hardly keep focused on the short remainder of my journey or the scheduled banking procedures. In fact, I told my monetary advisor the story and right then began consulting with her about how to start proceedings to finance my new business endeavor.

That Sunday, Easter Sunday, I went to the store and looked at it as I had never looked at it before. I swept a little feed from one side to the other. I rearranged a shelf of dog biscuits, stacked up some bird seed and again ran my fingers through the pail of tiny mustard seeds. I looked at the picture of my grandfather hanging above the cash register, and I told him I couldn't do it without his help. He just stared back at me with those kind eyes as if to say, "Don't worry, I'll be right here."

That was four years ago. My business is currently alive and well. Each day, it's truly a joy to go to work. Our customers are the greatest! It's especially rewarding when someone comes in who used to know my grampa. We both fondly remember a story or two together, which always brings a smile to our faces. Sometimes the conversation can go on until the next customer comes in. It's a real treat when that person, too, can share in the walk down memory lane. Then we're all laughing and swapping nostalgic tales of way back when.

Being a woman, owning a feed store is somewhat out of feminine character. Especially when fifty-pound feed bags need to be carried out or rearranged. But we manage. My mother is a huge help. Yes, she's still there. She doesn't have to be there. She just likes to be. I used to try and get her to go home and relax. Do things that she's always wanted to do in her retirement. But now after being at the store for four years I know why she's there. It's in her blood, and she loves it. And the customers love her! Someday, if I'm fortunate enough to have one of my children, grandchildren, nieces or nephews take over the business, I know that I will be there, too. It's just a place where your heart and soul find comfort.

By the way, I never saw that license plate again, even though I look for that car all the time!

Debby Kate Stahl Ramsey

Who Is Jack Canfield?

Jack Canfield is one of America's leading experts in the development of human potential and personal effectiveness. He is both a dynamic, entertaining speaker and a highly sought-after trainer. Jack has a wonderful ability to inform and inspire audiences toward increased levels of self-esteem and peak performance.

He is the author and narrator of several bestselling audio- and videocassette programs, including *Self-Esteem and Peak Performance, How to Build High Self-Esteem, Self-Esteem in the Classroom* and *Chicken Soup for the Soul—Live.* He is regularly seen on television shows such as *Good Morning America, 20/20* and *NBC Nightly News.* Jack has coauthored numerous books, including the *Chicken Soup for the Soul* series, *Dare to Win* and *The Aladdin Factor* (all with Mark Victor Hansen), *100 Ways to Build Self-Concept in the Classroom* (with Harold C. Wells) and *Heart at Work* (with Jacqueline Miller).

Jack is a regularly featured speaker for professional associations, school districts, government agencies, churches, hospitals, sales organizations and corporations. His clients have included the American Dental Association, the American Management Association, AT&T, Campbell Soup, Clairol, Domino's Pizza, GE, ITT, Hartford Insurance, Johnson & Johnson, the Million Dollar Roundtable, NCR, New England Telephone, Re/Max, Scott Paper, TRW and Virgin Records. Jack is also on the faculty of Income Builders International, a school for entrepreneurs.

Jack conducts an annual eight-day Training of Trainers program in the areas of self-esteem and peak performance. It attracts educators, counselors, parenting trainers, corporate trainers, professional speakers, ministers and others interested in developing their speaking and seminar-leading skills.

For further information about Jack's books, tapes and training programs, or to schedule him for a presentation, please contact:

The Canfield Training Group
P.O. Box 30880 • Santa Barbara, CA 93130
phone: 805-563-2935 • fax: 805-563-2945
To e-mail or visit our Web site: *www.chickensoup.com*

Who Is Mark Victor Hansen?

Mark Victor Hansen is a professional speaker who, in the last 20 years, has made over 4,000 presentations to more than 2 million people in 32 countries. His presentations cover sales excellence and strategies; personal empowerment and development; and how to triple your income and double your time off.

Mark has spent a lifetime dedicated to his mission to make a profound and positive difference in people's lives. Throughout his career, he has inspired hundreds of thousands of people to create a more powerful and purposeful future for themselves while stimulating the sale of billions of dollars worth of goods and services.

Mark is a prolific writer and has authored *Future Diary, How to Achieve Total Prosperity* and *The Miracle of Tithing.* He is coauthor of the *Chicken Soup for the Soul* series, *Dare to Win* and *The Aladdin Factor* (all with Jack Canfield) and *The Master Motivator* (with Joe Batten).

Mark has also produced a complete library of personal empowerment audio- and videocassette programs that have enabled his listeners to recognize and use their innate abilities in their business and personal lives. His message has made him a popular television and radio personality, with appearances on ABC, NBC, CBS, HBO, PBS and CNN. He has also appeared on the cover of numerous magazines, including *Success, Entrepreneur* and *Changes.*

Mark is a big man with a heart and spirit to match—an inspiration to all who seek to better themselves.

For further information about Mark write:

P.O. Box 7665
Newport Beach, CA 92658
phone: 949-759-9304 or 800-433-2314
fax: 949-722-6912
Web site: *www.chickensoup.com*

Who Is Patty Aubery?

As the president of Chicken Soup for the Soul Enterprises and a #1 *New York Times* bestselling coauthor, Patty Aubery knows what it's like to juggle work, family and social obligations—along with the responsibility of developing and marketing the more than 80 million *Chicken Soup* books and licensed goods worldwide.

She knows because she's been with Jack Canfield's organization since the early days—before *Chicken Soup* took the country by storm. Jack was still telling these heartwarming stories then, in his trainings, workshops and keynote presentations. And it was Patty who directed the labor of love that went into compiling and editing the original 101 *Chicken Soup* stories. Later, she supported the daunting marketing effort and steadfast optimism required to bring it to millions of readers worldwide.

Today, Patty is the mother of two active boys—ten-year-old J.T. and five-year-old Chandler—exemplifying that special combination of commitment, organization and life balance all working women want to have. She's been known to finish at the gym by 6:00 A.M., guest-host a radio show at 6:30, catch a flight by 9:00 to close a deal—and be back in time for soccer with the kids. But perhaps the most notable accolade for this special working woman is the admiration and love her friends, family, staff and peers hold for her.

Of her part in the *Chicken Soup* family, Patty says, "I'm always encouraged, amazed and humbled by the storytellers I meet when working on any *Chicken Soup* book, but by far the most poignant have been those stories of women in the working world, overcoming incredible odds and—in the face of all challenges—excelling as only women could do."

Patty is also the coauthor of several other bestselling titles: *Chicken Soup for the Christian Soul, Christian Family Soul,* and *Christian Woman's Soul, Chicken Soup for the Expectant Mother's Soul, Chicken Soup for the Sister's Soul* and *Chicken Soup for the Surviving Soul.*

She is married to successful international entrepreneur, Jeff Aubery and, together with J.T. and Chandler, they make their home in Santa Barbara, California. Patty can be reached at:

Self-Esteem Seminars
P.O. Box 30880
Santa Barbara, CA 93130
(805) 563-2935
fax: (805) 563-2945

Who Are Chrissy and Mark Donnelly?

Chrissy and Mark Donnelly are a dynamic married couple working closely together as coauthors, marketers and speakers. They began their marriage with a decision to spend as much time together as possible—both in work and in spare time. During their honeymoon in 1995, they planned dozens of ways to leave their separate jobs and begin to work together on meaningful projects. Compiling a book of stories about love and romance was just one of the ideas.

Chrissy and Mark are the coauthors of the #1 *New York Times* bestsellers *Chicken Soup for the Couple's Soul, Chicken Soup for the Golfer's Soul, Chicken Soup for the Sports Fan's Soul, Chicken Soup for the Father's Soul, Chicken Soup for the Baseball Fan's Soul, Chicken Soup for the Golfer's Soul: The 2nd Round* and *Chicken Soup for the Romantic Soul.* They are also at work on several other upcoming books, among them *Chicken Soup for the Friend's Soul,* and *Chicken Soup for the Married Soul.*

As cofounders of the Donnelly Marketing Group, they develop and implement innovative marketing and promotional strategies that help elevate and expand the *Chicken Soup for the Soul* message to millions of people around the world.

Chrissy, COO of the Donnelly Marketing Group, grew up in Portland, Oregon, and graduated from Portland State University. As a CPA, she embarked on a six-year career with Price Waterhouse.

Mark also grew up in Portland, Oregon, and unbeknownst to him, attended the same high school as Chrissy. He went on to graduate from the University of Arizona, where he was president of his fraternity, Alpha Tau Omega. He served as vice president of marketing for his family's business, Contact Lumber, and after eleven years resigned from day-to-day responsibilities to focus on his current endeavors.

Mark and Chrissy enjoy many hobbies together including golf, hiking, skiing, traveling, hip-hop aerobics and spending time with friends. Mark and Chrissy live in Paradise Valley, Arizona, and can be reached at:

Donnelly Marketing Group, LLC
3104 E. Camelback Road, Suite 531, Phoenix, AZ 85016
Phone: 602-508-8956
Fax: 602-508-8912
E-mail: *chickensoup@cox.net*

Contributors

Linda Apple lives in Springdale, Arkansas, with her husband Neal. They have five children and two grandchildren. She co-directs the women's ministry in her church, Christian Life Cathedral. She is an inspirational speaker and writer who had the honor of being published in *Chicken Soup for the Nurse's Soul*. e-mail: *psalm10218@cox-internet.com*.

Mickey Bambrick lives near LaConner, Washington, and she thanks God she could quit working in the "real world" a few years ago and now just sits at her computer writing stories all day. Or not. She loves being one of the ingredients in "Chicken Soup".

Nancy Bandy is managing director of Trainsitions, a consulting firm specializing in training and organizational design. She has held executive positions and is working on her first book, *The House that Service Built*. Degrees include a B.S. Ed. from Northern Illinois University and M.A. from Webster University. Reach her at *nbandy@trainsitions.com*.

Donna Barstow loves to draw and write cartoons. Her quirky drawings appear in over 200 publications including *The New Yorker*, *The L.A. Times*, *Readers' Digest*, *Harvard Business Review*, law publications, etc., and in many calendars, books and greeting cards, including Chicken Soup for the Soul. She has her own calendar, "What Do Women REALLY Want?" now available at Barnes & Noble. You may see more of her work at *www.reuben.org/dbarstow*, or contact her at: *dbarstow@hotmail.com*.

Barbara Bartocci is the award-winning author of six books and a popular keynote and breakout speaker for women's conferences, church conferences, and spouse programs. See more at *www.BarbaraBartocci.com*. Her story about Mother Teresa is also about Jim Siress, a speaker and corporate trainer who can be reached at *rhssvc@accessus.net*.

Peggy Bert is a graduate of CLASS Speakers, Certified Personality Plus Trainer, a private pilot and holds an M.A. in theological studies. She is a sought-after speaker for conferences, retreats and business seminars. Peggy also conducts customized programs to enhance communication, relationships and leadership skills. Contact Peggy at: *www.PeggyBert.com*.

Bits & Pieces is a monthly publication that has been motivating people for more than thirty years. Every issue is filled with inspiration and insights to help readers reach beyond the stress of daily life and improve any situation. Visit *www.ragan.com* to see a sample copy or call 800-878-5331.

Linda Blackman, CSP (Certified Speaking Professional designation, the industry's highest earned honor), sought-after speaker, trainer, author and award-winning television newscaster specializes in public speaking, presentational selling and crisis/media training. She coauthored *The Sales Coach* and is featured in other bestsellers. Linda is available to speak at your next event at *www.LindaBlackman.com* or *Linda@LindaBlackman.com*. 847-942-1888.

Virginia Boshears is married with two daughters, two sons-in-law and four grandchildren. She focuses on writing essays that detail everyday occurrences and has recently branched out into short fiction. She welcomes your e-mail at: *quotidianscribe@hotmail.com*.

Dianne Bradley spent ten years traveling in the Marine Corps. Once her daughter became school age, she left the Marines and became a full-time mother. She is now an executive secretary raising her daughter in South Florida. She enjoys running and rock climbing with her fourteen-year-old daughter.

Cynthia Briche graduated from high school with honors in 1972, has raised three children and married her soulmate in 1988. She enjoys snow skiing, cruises and fishing. She has only three years before retiring with thirty years of service with the Florida Retirement System. She is currently a casemanager for St. Johns County Social Services.

Beatrice E. Brown received her Bachelor of Science degree in biochemistry from Rutgers University in 1977. She currently lives in Tucson, Arizona ,where she is writing a novel about the African-American experience during the stock market crash of 1929. Please e-mail her at: *beabrown@Care2.com*.

Martin Bucella has sold over 20,000 cartoons to more than 500 magazines both here and abroad. His work can regularly be seen in *Better Homes & Gardens, National Enquirer, Woman's World, etc.* The artist's work can also be seen on greeting cards, T-shirts, books, calendars and in newspapers through syndication. Check out Marty's Web site at: *http://members.aol.com/mjbtoons/index.html*.

Gail Buchalter is a contributing editor for *Parade Magazine*.

Peyton Budinger was for many years a New York writer and editor producing work for such publishers Nast, Hearst as Condé, Avon Books and McGraw Hill. She is now a ceramic artist, dividing her time between Key West, Florida, and New York City.

Susan K. Burkholder's career was as a hospice home care nurse, then the director of a hospice home care agency. She retired a few years ago to travel, write and enjoy living in the southwest. Her favorite writing is non-fiction inspirational material. She can be reached at 2080 Flying Heart Lane, Tucson, AZ 85713.

Rachel Byrne received her bachelor's degree from Dartmouth College and her master's degree as a physician's assistant from the University of Colorado. Currently, she practices psychiatry and teaches infant care classes at a Denver hospital. She hopes to also pursue a writing career, focusing on fiction and medical articles.

Michele "Screech" Campanelli is a national bestselling author. She lives in Palm Bay, Florida, with her husband, Louis V. Campanelli III. She has written stories in over twenty-two anthologies and penned several novels including, *Keeper of the Shroud, Jamison and Margarita* published by Americana Books. Her personal editor is Fontaine M. Wallace. *www.michelecampanelli.com*

Martha Campbell is a graduate of Washington University St. Louis School of Fine Arts, and a former writer/designer for *Hallmark Cards*. She has been a freelance cartoonist and book illustrator since 1973. She can be reached at P.O. Box 2538, Harrison, AR 72602, (870) 741-5323 or *marthaf@alltel.net*.

Dave Carpenter has been a full-time cartoonist since 1981. His cartoons have appeared in a number of publications, including *Harvard Business Review, Barron's, Reader's Digest, The Wall Street Journal, Good Housekeeping, Better Homes and Gardens, Woman's World, First For Women, USA Weekend* and *The Saturday Evening Post*. Dave's cartoons also appear in many of the *Chicken Soup for the Soul* books. Dave can be reached at: *davecarp@ncn.net*.

Arlene Alice Centerwall is a retired registered nurse with many years experience in all fields of nursing including teaching and management. She won second place in the American Christian Writer's association Contest a few years ago and also second place at Cameron Press contest. She has been published numerous times in several anthologies and magazines and is also a poet. She presently is involved in writing a book for teenagers and to keep me busy, she volunteers in visiting the elderly and does pet sitting.

Joan Clayton has authored several books and around 450 published articles. She has been nominated three times in Who's Who Among America's Teachers.

Lisa Wood Curry writes copy for catalogs, brochures and direct mail and is currently working on a medieval mystery novel. Originally from Chicora, Pennsylvania, and an alumnus of Indiana University of Pennsylvania, she now lives in the suburbs of Pittsburgh with her husband, two sons and two dachshunds.

Joan C. Curtis manages a consulting business, Executive Expertise. She leads communication and motivation seminars. She holds a doctorate in adult education. Her writing credits include many stories and one book, Strategic Interviewing: Skills for Savvy Executives, published in 2000. Please visit her Web site *www.savvyinterviewer.com* or email her at *jcurtis5@charter.net*.

Renée Day received her bachelor of arts in political science in 1989, as well as her Single-Subject and Education Specialist credentials in 1998, from the University of California, Riverside. She teaches history and government to special needs students in California. Renée enjoys community activities with her family, gardening and writing.

Ellen Dietz is a freelance writer residing in Mesa, Arizona. She is the author of ten books and a former magazine editor. She is a contributor to *Chicken Soup for the Dental Soul*.

Kristin S. Door graduated from McGeorge School of Law with honors in 1978. She has been an Assistant U.S. Attorney since 1979. She and her husband have two teenagers. She enjoys horseback riding with her daughter, and is a "sometime" golfer with her husband and son. She can be reached at *kmarmee1@aol.com*.

Rayleen Downes is the mother of two girls, Breana and Kelsey. Both she and husband Gary are teachers. She holds a Masters in English literature and loves traveling with her extended family. She can be reached at *Raydelpew@ao.com*.

Andrea Durham is the proud mother of three adorable, precious children—Thomas, Alex and Natalie. Along with my husband Matthew, her family resides in Bethlehem, Pennsylvania. She graduated from Kutztown University with a bachelor's degree in social work. She works as a caseworker at Lehigh County Office of Children and Youth Services where she investigates cases of child abuse.

Colleen Eastman received her Bachelor of Arts in English from the University of California, Irvine. She works for a law firm in San Jose, California. She loves writing, not finishing her house and yard, and romantic trips to Home Depot with her husband. She has two children and is actively involved in the charity, "Help Save the Cancer Kids of America," set up by her oldest daughter who is a cancer survivor. You may contact her at *eastmans@hollinet.com*.

Benita Epstein's cartoons have been published in *The New Yorker, Reader's Digest, Barron's* and hundreds of other magazines. The National Cartoonist Society nominated her three times for Best Magazine Cartoonist and once for Best Greeting Card Cartoonist. Creators Syndicate distributes Benita's daily newspaper panel "Drawing a Crowd". *BenitaE@aol.com (www.reuben.org/benitaepstein/)*.

Paula Ferrato received her Bachelor of Arts from Washington and Jefferson College in 1983 and her Masters in Business from the University of Notre Dame in 1988. Paula currently lives in Rumford, Rhode Island with her husband Jim and daughters, Maggie, Katie and Anna. She is a self-employed marketing consultant.

Elaine L. Galit, coauthor of Exploring Houston with Children and Exploring Arts and Culture in Houston, is an award winning freelance writer. She's taught writing for the University of Houston, Cinco Ranch. Elaine lives in Houston with her calico cat, Juni, and a house full of books. Elaine can be reached at *EHWC123@AOL.com.*

Doug Garr is a journalist and author, most recently, of *IBM Redux: Lou Gerstner and the Business Turnaround of the Decade,* (HarperBusiness, 1999). He also is a speech-writer who has written for former New York Governor, Mario Cuomo and several prominent CEOs. He can be reached at *douggarr@yahoo.com.*

Susan Gilbert, nationally recognized as a Focus Strategist and is a successful entrepreneur.

Tony Gilbert is a writer, fitness consultant and marathon runner living in Albany, Georgia. His books, *Coincidental Encounters* and *Plastic Heroes,* are available at *www.invisiblerunner.com http://www.invisiblerunner.com.*

Randy Glasbergen is one of America's most widely and frequently published cartoonists. More than 25,000 of his cartoons have been published by *Funny Times, Woman's World, Cosmopolitan, America Online* and many others. His daily comic panel *The Better Half* is syndicated worldwide by King Features Syndicate. He is also the author of three cartooning instruction books and several cartoon anthologies. To read a new cartoon every day, please visit Randy's Web site at: *www.glasbergen.com.*

Nancy Harless is a nurse practitioner now exercising her menopausal zest through travel, volunteering in various healthcare projects, and writing about those experiences. Most of her writing is done in a towering maple tree, in the treehouse built specifically for that purpose by her husband, Norm. She is currently writing a book about some of the strong and beautiful women she has met along her journey. E-mail: *nancyharless@hotmail.com.*

Colleen Hartry began submitting stories when she was eight years old and continues to this day. She is pleased that her first submitted story is today being published in other languages.

Sara Henderson received her Bachelor of Arts from Illinois Wesleyan University and master of education from Bethel College in St. Paul, Minnesota. Sara was an elementary teacher for sixteen years. She is currently serving as the elementary principal at Maranatha Christian Academy in Minneapolis, Minnesota.

Connie Hill is President of TFC, Inc., a marketing support services company providing Fortune 1000 companies with web, data management, direct mail, print and fulfillment services. Connie grew from start up to a multi-million dollar corporation while raising two sons. She can be reached at *chill@tfcinc.com.*

Doris Iarovici, M.D., is a writer and psychiatrist at Duke University's Counseling and Psychological Services. Publications include articles in Parents, Newsweek, and Health and award-winning fiction in Crab Orchard Review. She lives with her husband and two children in North Carolina, and is at work on a novel. E-mail: *Doris.Monica@duke.edu.*

Jane Imber received her MBA from Wharton in 1980. She and her husband, Mitch, live in the mountains of Colorado where she skis, bikes and snowshoes. She is the author of *Barron's Dictionary of Marketing,* and is pursuing her second career writing fiction. Please email her at *Janeimber@yahoo.com.*

Ruth Reis Jarvis is a speech-language pathologist in Irvine, California. She has co-authored a four-volume educational series entitled "Strategies Offer Solutions" for Speech, Language, Cognition/Problem Solving, Classroom Success and Behavior. She lives in Tustin, California with her husband John and two daughters Carly and Janelle.

Marie Jones is a professional writer with over three dozen book credits, including *Looking For God in All the Wrong Places*, (Paraview Press, 2003). An ordained minister, she holds a Masters Degree in Metaphysics and lives in California with husband Ron, and toddler son, Max. Contact her at: *therevree@cox.net*.

Shirley Kawa-Jump sold the first of three thousand articles at age eleven. She writes romantic comedies for Silhouette Romance and is also the author of *How to Publish Your Articles* (Square One Publishers). A resident of Indiana, she spends her days being both mom and writer. For more information, visit: *www.shirleykawa-jump.com*.

Bil Keane created "The Family Circus" in 1960 and gathered most of his ideas from his own family: wife Thel, and their five children. Now read by an estimated 188 million people daily, nine grandchildren provide much of the inspiration for the award-winning feature. Web site: *www.familycircus.com*.

Cynthia Kersey is a nationally known speaker, columnist and author of the best-seller, *Unstoppable* and its upcoming sequel *Unstoppable Women*. Cynthia captivates audiences by delivering presentations on how to be unstoppable in their business and life pursuits. To learn more about joining the FREE "Unstoppable Community" or bringing Cynthia to your next meeting, visit *www.unstoppable.net http://www.unstoppable.net/*

Laura Kidder resides in Crosby, Texas, with her sixteen-year-old son, Bud, where she raises, trains and sells Tennessee Walking Horses. Laura has been a newsletter editor for several organizations, including the Association of Legal Administrators. She worked for a downtown Houston law firm for ten years, and finds that horses are a lot easier to take care of! See her horses at *www.cloud9walkers.com*.

Erin Kilby received her Bachelor of Science in English Education from Bowling Green State University in Ohio in 1994. She teaches Sophomore English in Kingwood, Texas. Erin enjoys spending time with her husband Michael and her stepson Tyler, writing and reading. She plans to continue teaching while pursuing her freelance writing career. Please e-mail her at: *erinkilby@hotmail.com*

Cheryl Kremer lives in Lancaster, Pennsylvania, with her husband, Jack, eleven-year-old daughter Nikki, and nine-year-old son, Cobi. In addition to writing, she enjoys crafts, being an aide in her church nursery, and watching her children play soccer.

Jeanne Marie Laskas is a columnist for *The Washington Post Magazine*, where her "Significant Others" essays appear weekly, and a contributing editor at Esquire. Her magazine pieces have been featured in numerous collections, including Best American Sportswriting. She received her MFA in nonfiction writing from the University of Pittsburgh, where she currently serves on the writing faculty as Assistant Professor. She is the author of *Fifty Acres and a Poodle* (Bantam 2000), *The Balloon Lady and Other People I Know* (Duquesne University Press, 1996) and *We Remember* (William Morrow, 1999). She lives and farms with her husband and daughters, along with their poodle, mutts, mules, sheep, and other animals at Sweetwater Farm in Scenery Hill, Pennsylvania.

Patty Lataille lives in a small artsy town in the Rocky Mountains and continues to run rivers, and teach skiing and snowboarding during the Colorado winters. Her freelance writing and editing as "Editor Extraordinaire" is inspired by her passion for the outdoors and animals. Patty can be reached at: *pattylco@caffee.net*.

Mary Dixon Lebeau is a freelance writer, newpaper columnist and employment counselor. She has written for numerous publications and has an essay in *Chicken Soup for the Romantic Soul*. Mary, her husband Scott, and their five children live in Woodbury, New Jersey. She may be reached at *mlebeau@snip.net*.

Delores Christian Liesner enjoys sharing the contagious joy and humor of God's workings in her life. Currently she is accepting stories for *Freedom's Price: Sacrifices, Joys and Inspiration from Lives of our Military and Their Families*. She also creates personalized poetry for gifts and special occasions. Contact her at: *godisgood@mygfa.org* or 262-634-8556.

Evelyn Lesch is a freelance newspaper columnist and filler writer, as well as a staff member of the New England Newspaper Association where she writes the advertising section of its montly *Bulletin* and edits a newsletter for classified advertising managers in the Northeast. She may be reached at: 28 Trinity St. Danvers, MA 01923.

Mark Litzler is a nationally published cartoonist whose work appears in *The Wall Street Journal, Barrons Financial Weekly, The Harvard Business Review, Saturday Evening Post* and *The Chronicle of Higher Education*. He attended Cleveland State University, where he earned his Bachelors Degree through the Business School and Case Western Reserve University, where he earned his Masters Degree in Public Administration. In the real work, Litzler is executive director of the Saint Luke's Hospital Foundation. He is married to Barbara Head, with whom he is the proud parent of nine-year-old triplets, Andrew, Peter and Molly.

Dian Tune Lopez is a mother of five children. She attended BYU for several years majoring in child development and family relationships and a minor in psychology. She is currently writing a book on living with the loss of a child and another titled *Doing the Tough Stuff*. It is her dream to be published by 2005. Please reach her at: *Youcanfindpeace@aol.com*.

Patricia Lorenz is a full-time freelance writer and speaker who works out of her home in Oak Creek, Wisconsin, and has a twelve-second commute to work. She is one of the top five contributors to the *Chicken Soup for the Soul* books with stories in over a dozen of them. She's the author of four books, over 400 articles, a contributing writer for fourteen *Daily Guideposts* books, and an award-winning columnist for two newspapers. To contact Patricia for speaking opportunities, e-mail her at: *patricialorenz@juno.com*.

Louise Moeri has been a writer all her life. Although she has written several adult novels, only her children's books have been published. She tries to present life as it is. When life gets hard, she thinks it's better to have a book of instructions than a book of magic.

Lisa Russell Motley received her A.A.S. degree in 1985. She is an elementary school instructional assistant. She is married and has two sons. Lisa enjoys playing piano, reading, writing, camping, working with children and spending time with her family. She enjoys writing poetry, children's books and short stories. Please e-mail her at: *shmlrm@aol.com*.

Wendy Natkong worked for thirty years in emergency medicine as a paramedic and instructor in Texas and Alaska. In 1999, she was diagnosed with progressive multiple sclerosis and now resides in her home state of North Carolina with her husband Don.

Judith Newman is a freelance writer based in New York. She is a contributing editor for *Allure* and *Self*, and also writes for *Vanity Fair, The New York Times, Ladies' Home Journal* and many other publications. Her book, *Diary of an Old Mother*, will be published by Miramax in May, 2004. She can be reached at: *judithn@compuserve.com*.

Amy Ash Nixon has been a journalist since 1985, when she graduated with a degree in print journalism from Emerson College. Since 1988, she has written for *The Hartford Courant*. Amy also has taught writing at the college level and is now a certified language arts teacher for middle school students in Connecticut.

Brenda Nixon, M.A., is a parenting speaker, author, and educator specializing in early childhood. She is married and the mother of two teenagers whom she hugs regularly. Brenda offers practical parenting tips, articles, and information about her books and tapes on her Web site *www.parentpwr.com.*

Sybella Ferguson Patten is a software engineer. Her community activities include project director for a women's health symposium project, grant writer, career speaker, and mentor. Sybella is a contributing writer for her church's newsletter and also enjoys gardening, sewing, and reading. Please e-mail her at *aggiesvfp@aol.com.*

Laurie Patterson is the associate publisher of Heartwarmers.com. Sadly, her daughter, mentioned in this story, passed away on December 24, 2001. Laurie can be reached at: *Patterson1@adelphia.net.*

Ava Pennington is a Bible study teacher, public speaker, and former human resources director. With an MBA degree in Management from St. John's University in New York, and a Bible Studies Certificate from Moddy Bible Institute in Chicago, Ava divides her time between volunteering, teaching and writing. Contact her at: *rsuavapen@yahoo.com.*

Russ Perman is a vocational teacher and technical writer living in the Northwest with his wife and inspiration, Diane. He likes camping, motorcycling, and tennis as well as computers and the Internet. His work has appeared in the *Reader's Digest,* trade journals and local classified ads. Contact him at: *RPerman@NCPlus.Net.*

Teresa Pitman is the author or coauthor of eleven books, all on parenting topics. Her articles also appear in magazines such as *Today's Parent* and *Mothering.* Teresa has four children and one grandson.

Kimberly Porrazzo is an author and award-winning columnist. A graduate of California State University Long Beach with a degree in journalism, she is a regular contributor to several publications. She and her husband Keith enjoy watching their two teenage sons play baseball in their free time. E-mail: *kimberlyporrazzo@cox.net.*

Debby Kate Stahl Ramsey is a mother of three and owner of the IUP General Feed Store in Zion, Illinois. 847-731-3333 (FEED). After her kidney transplant in 1984, she regards each day as a gift. She hopes to share this gift by becoming a better writer and eventually a published author.

Elizabeth Rand is a fiction and freelance writer who has never regretted her decision to leave the practice of law for the more rewarding life of a writer.

Deborah Ritz is a writer and educator. She received her bachelor of arts from Dickinson College and Master of Teaching from University of Richmond. She facilitates creative writing workshops for children and teachers in Virginia, and has served as a writer-in-residence. Deborah can be reached at *dr@moonlitwaters.com.*

Gail Rosenblum is an editor, essayist and script writer, and the mother of three children, ages thirteen, eleven and four. Her previous essays have been published in *Chicken Soup for the Writer's Soul* and *A Second Chicken Soup for the Woman's Soul.* She lives with her family in Minneapolis and can be reached at *gail@roseberrymedia.com.*

Julia Rosien lives in Ontario with her husband and four children. Her essays and articles appear in magazines and newspapers across North America. She can be reached at *juliarosien@rogers.com.*

Elizabeth Schorr has been married for twenty-one years to Marc. They have three teenagers; Nicholas, Kyle and Jacqueline. She continues to work part time for their drywall company and enjoys volunteering for her children, their schools and her church. She has a BA in journalism-public relations and is a freelance writer.

Denise Schupp was raised and continues to live in Colorado, where she enjoys all outdoor activities—hiking, biking, skiing. After receiving her degree from CSU, she worked for fifteen years as a personal trainer before retiring to raise her two children. In addition to her current roles as wife and mother, she works as a freelance writer.

Harley Schwadron's cartoons appear in such diverse publications as *Barron's, Wall Street Journal, Readers' Digest, Harvard Business Review* and *Woman's World.* His specialties are business and topical cartoons. He can be reached at: P.O. Box 1347, Ann Arbor, Michigan 48106 or tel/fax: 734-426-8433.

Jodi Severson earned a bachelor's degree in psychology from the University of Pittsburgh. She resides in Rice Lake, Wisconsin, with her husband and three children, and is employed by the State Public Defender's Office. She has had several short stories published including one in *Chicken Soup for the Sister's Soul.* E-mail: *jodis@charter.net.*

Deborah Shouse is a Kansas City area speaker, editor and writer who believes in celebrating the extraordinary in everyday life. Her latest book is *Making Your Message Memorable: Communicating Through Stories* (Crisp Publications). Her work has appeared in *Reader's Digest, Newsweek, Family Circle* and *Ms.* Visit Deborah's Web site at *www.thecreativityconnection.com.*

Jenna Skophammer is a junior at Fort Dodge, Iowa Senior High School. Her interests are writing, art, music, travel and her cat Harley. Jenna has a part-time job at Target and volunteers at the public library. She lives with her parents, Karen and Tom and brother Scott.

Patricia Dillon Sobczak is campus director and adjunct professor at Chapman University Irvine. She holds on MBA from Pepperdine University and an MLS from San Jose State. Patricia resides in Orange County, California, with her husband Bruce, children Kyle and Jessica and basset hound Murphy Louise. You can contact her at *pdillon@chapman.edu.*

Susan Stava has been a registered nurse in various capacities for over eighteen years. This is her first published work. She dedicates her story to the memory of her patients who never made it home for Christmas.

Ken Swarner is author of *Whose Kids Are These Anyway?* on Pedigree Books. He writes the syndicated humor column, *Family Man.* He can be reached at *kenswarner@aol.com,* or seen at *www.kenswarner.bigstep.com.*

Linda Tuccio-Koonz followed her father, Martin Buskin, into journalism, and is Entertainment-Features editor at *The News-Times,* in Danbury, Connecticut. She and husband Brian have their hands full with two boys who believe in magic. Her writing has also appeared in *Newsday* and *The New York Times.* Contact her at *briankoonz@aol.com.*

Rosalind Turner is the news editor at a weekly newspaper in Harrodsburg, Kentucky. She has a Bachelor of Arts degree in journalism. She enjoys doing volunteer work with involvement in a preservaton society, civic groups and theater. A goal is to write stories that nieces, Mika and Shania will enjoy.

Eileen Valinoti has had a long career in the health care field and is a freelance writer. Her work has appeared in *Glamour, Parents, American Health, PTA Today* and in numerous professional journals.

Diane M. Vanover is a freelance writer residing in Tucson, Arizona. Writing is her "soul food." Her works in progress include a novel set in Lithuania, nonfiction animal stories, and wildlife articles. She may be reached by phone at 520-296-7344 or e-mail: *dmvanover@aol.com.*

Carolee Ware is retired from the travel industry and enjoys the many benefits of living in Colorado, at the base of the beautiful Rocky Mountains. Family, friends, travel and a love of writing fill her everyday life. Currently she is writing her memoirs in the form of several short stories. She can be reached at 303-936-3223.

Maggi White is the founding editor of two Portland weeklies, *Downtowner* and *Ourtown*, from 1973-2000. She was also editor of *This Week*. She currently writes a column for *Northwest Senior Life* and articles for *The Columbian*, a daily in Vancouver, Washington.

Roger Wilkins is a professor of history at George Mason University. He has worked in the federal government, in philanthropy and in journalism—having been on the editorial boards of the *Washington Post* and *The New York Times*. He has a wife, three children and one grandchild.

Celeste Winters earned BA and MA degrees in journalism from Marshall University in West Virginia. Her consulting company—Calliope, Inc. of Phoenix, Arizona—provides copywriting; publicity; speaking; market research; media training; and arts marketing. Celeste is also a University of Phoenix faculty member and an animal lover. E-mail *celestewinters@cox.net*.

Bob Zahn has had thousands of his cartoons published in all the leading publications. His e-mail address is: *zahntoons@aol.com*.

Permissions

We would like to acknowledge the following publishers and individuals who granted us permission to reprint the following material. (Note: The stories that were penned anonymously, that are in the public domain, or that were written by Jack Canfield, Mark Victor Hansen, Patty Aubery or Mark and Chrissy Donnelly are not included in this listing.)

The Interview. Reprinted by permission of Nicole Jenkins and Michele "Screech" Campanelli. ©1999 Michele "Screech" Campanelli.

Ask and You Shall Receive. Reprinted by permission of Jane Imber. ©2002 Jane Imber.

Love and War. Reprinted by permission of Elizabeth Rand. ©2002 Elizabeth Rand.

The Commanding Secretary. Reprinted by permission of Russel M. Perman. ©2002 Russel M. Perman.

Getting Away. Reprinted by permission of Kimberly Ann Porrazzo. ©1999 Kimberly Ann Porrazzo.

Career Day. Reprinted by permission of Mary Dixon Lebeau. ©2002 Mary Dixon Lebeau.

The Birthday Tiara. Reprinted by permission of Deborah Ritz. ©2002 Deborah Ritz.

Not Just Another Rat. Reprinted by permission of Ava Marie Pennington. ©2002 Ava Marie Pennington.

Trooper. Reprinted by permission of Laura Kidder. ©1998 Laura Kidder.

The Lady Behind the Slinky. Reprinted by permission of Jeanne Marie Laskas. ©1993 Jeanne Marie Laskas.

A Speedy Job. Reprinted by permission of Evelyn L. Lesch. ©1980 Evelyn L. Lesch.

The Real Lesson. Reprinted by permission of Ruthann Reis Jarvis, M.A., C.C.C. ©2002 Ruthann Reis Jarvis, M.A., C.C.C.

The Red Purse. Reprinted by permission of Louise Moeri. ©1990 Louise Moeri.

Getting My Priorities Straight. Reprinted by permission of Sybella V. Ferguson-Patten. ©2002 Sybella V. Ferguson-Patten.

Just a Few More Minutes. . . . Reprinted by permission of Sara Lynn Henderson. ©2001 Sara Lynn Henderson.

A Working Mother's Prayer. Reprinted by permission of Cheryl M. Kremer. ©2000 Cheryl M. Kremer.

Leaving My Ego at the Door. Reprinted by permission of Patricia Dillon Sobczak. ©2002 Patricia Dillon Sobczak.

The Back Corner Booth. Reprinted by permission of Celeste Winters. ©2002 Celeste Winters.

The Best Sales Bonus. Reprinted by permission of Beatrice E. Brown. ©2002 Beatrice E. Brown.

A "Dish" with Integrity. Reprinted by permission of Erin Kellie Kilby. ©2002 Erin Kellie Kilby.

The Monday Good News Lunch Club. Reprinted by permission of Mickey Bambrick. ©2002 Mickey Bambrick.

More Time for Mom (to be). Reprinted by permission of Ellen Dietz. ©2002 Ellen Dietz.

The Gift of Understanding. Reprinted by permission of Susan Stava. ©2002 Susan Stava.

Little Amigo. By Deana Ward, LVN. Reprinted by permission of Lippincott, Williams & Wilkins. From NURSING2000, Vol. 30, November 11, 2000; p. 96.

The Hammock and *Letters from My Daughter.* Reprinted by permission of Patricia Lorenz. ©1984, 1989 Patricia Lorenz.

Respect and Pride. Reprinted by permission of Dianne C. Bradley. ©2002 Dianne C. Bradley.

A First. . . . Reprinted by permission of Rachel Byrne. ©2002 Rachel Byrne.

Any Regrets? Reprinted by permission of Lisa Russell Motley. ©2002 Lisa Russell Motley.

Performance Under the Stars. Reprinted by permission of Rayleen Downes. ©1996 Rayleen Downes.

The Other Side of the Glass Ceiling. Reprinted by permission of Nancy Michel Bandy. ©2002 Nancy Michel Bandy.

Standing Firm. Reprinted by permission of Virginia Boshears. ©2002 Virginia Boshears.

She Believed in Herself—Not the Experts, She Gave New Shape to the Shoe Business Then She Added Soul and The Creation of a Caring Corporation. Reprinted by permission of Cynthia Kersey. ©1998 Cynthia Kersey. Excepted and adapted from Unstoppable.

Discovery Toys. Reprinted by permission of Doug Garr. ©1990 Doug Garr.

The Damn Cape. Reprinted by permission of Colleen Eastman. ©2001 Colleen Eastman.